7/4·91

Palo Alto City Library

Freud's Vienna and
Other Essays

BRUNO BETTELHEIM

Freud's Vienna and Other Essays

ALFRED A. KNOPF   NEW YORK   1990

THIS IS A BORZOI BOOK
PUBLISHED BY ALFRED A. KNOPF, INC.

Copyright © 1956, 1962, 1977, 1981, 1983, 1985, 1987,
1989 by Bruno Bettelheim
All rights reserved under International and Pan-American
Copyright Conventions. Published in the United States
by Alfred A. Knopf, Inc., New York, and simultaneously
in Canada by Random House of Canada Limited, Toronto.
Distributed by Random House, Inc., New York.

Owing to limitations of space, all acknowledgments
of permission to reprint previously published material
will be found following the index.

Library of Congress Cataloging-in-Publication Data
Bettelheim, Bruno.
Freud's Vienna and other essays / by Bruno Bettelheim.—1st ed.
p. cm.
ISBN 0-394-57209-2
1. Psychoanalysis.   I. Title.
RC504.B35   1990
150.9′52—DC20   89-45286
CIP

Manufactured in the United States of America
First Edition

To Trude Bettelheim

in loving memory ·

Contents

Introduction

Many times during my life, I have been asked what were the major influences which shaped me and my work. Obviously the most important influences are one's parents and family, but if I centered on them, I would have to write an autobiography. As a Freudian, I believe what Freud said about biographies applies even more to autobiographies, namely that the person who undertakes such a task "binds himself to lying, to concealment, to flummery." And when I made efforts to recollect major events in my life, I became aware of my tendency to overstress the importance of some events and conveniently to forget others, just as Freud had warned.

Thus if I were to present personal material in a book, it would have to be done in some other form. The one I decided to use was a collection of essays which had been written over some time but had not yet been published in book form. These, in themselves and by their selection for inclusion, would permit the reader to arrive at his own ideas concerning the major influences on me.

The most important person in my life has been my dear wife, to whose memory this book is dedicated. The details of her impact on me belong to that most private world which I believe best remains private.

This book begins with an essay about the most public influence on my life and work, that of my native city. In "Freud's Vienna," I talk about why I believe that there were specific features in the ambience of Vienna that were particularly conducive to the creation of psychoanalysis. In the next essay, "Berggasse 19," I speculate on why Freud may have chosen this particular location for his home and place of work.

"How I Learned About Psychoanalysis" tells about some significant happenings in my early life. It is included because it suggests how very differently one came to psychoanalysis in those early days, when common knowledge about it was not yet as widespread as it is today. "Two Views of Freud" expresses the reasons for my dissatisfaction with Ernest Jones's biography of Freud, which was accepted as the standard one for over thirty years. The appearance of Peter Gay's new biography in 1988 was a happy event, for it gives a much fuller picture of Freud than have any previous works.

In "A Secret Asymmetry," an effort is made to throw light on a complex triangular relationship, previously suppressed, that seems to have had an important impact on how the Freud-Jung relationship developed, a relation which was so significant in the history of psychoanalysis.

In "Lionel Trilling on Literature and Psychoanalysis," I try to show how important this great literary critic was in making psychoanalysis a significant part of the intellectual life of the United States.

The second part of this collection begins with "Essential Books of One's Life," a highly personal discussion of which books shaped much of my thinking and why. The essays that follow it also relate some of my personal experiences, and deal with topics reflecting my life's work with children, particularly the rehabilitation and education of severely disturbed children. In "The Art of Motion Pictures," I speak about what the movies have meant to me, but this is somewhat incidental to my thoughts on what they could mean to all of us. In "The Child's Perception of the City," I again draw on my own childhood experiences in an effort to illustrate how important our early experiences are in shaping our views of the world in which we live.

In "Children and Museums," I reflect on how art came to play such an important role in my life, and how it could do the same in the lives of most children. In "Children and Television," I attempt to help parents get a better and more useful understanding of what is certainly today an important experience of children.

I was deeply moved when I came to realize that the practice of milieu therapy, which I named and which I was instrumental in gaining acceptance for as a method for helping the most disturbed children, had been invented and applied by Anne Sullivan in her treatment of Helen

Keller long before I was born. A result of this realization is the essay "Master Teacher and Prodigious Pupil," which examines what lies behind such "miracles." The myth of wolf-children is explained in "Feral Children and Autistic Children," which is the direct result of my work at the Sonia Shankman Orthogenic School at the University of Chicago.

This book's third and last section represents one Jew's efforts to cope with the destruction of European Jewry under Hitler. This is, of course, a nearly impossible task, particularly for a person who, as I did, spent a year in two German concentration camps and then was one of the lucky ones set free. The first essay, "Janusz Korczak: A Tale for Our Time," has been superseded by a more complete biography of Korczak, *The King of Children* by Betty Jean Lifton (published by Farrar, Straus & Giroux, which also published Korczak's *King Matt the First,* to which I contributed an introduction). Nevertheless, after some deliberation I decided to include my much shorter appreciation of this great educator in this book, since I believe that everything possible should be done to bring this great man to public attention.

The next piece, "Hope for Humanity," is included because Miep Giese is one who gave hope to me, and I hope she will also affect my readers. "Children of the Holocaust" shows how deeply hurt were even those children who survived the Holocaust, and suggests how problematic such survival is. "Returning to Dachau," once more a highly personal recollection, centers on the continuing difficulty of coping with the experience of the Holocaust, despite the passage of years.

The last essay, "Freedom from Ghetto Thinking," asks once more what factors may have contributed to making the destruction of millions of Jews possible, and what may be needed to prevent any repetition of such a catastrophe.

My hope in publishing this book is that it may contain matters of sufficient interest, both personal and general, to make it worthwhile reading. I find that at my age (I am now in my eighty-seventh year) one no longer fully trusts one's own judgment, particularly where personal matters are concerned; one needs encouragement. I was encouraged to publish these essays by my good friend Theron Raines, and I am very grateful to him for this, as well as for much else. My dear friend and editor Joyce Jack, whose good judgment I learned to trust as she helped to create many of my previous books by working with me, did the same for this book. Whatever may be the fate of this book, I am deeply grateful to her for her efforts to make it readable.

PART I

On Freud and Psychoanalysis

Freud's Vienna

I t is not by chance that psychoanalysis was born in Vienna and came
of age there. In Freud's time, the cultural atmosphere in Vienna
encouraged a fascination with both mental illness and sexual problems in a way unique in the Western world—a fascination that extended
throughout society, even into the imperial court which dominated Viennese social life. The origins of this unique cultural preoccupation can
be traced to the history of the city itself, but most especially to the concerns and attitudes foremost in the minds of Vienna's cultural elites just
before and during the period in which Freud formed his revolutionary
theories about our emotional life.

Freud was by no means the only innovator in Vienna who brought a
change in our view of sexuality in general and sexual perversions in
particular, and of the treatment of insanity. For instance, Baron Richard
von Krafft-Ebing, a professor of psychiatry at the University of Vienna,
first gave a name to paranoia and brought it into common discourse. His
clinical accounts of sexual pathology showed in a lively way the many
forms the sexual drive may take, years before Freud undertook his stud-

This essay appeared in French in somewhat different form with the title "La Vienne de Freud," in
Vienne, l'apocalypse joyeuse (Paris: Editions du Centre Pompidou, 1986). It appears here in English for the first time.

ies of sex. Krafft-Ebing's most important work, *Psychopathia Sexualis*, published in 1886, revolutionized the world's ideas about sexual perversions, a subject completely ignored by scientists up to that moment. This book led to the decriminalization of sexual perversions in Austria, long before such a sensible view spread to other countries. Krafft-Ebing led the way to an era of changed attitudes toward sexuality in Vienna and Austria, and in a sense he prepared the environment that made Freud's work possible.

In addition to psychoanalysis, other modern methods of treating mental disturbances were created and developed by doctors in Vienna. Wagner von Jauregg, who followed Krafft-Ebing as head of psychiatry at the University of Vienna, and who as such was Freud's chief while he taught there, discovered the malaria treatment of general paresis and the fever treatment of the same disease; for this he won in 1927 the first Nobel Prize in medicine that was awarded for a psychiatric discovery. His work can justly be seen as the beginning of chemical treatment for mental illnesses. In the same direction, Manfred Sakel, another Viennese physician, discovered in 1933 the insulin-shock treatment for schizophrenia. It is almost astonishing to note that *all* modern methods of treatment for mental disturbances—psychoanalysis, chemical treatment, and shock treatment—were brought into the world within a few decades in one and the same city.

To understand the unique form that Vienna's culture attained during the late-nineteenth and early-twentieth centuries, one must recognize that Vienna had been, as it was called with some affection, *die alte Kaiserstadt*—the old Imperial City. The Hapsburg name does not now carry the aura and glamour it once did, but for many centuries the vast Hapsburg Empire, of which Vienna was the capital, was the greatest the world had ever known, surpassing in extent the ancient Roman Empire, of which it saw itself the rightful heir: the Hapsburgs were rulers of the "Holy Roman Empire of the German Nation."

In the sixteenth century a Hapsburg emperor, Charles V (also Charles I, as King of Spain), could make the claim (later borrowed by the British) that since his empire circled the globe, the sun never set upon it. After Charles V, a gradual but steady decline of the Hapsburgs and their power set in. The empire almost perished during the Napoleonic Wars. But at the end of this episode, Vienna hosted the Congress of Vienna in 1814–15, which determined the geography and future of

Europe. After this, the Viennese could look upon theirs as the preeminent city of Europe, for the Hapsburg emperor and his realm once again dominated the continent, this owing to the skill of Austria's chancellor, Prince Metternich.

However, this changed once and for all with the revolutions of 1848, when the aged Metternich was forced to resign and Franz Joseph began his long reign (1848–1916). Even in its reduced form after the Napoleonic Wars, and in the absence of the title "Holy Roman Empire," the Hapsburg realm remained Europe's foremost imperial presence, dominating an assortment of German principalities before modern Germany was formed; and it held sway in all of Central Europe and much of Italy and Eastern Europe as well. The Hapsburg state was thus a multinational one, inhabited by many different language groups, of which the most important were the Germans, Italians, Poles, Czechs, Hungarians, Slovaks, Croatians, Slovenes, and Ruthenians. In 1848 and afterward, with the tide of nationalism rising, these various peoples forming the empire began to demand self-determination and soon absolute independence, threatening the empire with what seemed like chaos. These powerful forces in the minds of ordinary people were counterbalanced and kept in check by the presence of the emperor's army, which was made up of all nationalities, and by the reverence accorded the emperor himself, which he worked constantly to maintain.

In addition, the capital city of Vienna continued to grow in cultural influence over the intelligentsia of the entire empire, as well as much of the rest of Europe, such as the German states and the Balkans. It might be said that in Central and Eastern Europe, all roads led to Vienna; not only was it the seat of empire and of the most important cultural institutions within its sphere of influence, but it was by far the largest city in this vast geographical area. In fact, it was the second-largest city on the continent of Europe (after Paris), and so it naturally attracted those who wished to leave the provinces in favor of life at the center of things. Throughout the nineteenth century, Vienna continued to grow in size, in cultural opportunities, in scientific renown, and in economic importance. And all this time the emperor held his place, growing more revered as he grew older.

Most of those who contributed to Vienna's cultural greatness in these years were not born there, but came from the empire's near or distant provinces. They were drawn to Vienna either as immigrants to the cultural center, or because they had already been educated there. Many were brought to Vienna in childhood by their parents, who wanted their children to have the best. Sigmund Freud was one of these, as was Theodor Herzl, the founder of Zionism. Others came to Vienna as adults, such as the musicians Gustav Mahler and Johannes Brahms, the painter Oskar Kokoschka, the early modern architect Josef Hoffmann, and the educator Franz Cizek, who was the first to discover and nurture the art of children.

A culture has power to draw talented people to its center, and one example of Vienna's attraction in our own century is that of the Nobel Prize winner for literature Elias Canetti. In one volume of his autobiography, entitled *Die Fackel im Ohr (The Torch in My Ear)*, he tells how he came to Vienna from the Balkans and was influenced by the cultural climate he found there. He pays particular note to the critic and political writer Karl Kraus, whose ideas, as expressed in his magazine, *Die Fackel* ("The Torch"), were crucial to Canetti's own development.

But what gave this Viennese culture its true uniqueness was the luck of history, by which the culture's greatest flowering came about simultaneously with the disintegration of the empire which had made Vienna important in the first place, and of which it was still the capital, the seat of government—and, most important of all, its emperor's residence. Franz Joseph, as emperor, was not only the ultimate symbol of the empire, but also the person who actually held it all together. Things had never been better, but at the same time they had never been worse: this strange simultaneity, in my opinion, explains why psychoanalysis, based on the understanding of ambivalence, hysteria, and neurosis, originated in Vienna and probably could have originated nowhere else. And psychoanalysis was but one of the major intellectual developments of a time when a pervasive awareness of political decline led Vienna's cultural elites to abandon politics as a subject to take seriously, to withdraw their attention from the wider world and turn inward instead.

The decline was noticeable to all concerned after the events of 1859 (only three years after Freud's birth), when the empire suffered the first of a series of blows to its eminence (and image) as a world power. In that year, it lost its most prosperous and advanced provinces: most of northern Italy, including Lombardy and the all-important Milan, Tuscany with Florence, Parma, Modena. Only Venice and the Veneto still remained Austrian, and this only for a few more years. Seven years later, in 1866, as a result of war with the upstart Prussia, there was a devastating defeat in the battle of Königgrätz; the last Italian territories were lost, and Prussia became the dominant power over the other German states. This deprived Austria of the hegemony it had held over Germany for some six hundred years. Four years later, when Prussia defeated France in 1870, Germany became united under the leadership of Prussia. With this, Berlin began to replace Vienna as the center of the German-speaking world, and it could boast a young emperor more impressive and dynamic than the fading Franz Joseph.

One way to cope with these losses which presaged the doom of the empire was to use denial as a kind of defense. Thus the Viennese intelligentsia might say, "While the situation is desperate, it is not serious." In this mind-set, which was very common for many years in Vienna, external reality is discounted and all mental energy is turned inward: only the inner life of the individual is allowed to matter. At the same time when the new, unified Germany (with its capital, Berlin) was turning its enormous energies toward empire-building, Vienna's cultural elites became centered upon discovering and conquering the inner world of man. This withdrawal was made easier and more certain by new disappointments which rose up on the heels of the old.

There were official efforts to counteract this feeling of decline, but nothing worked quite the way it was expected to. For instance, to counteract the military defeat of 1866, the government went to great lengths to reassert Vienna's cultural and economic importance. A world's fair was planned for 1873, with the aim of bringing Vienna once more to the admiring attention of the world. The expectations of prosperity that the fair would bring to Vienna led to a building boom; and many grandiose structures, both public and private, rose up on both sides of the newly created Ringstrasse. This avenue circled the inner city and was intended to outshine the world-famous Haussmann boulevards of Paris, because the buildings on the Ringstrasse would be even more splendid than those gracing the Paris avenues.

Historically, Vienna had been a city of the baroque; it was the grand baroque churches and palaces that had given the city its character. Now the modern buildings of the Ringstrasse gave Vienna a double and somewhat contradictory character: that of both an old imperial capital and a center of modern culture. It was as if the city could not decide which way to turn: toward the glorious (though receding) past, or toward a new and modern future.

Great expectations for the World's Fair also led to wild speculation on the stock market. Nine days after the fair opened, the stock market crashed. On Vienna's "black Friday," 125 banks went bankrupt, and many other enterprises failed, in a widening shock that brought about a deep depression. The financial crisis in Vienna spread all over Europe and even affected the United States.

As mentioned, Vienna's cultural elites rejected the importance of the events occurring around them and turned their attention inward, to the previously hidden and unrecognized aspects of man. However, this was a solution to the haunting contradictions of Viennese life for only a few. The vast majority of Vienna's population had to find another way to escape the unease they felt in a time when the secure, traditional world they and their ancestors had known was falling apart. The answer was lighthearted entertainment. True, the World's Fair of 1873 had failed, but with the premiere of *Die Fledermaus* in 1874, Vienna began once more to rule the world—the world of the operetta. Once the center of the old high culture—grand opera and serious theater, the greatest in the German language—Vienna now rose to preeminence in light opera and most of all in dance music. The Viennese waltz in a few short years had conquered the globe; besides the waltzes, there were the many operettas of Strauss, Lehár, Suppé, and others. As we look back, it seems as if the Viennese of that time never stopped dancing: masked balls, the antics of the carnival (the *Fasching,* in which nearly all of Vienna participated), and splendid dancing halls in all parts of the city. Some of these occasions, such as the great balls at court, were only for the upper classes; but many more were for the lower classes, as well as many in which the classes mixed freely. In addition, Vienna was a great city for pageants, with many floats for everybody to admire when celebrating court events, royal marriages, or anniversaries of the emperor. These were occasions upon which artists could display their talent and imagination as they entertained the populace. Through these continual celebrations, the decline of the empire was denied any seriousness.

In the realm of politics and world events, catastrophes periodically shook the empire to its roots and hastened its disintegration. But this was not all: equally disastrous were the catastrophes which took place in the heart of the city's personal world—within the imperial family at the court which was the city's true center, its *raison d'être.*

Emperor Franz Joseph's marriage to Elizabeth, a very young and very beautiful Bavarian princess, was one of great love and devotion on his part, and this love continued all through his life. However, despite the emperor's efforts to please Elizabeth and make her happy, she soon distanced herself from him and from the court, a process which became ever more extreme until she spent hardly any time with him, or in Vienna.

We can now see Elizabeth as hysterical, narcissistic, and anorexic. At the time, however, she was acclaimed, with much justification, as the most beautiful woman in Europe. To retain her distinctive beauty, the attribute responsible for her rise to empress, she starved herself on various extreme diets, such as having nothing except six glasses of milk in a day, for days on end. On frequent walking tours, she marched at such a brisk pace that her companions fell behind her in exhaustion, as she continued on for seven, eight, even ten hours.

Like some hysterics, such as the one Schnitzler later described in his novel *Miss Else,* the empress—who always traveled with enough trunks to fill many railway cars, so that she had always at her disposal a vast array of the costliest and most beautiful clothes—at last took to going out for her walks wearing only a dress, a single garment to cover her naked body. She wore no underclothes and, to the horror of her companions, no stockings. Nevertheless, she often wore as many as three pairs of gloves to protect her beautiful hands.

Possibly one of the clearest symptoms of her neurosis was her endless and aimless traveling all over Europe. In the words of the French writer Maurice Barrès: "Her voyages did not resemble the peaceful and deliberate regularity of migrating birds; they were rather the planless darting to and fro of an unanchored spirit which beats its wings, allowing itself neither rest nor design."

In 1871, when the emperor wrote to Elizabeth, who, as nearly always, was not in Vienna, asking what gift she would like best to receive on her name day, she wrote back, probably in a spirit of self-mockery, "What I would really like best would be a completely equipped insane asylum."

Madness held a particular fascination for Elizabeth, possibly because it was not uncommon in her family, the Wittelsbach rulers of Bavaria. She frequently visited institutions for the insane, for example in Vienna, Munich, and London. She extolled both death and madness in remarks such as "The idea of death purifies" and "Madness is truer than life"—evidence of her profoundly melancholic disposition long before the terrible events of Mayerling, after which it became even more intense. At last, in 1898, on one of her trips to Geneva, she was assassinated by an anarchist. Her murder made as little sense as had her life before it.

Thus, an interest in insanity and examples of the devastating impact of neurosis and the destructive results of hysteria could be found at the imperial court which dominated all that went on in Vienna, long before Freud decided to devote his life to a deeper understanding of the inner and so far unknown forces in man which cause these disturbances.

In 1889, Franz Joseph had been emperor for over forty years; the continuation of the empire depended upon Rudolf, his heir and only son. Rudolf led a lonely existence; his mother, Elizabeth, was distant and mostly unavailable to him. He and his father had little mutual sympathy, and no love existed between him and his wife, a Belgian princess. By the age of thirty, he had had many affairs, which were meaningless to him. Depressed and lonely, feeling totally useless at this young age, Rudolf formed and carried out a suicide pact with one of his lovers, a Baroness Vetsera: he killed her and then committed suicide at his hunting lodge at Mayerling, in the heart of the Vienna Woods, fifteen miles from the city itself.

Oedipal conflicts between rulers and their sons were nothing new in history—or in the house of Hapsburg. The conflict between Philip and Don Carlos not only made history but became the subject of one of the world's greatest dramas and then a great opera. But Rudolf's act seems unique: the heir of a great empire committing homicide and suicide, immediately after having sex with a woman of his choice, who also had clearly chosen both sex and death. The psychological climate of Vienna during the empire's decline and the morbid feelings which pervaded the city as a consequence in this period are the fitting and even necessary background for such an extreme example of a severe oedipal conflict with a father—neurosis, sex, murder, and suicide. It was a shockingly vivid demonstration of the destructive tendencies inherent in man which Freud would investigate and describe later. It also reflected the intimate relationship between the sex drive and the death drive—a connection Freud sought to clarify in his explorations of the darkest aspects of man's psyche.

The emperor himself sought to cope with these personal and familial tragedies through an aggravation of his work neurosis; he immersed himself in his paperwork tirelessly for some sixteen hours a day, as if he were some mere subaltern of the empire rather than its supreme ruler. Compulsively, he insisted on court etiquette and had adopted the famous (or in truth infamous—because it denied any place to human emotions or spontaneity in human relations) Spanish Court Ceremony, which did not permit personal contact of any nature. Interestingly, however, after Elizabeth's estrangement became permanent, and even more after her death, he sought solace in the company of a young and beautiful actress who had been her reader. Because of Rudolf's suicide, the Archduke Francis Ferdinand—a man with whom the Emperor was in deep conflict—became heir to the throne. It is reported that when Ferdinand was assassinated in 1914—the event which led to the First World War—Franz Joseph remarked that he was relieved, because this murder had rectified a situation which was much in need of it.

Sex and destruction shared a strange coexistence in much of Vienna's culture during this period of the slow demise of the empire. Even leading politicians were preoccupied with ideas of death, as suggested by the remark "We have to kill ourselves before the others do it," made by the Hungarian foreign minister around 1912. This interconnection between sex and death formed a main underlying topic of Viennese art, literature, and psychoanalysis. It permeated the work of many, such as the young and brilliant philosopher Otto Weininger, who in 1903, at the age of twenty-three, committed suicide at the place where Beethoven had died. His *Sex and Character,* with its deeply pessimistic view of sex, had tremendous influence on the intelligentsia of Vienna.

Early in his own life, Sigmund Freud made a choice that seemed to presage his later recognition of the importance of the death drive in his mature system. In December of 1881, Vienna's Ring Theater had burned down with a great loss of life, another tragic catastrophe which shook the city. The emperor, always putting the best face on disaster, decreed that on the site of the destroyed theater there should rise a new residential and commercial building to be called the Sühnhaus ("House of Atonement"). The architect would be the man then deemed Vienna's greatest, F. V. Schmidt, and because of the excellent location on the

Ringstrasse, the new building would be able to charge high rents; a part of the income thus derived would go to support the children who had been orphaned by the fire.

At first, it was difficult to find tenants for the Sühnhaus's splendid apartments: people were reluctant to move to a place where so many others had lost their lives. But it was in this "House of Atonement" that Freud—although the rent was far beyond his means—took an apartment when he married, and there he conducted his practice. More significantly, he did not consider that his patients, suffering from debilitating nervous disorders, might be hesitant to go for treatment into a building with morbid associations. For reasons we do not know, Freud not only did not mind these associations, but obviously cherished them. Perhaps even at that time ideas about the morbidity of neuroses were in his unconscious, bringing him to choose this ominous building as the place for his life and work. The Freuds were such early tenants in the Sühnhaus that their first child was also the first baby to be born there. On this occasion, Freud received a letter from the emperor, congratulating him as father of the first child born in the building, bringing life into the world at a place where so many lives had been lost.

This letter is the only direct connection between the emperor and Freud of which we know. But the emperor, and what he stood for, was never far from Freud's awareness. He said many times that an emperor was a symbol for the father and the superego, and that therefore the figure of the emperor played an important role in the conscious and unconscious of everyone.

Events, however, had made clear that even Vienna's emperor was not master in his own house; and this fact may have inspired Freud to develop the idea that the ego was not master in *its* own house—a realization Freud calls a severe blow to our narcissism (as it must have been destructive to the emperor's narcissism that he was rejected by son and wife). Work neurosis as the emperor's defense against the many blows to his self-esteem probably was not lost on Freud as he studied the neuroses and discovered that they were defenses against sexual fears and against attacks on one's self-love.

In this unique Viennese culture, the strongest inner powers were thanatos and eros, death and sex. The formulation looks simple, but the interplay of these powers is anything but simple; on the contrary, it is most complex, creating far-ranging and intricate psychological problems. Viennese culture liked to explore these psychological complexities and embodied them in its creations. To tease out the meaning of these hitherto unknown, dark and hidden, most complex psychological phenomena so that one might be able to understand and perhaps even master them was the central problem of Viennese culture. Freud was not alone in devoting his life to the struggle with these taxing problems. The Viennese Arthur Schnitzler, whom Freud called his alter ego, had been, like Freud, trained as a physician; and also like Freud, Schnitzler exercised this craft for a relatively short time. Then he too turned to the study of man's psyche, not as a psychiatrist, but as a writer.

Schnitzler was far and away the leading literary figure of Vienna in his time, and was recognized as such; his novels were widely read and admired, and his plays were those most frequently performed on the German stage, particularly in Vienna, a city where the theater had always been held in esteem. This is not the place to analyze Schnitzler's work in any detail, but at least two of his most important plays should be mentioned to make the point that in his mind too, sex and death were inextricably interwoven. The title of one of these plays may be freely translated as "A Little Love Affair" (*Liebelei*). A young man of the upper class has an affair with a lower-class girl who loves him deeply. But their relation is of little importance to him, compared with his interest in seducing the wife of a prominent citizen. He is not truly in love with her, either, but the challenge of seducing her appeals to his vanity. The lady's husband feels obliged to challenge him to a duel, in the course of which he kills the young man. The girl who has loved him so much is not even permitted to attend the funeral, and this fact impresses her with how little she had meant to him; in desperation, she commits suicide.

The other play is *Das Weite Land*, "The Enormous Country." This enormous and unknown country is, of course, man's psyche. In this play a married upper-class lady has an affair—we must assume for the first time in her life—with a young naval officer on leave. Her husband has had many affairs himself, none of which have meant much to him, but nevertheless takes offense at his wife's affair because it hurts his pride. He challenges the naval officer to a duel and kills him. In consequence, not only is this life destroyed but also those of both the husband and the wife, since their lives have now lost all meaning. Thus in both plays, as in many of Schnitzler's other writings, sexual involvement leads to destruction. This is also the theme of one of his best-known novels, *Fräu-*

lein Else ("Miss Else"), in which a clearly neurotic and probably hysteric young girl, to save her father from being disgraced, accedes to the desire of an older man that she come to him naked, only to kill herself as she does so.

In a conversation with Martin Buber—another extraordinary man whose personality was formed during those years in Vienna, where he was born and where, through his association with Herzl, he decided to devote his life to the study of Hasidism—Schnitzler said about the figures he had created, who were so typical of Vienna at this time, that a sense of the end of their world envelops them, and that the end of their world is near; as indeed it was.

Rilke, in his *Tale of Love and Death of Cornet Christoph Rilke,* projects into Austria's past the idea that death immediately follows sexual experience, but the theme was clearly a contemporary one, as the tragedy of the Austrian crown prince so clearly showed.

That eros and thanatos are the deepest and strongest drives in man was an insight achieved by others besides Freud and Schnitzler. One of Brahms's greatest works, his *German Requiem,* has a central theme that "in the middle of life we are surrounded by death." Mahler wrote songs on a child's death, a resurrection symphony, and, as his crowning achievement, the Eighth Symphony, in which he combines a medieval mass with the last part of Faust—his apotheosis, where in death he is saved by the love of woman, suggesting that only in death is true fulfillment possible.

Freud began his investigation of the hidden forces which underlie man's actions with his study of hysteria, which he was still working on when the Mayerling tragedy occurred. Through his study he discovered how powerful and all-encompassing a force the sexual drive is, and what strange forms of behavior it could produce when inhibited and/or repressed. His (and Breuer's) *Studies on Hysteria* appeared in 1895, to be followed the next year by Freud's paper on the etiology of hysteria and by that on sexuality in the etiology of neuroses. How deep an impression these studies made on Vienna's literary world may be illustrated by Hugo von Hoffmannsthal's remark that while he was writing the libretto for Richard Strauss's opera *Electra,* he consulted them again and again. Electra is indeed portrayed as a hysterical woman.

With the appearance of *The Interpretation of Dreams* in 1900, psychoanalysis became established. This greatest of Freud's works is one of introspection; in it all interest is devoted to the innermost self of man, to the neglect of the external world, which pales in comparison to the fascination of this inner world. That this turn-of-the-century Viennese *chef d'oeuvre* was indeed the result of desperation at being unable to change the course of the external world, and represented an effort to make up this deficiency by a single-minded interest in the dark underworld, is attested to by the motto which Freud put at its beginning: Virgil's line *Flectere si nequeo superos, Acheronta movebo* ("If I cannot move heaven, I will stir up the underworld"). This motto was a most succinct suggestion that turning inward toward the hidden aspects of the self was due to a despair that it was no longer within one's ability to alter the external world or stop its dissolution; that therefore the best one could do was to deny importance to the world at large by concentrating all interest on the dark aspects of the psyche.

These preoccupations with sex and death are found to a very marked degree in the work of Vienna's greatest artists of the period, most notably Gustav Klimt and Egon Schiele. Klimt's early work had been quite conventional, but upon reaching maturity around the turn of the century he began to paint and draw hysteric nude women. For example, some of his studies for his large paintings which were to decorate the University of Vienna showed nude women in the typical hysterical *arc de cercle* posture, a motif he repeated many times. In fact, as early as 1902 an inimical critic referred to Klimt, not without reason, as "the painter of the unconscious." The role of eros in Klimt's painting can hardly be disregarded, so dominant are erotic themes in most of his paintings, with the exception of the landscapes. Klimt's paintings *Danaë, Water Serpents, Fulfillment,* and various parts of the Beethoven Frieze, such as *Hostile Powers,* should be mentioned here, as well as his *Leda* and *The Kiss.*

Klimt's most gifted student, Egon Schiele, carried this development much further. As soon as he reached artistic maturity he painted and drew mainly the inner world of man, especially man's neurotic aspects. One important precept of Freud's that seems to have influenced Schiele is that self-analysis must precede the analysis of others; in order to understand the unconscious fully, one must study one's own unconscious first. In his self-portraits Schiele analyzed his own personality as penetratingly and as mercilessly as Freud had analyzed himself. The two paintings he did in 1910 and 1911 entitled *The Self Seers* are typical of Schiele's ability to give us visions of a person's unconscious life. In the double portrait *Inspector Benesch and His Son,* he painted not only the hidden aspects of the psyches of these two people but their oedipal conflict. Here a picture does indeed convey the essence of an oedipal conflict as eloquently as Freud's own writings.

What has been said above concerning the portraits and self-portraits by Schiele can be said with equal justification about those by Oskar Kokoschka. And Arnold Schönberg, who created in Vienna the foundations of modern music, also painted; his *The Red Stare* and *The Vision* let us see the inner life of the person represented more clearly than the external appearance. But ultimately, pictures speak directly to us, and the messages these paintings convey about man's innermost secrets should be found in them—in our own responses to them—and not in what may be said or written about them.

There is an eloquent footnote to the story of Empress Elizabeth and her desire for a "completely equipped insane asylum." In the decade after her death, an institution was built to house the insane of Vienna. The greatest artistic talents available were called upon to create the most modern and most beautiful building for the sole use of mental patients. One of Vienna's most distinguished architects, Otto Wagner, was commissioned to design this structure, the Church of St. Leopold on the Steinhof, a place devoted to serving the spiritual needs of patients who suffered the most severe inner disturbances. Wagner conceived of this church as a total work of art, a *Gesamtkunstwerk,* and he invited many of the best young artists of Vienna—Kolo Moser, Richard Luksch, Othmar Schimkovitz, and others—to participate in decorating it. One of the most splendid features of the church, begun in 1905 and completed in 1907, is its golden cupola, a cupola covered with gilded bronze, which glows beautifully when the rays of the sun are reflected by it. This church dominates not only the entire institution but the surrounding districts; it has become one of the great landmarks of the city.

Thus during the last years of the disintegration of the great Hapsburg Empire, its capital paid tribute to the importance of madness with a beautiful and impressive monument. Its greatest writers and painters, too, explored the nature of madness in their work, and its best scholarly minds devoted their energies to discovering and understanding the deeply hidden, innermost mind of man, that "enormous country" of

Berggasse 19

I n June of 1938, a few days before the Freud family left Vienna for London, Freud's friend August Aichhorn asked a young photographer, Edmund Engelman, to take some pictures of Freud's place of residence, so there would be a visual record of the locale where psychoanalysis came into being. The plan was to take the photographs without Freud's knowledge, so as not to further disturb an old, gravely ill man at a moment when he was deeply worried by the Nazis' harassment of him and his daughter and by concern over their impending departure. But by chance Freud encountered Engelman while he was taking the pictures and agreed to sit for some portraits, which add greater meaning to the photographs presented in the book *Sigmund Freud's Home and Offices, Vienna 1938*.

The photographer was handicapped by the fact that he could not use flashbulbs; he had to avoid attracting the attention of the Gestapo, which had the Freud home under close surveillance. This had started when Freud, through the intervention of influential foreign friends, was given permission to ship abroad his possessions, the most important of

This review of *Sigmund Freud's Home and Offices, Vienna 1938: The Photographs of Edmund Engelman* (New York: Basic Books, 1976) appeared under the title "Where Psychoanalysis Was Born" in *The New York Times Book Review*, January 2, 1977.

Schnitzler's play, and to deciphering the sources of hysteric and rotic behavior.

Because of what took place in Vienna at that extraordinary time, now have the means of mastering—or at least understanding—some the darkest forces of our minds, and so finding it possible—even wher surrounded by disintegration—to extract meaning from life and, as Freud taught, to be master in our own house.

which to him was his art and antiquities collection. The Gestapo's surveillance was intended to prevent others from smuggling additional valuables into the apartment and thus circumventing their confiscation by the Nazis.

Half a year later, Engelman too left Vienna. He did not dare take the Freud negatives along, fearing that when his luggage was inspected they might arouse suspicion and prevent his departure. He left them behind with Aichhorn for safekeeping. When Aichhorn died after the war the negatives were sent to Anna Freud in London, and she eventually returned them to Engelman. Thus this book came about, as Engelman relates in a concluding memoir.

Beginning in 1891, a nondescript four-story apartment building at Berggasse 19 housed Freud's combined home and workplace on its mezzanine floor. Here Freud would have remained, had not the Nazis—much against his desires—forced him to leave Vienna a year before his death. At Berggasse 19, Freud achieved the startlingly new, deeply troubling insights into himself and others that have reshaped our views of man. Here he treated patients, wrote nearly all his most important works, and met with the Wednesday discussion group on whom he used to test his new ideas—the first, and for a long time the only, psychoanalytic society. It was here that Freud met his friends, and later his followers, who came from all over the world to see him. Here he lived with his family for nearly half a century. How natural it is for us to wonder, then, whether the setting permits insights into some of these famous events in the history of psychology.

But I doubt that these photographs, showing the typically Victorian surroundings in which psychoanalysis began, help to shed light on it. Studying the psychoanalytic couch in detail does not necessarily give any inkling of what psychoanalysis is all about, nor does viewing the settings in which it all happened explain the man, or his work. Still, the physical environment within which a man chooses to live, and that which he created for himself, does tell something of his style of life, of his interests and preferences. Without explaining Freud or his creation, the photographs permit some intimate glimpses into his way of life, at least as far as externals are concerned. And, as not only the psychoanalyst knows, different though the exterior may be from the interior, it is not unrelated to it.

Berggasse, "Mountain Street," is a misnomer, calling exaggerated attention to the short steep hill at one end. For most of its length the street is flat and fairly wide, and number 19 is located on this flat stretch. While the street conveys middle-class respectability, it is not that of the upper or of the intellectual middle classes. Berggasse is a dull and undistinguished street in a nondescript part of the ninth district of Vienna. And what goes for the street also holds true of number 19, as we can see in the photographs of the building's entrance and stairway, and the door to Freud's office.

As a young man I used to walk by the building, more often than not choosing to use this hilly, unattractive street to where I was going only because Freud lived there. Upon looking up at his quarters, I always wondered why this great man chose to live there, when Vienna had so many other streets that were either more attractive in themselves, had more beautiful buildings, or at least offered charming or historically interesting vistas.

Only now, from the distance of a lifetime and a continent, it occurs to me that one might well view the location of Freud's home as a symbol of the course of his life. The street's flat beginning was at the permanent Vienna flea market, the Tandelmarkt, a jumble of junk shops most of which in Freud's time were owned by poor Jewish storekeepers. Close to Berggasse's other end, on top of the hill, were the University of Vienna clinics, the university itself, and some of the choicest upper-middle-class quarters around the city hall, from which most of Freud's patients and visitors came.

Did the location of his home reflect Freud's feeling about his life? He began as the son of a Jewish merchant of quite limited means, who had had limited success in what he did. During his youth, Freud lived and went to school in Vienna's second district, as did most of Vienna's poorer Jewish population. It is quite close to this second district, in which Freud's parents continued to live, that Berggasse begins. Freud clearly left behind the life that went on in the second district, but he never gained the full professorship at the university that had long been his ambition, nor was he ever really accepted into the circles of the upper-class bourgeoisie of Vienna. There on the flat part of the street, halfway between his Jewish beginnings and the affluent and intellectual hill neighborhoods, Freud made his home. It never made sense to me as the abode of the world-famous genius who had discovered psychoanalysis, but perhaps it was the place in which he felt most comfortable because it reflected something about his external life, and the progression of his career.

The choice of his home's location may also have reflected Freud's belief in the relative unimportance of surface appearances—his perception that behind commonplace externals, much more important secret meanings may be hidden; and the more ordinary the surface, the more successfully so. Then Freud's residence in this bland, respectable, ordinary house may not have been due just to his conviction that true originality eschews its trappings—protected against unwarranted interference when hidden behind the commonplace—but also to his conviction that if we wish to understand a man, we must search for what lies behind the surface. With this in mind we are ready to appraise from Engelman's photos that which may be hidden from the eyes of the casual observer in the apartment on the mezzanine floor of Berggasse 19.

If one has not previously seen Freud's working quarters, one's curiosity immediately centers on the psychoanalytic couch as Freud devised it, his chair that stood behind it, and the desk on which he did his writing—where he composed his works and carried on the vast correspondence that, in its own way set the stage for the future of psychoanalysis. So Engelman focused his camera mainly on these three objects.

Among the innumerable objects filling the treatment room and the study, the couch is one of the central, but least interesting, features. The couch itself is covered with an oriental rug, while another hangs on the wall against which one of its long sides is pushed. Oriental rugs cover the floors—as was customary in bourgeois Vienna at that time—but they are also spread over the tables, which was less so. This would enhance the room's comfortably warm, almost cozy, atmosphere. What might be surprising is that the couch is piled high with pillows, so that the patient would rest on it in a half-sitting position, rather than a supine one. In this posture, the patient could not help taking in—unless he kept his eyes closed—a very comfortable, but extremely crowded room that everywhere reflected his analyst's highly personal—even idiosyncratic—antiquarian interests. The rooms are entirely dominated by a profusion of antiquities, a collection which he said gave him "unsurpassed comfort."

One has only to observe these photos to believe it; there are antique objects everywhere in these two rooms. They fill the walls, are crowded several rows deep on tables, on shelves, in showcases. Some twenty statuettes are even arranged on Freud's desk, so as to face him as he worked. Wherever he looked they were always before his eyes. The objects are not arranged in any systematic way, not by subject or by period or by culture. Ancient Greek and Roman objects are placed next to Egyptian and Chinese ones. (It is noteworthy that despite Freud's strong sense of Jewish identity, there are no Jewish antiquities in his collection—an understandable omission, perhaps, for a man who viewed Moses as an Egyptian. Egyptian pieces have a dominant place in the collection.) One feels that in Freud's mind each object had its assigned place in accordance with what its meaning was to him. One longs to understand why and how the very diverse objects Freud placed together fitted together in his mind.

It was not unusual in Freud's time for members of the cultivated Viennese middle class to collect art, or to limit such a collection to objects of the past. The humanistic education to which this class was exposed, with its emphasis on Roman and Greek culture, blinded many of them to the merits of the art of their own times which was being created around them; and Freud would seem to have shared this attitude. Nonetheless, there are unique aspects to his collection worth reflecting on. First, he much preferred complete objects, eschewing fragments or damaged ones. Second, his interest was essentially archaeological, not aesthetic. As Freud himself stated, formal qualities did not interest him: what mattered was what the object told about man's past, not what it revealed about man's sense of beauty.

Finally—most remarkable and, compared to the practice of other collectors, most unusual—all these many, many objects were crowded into his treatment room and study; none of them spilled over into the many rooms next door which formed the family living quarters. What more definite statement could Freud have made that his collection was part and parcel of his psychoanalytic interests, and not at all of his life as paterfamilias? It is a contrast that seems to declare: "Unique though my life as the discoverer of the unconscious is, my life with my family is ordinary." (Thus, it hardly seems worth discussing the photos of the family's quarters; they show unremarkable interiors typical of the residence of any well-off Viennese middle-class family of the time. All the furnishings we see, including the objects in the one showcase of the living quarters that is reproduced, are lacking in distinction. In the showcase are family photos and other mementos such as one would find in most rooms of the other buildings along Berggasse, or wherever a Victorian way of life prevailed.)

Because they were symbolic of his psychoanalytic work, Freud was more than ready to share his "archaeological" interests with patients and fellow analysts. Thus we can understand why the pieces Freud collected had to be ancient, why they had to have been hidden from view for a long time, had to have been "unearthed" in exactly the form in which they had been buried long ago. If these objects were important for Freud as symbols of his life's work, then we can understand why they were so crowded together in small spaces, in a seemingly disorganized jumble, just as repressed events are jumbled and crowded in the unconscious. We can also then comprehend why their aesthetic merits did not matter to Freud. For the psychoanalyst, beauty lies in the complete and undistorted recovery of what has long been buried in the unconscious, and not in whether what has been "unearthed" has any particular artistry. The deeper and longer something has been buried, the more carefully it has been made inaccessible (like objects in Egyptian graves), the greater the psychoanalytic achievement in its complete recovery. If this was the symbolic meaning of his antiquities collection for Freud, we can understand why most of the objects are of funerary origin. Not because, as has sometimes been proposed, of some connection to a death instinct, or any morbid interests centering around death. On the contrary, it may be surmised that these once-buried little treasures symbolized things deeply hidden, things not even known to exist, which nevertheless had reality and could be completely recovered, thereby adding to the enjoyment of life.

If so, one might hope that besides giving Freud a collector's joy, his assemblage, certainly an unusual one for a private man who had little time and often little money to spare, also pleasurably reminded him that he had unearthed treasures far superior even to those Schliemann had discovered. While other archaeologists have enriched our knowledge of history, made available to us objects that give aesthetic pleasure, Freud all by himself unearthed that which can free us of repression and anxiety, and thus not only give us knowledge and pleasure but also make us masters of ourselves.

How I Learned About Psychoanalysis

Seventy years ago, in the early days of psychoanalysis, one's introduction to it was likely to be very different from what it typically is today. It was usually a highly personal matter, rather than a chosen course of study.

I did not come to psychoanalysis originally because of what it had to offer people in need of therapy, nor out of intellectual curiosity, nor as part of my academic studies. Least of all did it occur to me that psychoanalysis could become my vocation. Although it eventually became the most important ingredient of my intellectual life and my main profession, this was actually a matter of pure chance and due to most personal experiences.

In the spring of 1917, the third year of the First World War, I was thirteen years old and I joined the Viennese radical youth movement called Jung Wandervogel, which was both socialist and pacifist. The group called itself the "Young" Wandervogel to emphasize its divergence from the prewar German Wandervogel movement, which had been strongly nationalistic and patriotic. But the Jung Wandervogel shared with the older youth movement an interest in radical educational reform. Ours was a small group of some fifty to a hundred adolescents. An important part of our activities during these war years was regular Sunday outings into the Viennese woods, excursions which were equally conducive to play and to the exploration of radical ideas concerning politics and human relations, including those within the family. From exploring what seemed to us new ideas about human relations, it was only a short step to forming affectionate attachments, the nature of which we so earnestly discussed.

It was in this context that I formed my first adolescent attachment to a girl my age. All seemed to go well, until one Sunday when a young man in uniform named Otto Fenichel joined our group, of which he had been an important member before he was drafted into the army. He was only a few years older than we, and had been given leave from military duties to finish his study of medicine. Much to my dismay, he concentrated his interest on the girl whom I considered to be my own.

Otto was at the time attending Freud's lectures at the University of Vienna. They were the lectures which under the title *Introductory Lectures on Psychoanalysis* subsequently became world-famous. These lectures had fascinated Otto. Like many new converts, he was not only all excited about the arcane doctrines of Freud, but felt obliged to propagandize them. While we had heard vaguely about these theories in our circle, which was eagerly taking up all new and radical ideas, we knew nothing of substance about them. So what Otto told us about Freud's teachings was all news to us.

Mostly Otto asked us about our dreams and tried to tell us their meanings, very much including their sexual meanings. This was a most alluring topic to his young listeners, particularly in view of our ambivalent attitude toward sex, characteristic of the youth movement in that period. Rejecting what we considered the stuffy bourgeois prejudices about sex of our parents' generation, and the prevailing double standard in regard to it, we were committed to sexual freedom in theory. In actuality, we repressed our sexual strivings, pretending that in doing so we were following the principles of a superior morality, thus hiding from ourselves our sexual anxieties. Holding such ambivalent attitudes about sex, we found what Otto told us of Freud's ideas concerning sex and its important role in man's life both exciting and perturbing.

The situation that day was particularly perturbing to me, as I observed that the girl I had considered my "girlfriend" gave apparent signs of being more and more interested not only in what Otto had to say but also in him as a person. The more captivated she seemed, the more furious I became, feeling badly outclassed by all the new and exciting knowledge the young medical student spouted. But since my self-love did not permit me to believe that Otto might be more interesting to her than I was, I attributed all his success to his knowledge of psychoanalysis, which by the end of the day I thoroughly hated and despised. It was psychoanalysis which I thought had alienated my girl and made her turn her affection toward my competitor. Thus we parted at the end of this, for me, fateful Sunday.

My intense anger at and scorn for psychoanalysis prevented me from falling asleep that night until finally, early in the morning, I hit on a solution. I decided that if Otto F., as he was known in the circle of the Jung Wandervogel, could win my friend by talking about psychoanalysis, I might be able to beat him at his own game by winning her back with the same method. All I had to do was to become knowledgeable about psychoanalysis, and this I would do. The decision made, I finally could fall asleep.

On Monday as soon as school let out, I went to the only bookstore in Vienna which stocked psychoanalytic publications, since it was also their publisher, and bought as many of them as I could afford. I acquired some monographs and current psychoanalytic journals and immediately began reading them. The more I did, the more surprised I became at what I was reading. I soon realized that my Victorian family, although personally acquainted with members of the Freud family, would be utterly shocked to find me perusing such obscene literature. My solution was to hide it from them by taking it to school and reading it there surreptitiously while I was supposed to be attending to studies which, by comparison, were utterly boring.

The works that impressed me most were *The Psychopathology of Everyday Life, Wit and the Unconscious,* and, because of my interest in art, the papers on Leonardo and Moses. The two first mentioned are still those of Freud's writings which are most easily accessible, so it was a fortunate chance that I was able to acquire them. *The Interpretation of Dreams* was not available to me; I do not recall whether it was out of print at the time, or if it was too expensive for me to buy. But the more I read of Freud, the more interested I became, and the more convinced that through my reading I was gaining an entirely new and most important understanding of man's psyche.

Such was my introduction to Freud and psychoanalysis. While hating it as much as I was able to hate anything because I blamed it for the loss of my girl, I was at the same time utterly fascinated by what I learned from it and certain that by becoming knowledgeable about it I could win her back. I do not know whether one could call this a belief in the practical value of psychoanalysis, but during this week in which I became converted to it, I believed in its power to gain for me what at that moment seemed the most desirable goal. So hatred of psychoanalysis and simultaneous belief in its extraordinary power stood at the beginning of its becoming an important part of my life.

Now I believe that coming to psychoanalysis in such a personal way, becoming so deeply involved emotionally and yet so ambivalently, was a most auspicious beginning.

To finish this part of my story, there was a happy ending in all respects, not just in regard to psychoanalysis gradually becoming my lifelong vocation. The next Sunday, my girlfriend and I got together again to go with the youth group to the Vienna Woods. When I began to unpack my newly acquired knowledge of psychoanalysis, she told me that this subject had been fine for one Sunday, but now we should talk about ourselves. She assured me, to my great relief, that while she had been very interested in what Otto had said about psychoanalysis, not for a moment had she been interested in him as a person or wavered in her affection for me. So now there was no reason for me to go on with psychoanalysis so far as my relation to this girl was concerned. But there was no longer any getting away from it for me. One week of complete concentration on psychoanalysis and I was hooked for life.

The young lady and I lost our romantic interest in each other a while later, but remained good lifelong friends. The reason I recount this story is to highlight the result of our different types of interest in psychoanalysis. Because this young woman's interest in psychoanalysis had been theoretical and more or less abstract, it did not take deep roots and played no significant part in her life. My interest had been anything but theoretical—from the very beginning it had been personal and very emotional, characterized by a belief that psychoanalysis could make a most important difference in one's life; and so it did in mine.

As far as I know, the pioneers of psychoanalysis came to it in quite different but more or less equally personal and emotionally conditioned ways, and psychoanalysis flourished under their influence. Hardly any of them came to it with plans to make it their profession, nor did they have any formal training in it beyond their own psychoanalysis. It was all a matter of very personal experience, not of any formal training. Today an elaborate course of study is required of people wishing to become psychoanalysts and much of the highly personal excitement psychoanalysis once created is gone; it has become an institutionalized discipline. To point out this difference and what has followed from it for the therapeutic practice of psychoanalysis, as well as for its theoretical development, is the reason I have written this brief personal history.

Some twelve years after the events just described, I entered psychoanalysis myself. In the meantime my interest in it had not flagged or changed, but I had become dissatisfied with many aspects of my life, more than I consciously realized, and I wished to gain clarity about what I wanted to do with it. Although I desired an academic career, at this time a Jew had no hope of becoming a university professor in Austria. I had begun my university studies by concentrating on literature and Germanics. After several years I found them less and less engrossing, so I changed my study emphasis to philosophy and art history. These I found more interesting and satisfying. But the question of how to spend my life remained open, since these studies did not seem to offer a chance of making a living through them.

While I was able to earn a good living from an inherited business, I found the business boring and disliked many aspects of it; it was not at all to my taste. Although some of my closest friends had become psychoanalysts, I had hesitated to follow their example, partly because I did not wish to be a copycat, and partly because I was not impressed by what becoming psychoanalysts had done for them personally. That the latter view was due to my resistance I am now quite ready to acknowledge, but did not realize then.

Thus the influences that brought me to consider going into psychoanalysis were events in my private life, a dissatisfaction with the way I was living it, and feelings of inferiority and depression which, although not very serious, I knew rationally had no objective cause but must come from my unconscious. Despite these factors it was finally a crisis in my married life which convinced me to give psychoanalysis a try, thinking it might not be a bad idea to discover what it could do for me.

Being good friends with so many of the small group of younger Viennese analysts proved to be a problem, because I had to find one with whom I was not well acquainted. But there was at least one among them—Dr. Richard Sterba—who was well recommended to me by an analyst friend whom I trusted. So with some hesitation I made an appointment to see him to discuss matters.

At that time, the practice in Vienna was to meet your future analyst for the first time in a more or less social setting, to discuss practical matters, such as the time of the daily sessions, the fee, and whatever other issues needed to be clarified. If the decision was then to begin psychoanalysis, on the very next meeting you had to lie down on the couch to engage in free associations, with the psychoanalyst sitting behind the couch in a formal, professional situation.

On this first meeting, after we had discussed the time of the sessions and the fee I was to pay, I revealed my doubts about going into analysis. I first asked Dr. Sterba whether he thought I really needed to do so. His answer was that he had not the slightest idea now; he might know whether or not I needed it in perhaps a year, or possibly two, but by then I would know it too, and would not need to be told by him. This hardly reassured me about my question, so after some further small talk I asked him whether psychoanalysis would help me. To this his answer was pretty much the same as before; at this moment he had no idea, and he would not know any sooner than would I.

These answers failed to reduce my doubts, so, with some desperation, I finally asked him what reason there could be for me to go into psychoanalysis. To this he replied that from our conversation he had learned that for many years I had been interested in psychoanalysis. Because of this, the only promise he felt able to give me was that I would find the experience very interesting because I would discover things about myself that I had not known before. This would permit me to understand myself better and would make many aspects of my life and behavior more comprehensible to me. Since I had the time and the money to undergo psychoanalysis, why not find out more about myself?

At that I decided here was a man whom I could trust, because he did not make promises when there was no certainty he could keep them, even though, as I knew, he was interested in my entering analysis with him. His candor made me entrust myself to him.

Very recently I was invited to present a lecture in honor of Dr. Sterba's ninetieth birthday. I began by telling about our first meeting. In response to this, he said that he had not the slightest recollection of it, something I had expected. He did not remember having said these things, because they came quite naturally to him; our interchange had not seemed remarkable to him, only to me. His refusal to make empty promises, much as I wanted to hear them, had made me trust him and his psychoanalytic skills. It was something I never regretted, as it changed much of my life for the better.

Today, all too often, psychoanalysts with the best of intentions give their patients the impression that they have superior knowledge about what ails the patient and why. Sometimes they even permit themselves to be seduced into making promises to their patients. That is to say, they essentially adopt the classic medical model, according to which the doctor knows things the patient does not, and so can, indeed must, tell the patient what to do. It was my own analyst's determined refusal to follow this model—his insistence that he had no idea how my analysis would proceed or what it would achieve, his statement that if he did find out important things about me, he would certainly not find them out any sooner than I did—that placed psychoanalysis for me into a quite different and more humane perspective. For what he thereby made clear was that psychoanalysis was not something he would unilaterally do *to* or *for* me, but rather a joint undertaking in which the participation of both of us was critical; we were two human beings about to engage in a voyage of discovery which would be of great and common interest. To be sure, we were not really equal partners in this enterprise, since, as he pointed out, he had knowledge superior to mine about psychoanalysis and, more important, skill and experience in it. (And, indeed, why else would I be consulting him?) But we *were* equal in our efforts to learn significant things about me. This I found most reassuring, since it allayed my anxiety that things might be done *to* me without my knowing what they were or having any power to influence, shape, or prevent them.

Maybe the popular American view of the psychoanalyst as a "headshrinker" highlights best the difference between how things are done today in America and how they were done then in Vienna. The reason this headshrinker image is so widely accepted in America (although it is always recognized as a funny and ironic image that puts the psychoanalyst down a few pegs) is, I believe, that it represents the patient's reaction to the psychoanalyst's belief that he is superior to the patient. The very notion of a headshrinker clearly implies that the therapist does to the patient what he decided needs to be done in the patient's best interest (that is, once again, the medical model).

I am not suggesting that today's analysts approach their patients differently than mine did me because they lack human decency. I believe, rather, that their attitudes largely reflect the institutionalization of psychoanalysis as a highly skilled therapeutic specialty, and by certain rigidities resulting from the long, demanding, and complex training psychoanalytic institutes require of candidates.

In Vienna, it should be noted, while a majority of the psychoanalysts were physicians, a number of prominent ones were not. In the beginning days of psychoanalysis, analysts treated patients in their homes and not in offices, six sessions a week at exactly the same time each day. Freud did this, and so did nearly all the other Viennese physicians. Characteristically, Freud's treatment room, in its furnishings, especially the collection of archaeological artifacts which filled it, was testimony to his dominant interests and also a clear and definite expression of his personality. (This is discussed in some detail in the essay "Berggasse 19.") Thus the original setting in which psychoanalysis took place was a very personal one, reflecting the individuality and interest of the therapist. This contrasts strongly with the impersonal and rather sterile settings which most present-day American psychoanalysts prefer for their work.

During their working hours, most Viennese analysts used their living rooms as the waiting room for their patients; thus it, like the treatment room, was an integral part of the analyst's home. This was true also of my analyst, and since his wife was one of the earliest child analysts, her patients used the same waiting room as did his. Both husband and wife did try to arrange things so that their patients would not meet; but if one patient came a bit earlier than scheduled or another ran late, then patients whose session times overlapped sometimes encountered each other in the waiting room. Such meetings were awkward, and yet curiosity tempted one to become acquainted.

Around the same time of day I saw my analyst, his wife treated a psychotic child whom I shall call Johnny. It was many years before such specific diagnostic terms were used for children, so at the time his disturbance had no name. Without worrying about etiology or classification, one called such children abnormal and attempted to help them analytically. Johnny's utterly withdrawn and bizarre behavior did not invite interactions. Still, when we met from time to time, I tried to say a few friendly words to this obviously terrified child. He either did not react or responded with a monosyllable.

On the windowsill of the waiting room stood some small potted cacti, fashionable in Vienna at the time. Johnny had the disconcerting habit of plucking one of the leaves full of sharp thorns, putting it into his mouth, and chewing it. The spines must have hurt his lips, gums, and tongue; occasionally I saw his lips bleed. Watching him hurt himself in this way always upset me, but for a long time I did not openly react.

One day, however, when I had been in analysis for about two years, I could not restrain myself and, although knowing it was wrong, I blurted out: "Johnny, I don't know how long you have been seeing Dr. Sterba, but it must be at least two years, since I have known you for that long, and here you are still chewing these awful leaves!" In response, this scrawny little boy suddenly seemed to grow in stature—I still do not know how he managed to give me the impression that at this moment he was looking down on me—and said with utter disdain: "What are two years compared with eternity?" It was the first time he had uttered a full sentence, and it left me flabbergasted.

While I was still trying to recover and make sense of what Johnny had said, my analyst ushered me into his office. As soon as I lay down on the couch I realized that what I had said to Johnny had not been motivated by unselfish concern about the pain he was inflicting on himself, as I had thought when I made the remark. On the contrary, my involvement had been entirely with myself. For some time I had been worrying whether there was any point to my analysis. Because of this worry, watching Johnny chew cactus leaves made me wonder whether his analysis was doing him any good and by implication whether analysis was doing anybody any good. This is why I had framed my remark so as to suggest that he had made insufficient progress in the years I had known him.

Unconsciously, I had hoped that Johnny's answer would either make it clear that we both were wasting our time by being in analysis or convince me that his analysis was doing him some good, despite his continuing to chew cactus leaves, suggesting that my analysis also probably was doing me some good, although I felt I could discern no signs of it. Having thought this through in silence helped me to overcome my strong resistance against talking about my doubts concerning whether analysis was helpful to me, and I began to analyze what was behind them. But I could not get Johnny's remark out of my mind, partly because of my guilt for having pretended concern with him when in fact I had been selfishly trying to use him to solve one of my own pressing problems, and by doing so had tried to put the value analysis had for him into question.

Intuitively, Johnny must have understood what I was up to: that I was dissatisfied with the comparatively long time—or what seemed to me too long a time—I had by then spent in analysis, and that I was using him to unload my dissatisfaction. He put me in my place by, in effect, telling me that my judgment of time was all wrong, that it did not apply to the work involved in psychoanalyzing oneself. Johnny's intuition had permitted him to perceive that what I needed at the moment was to gain a better perspective on time, if I wanted to derive the best results from my analysis. It was his intuition, and the concise way in which he expressed it, which permitted me to learn to be patient, first about my own analysis, and later about the time required by others to reshape their personalities.

Actually, with his seven short words, Johnny taught me many things—some of which I understood right away, others which took years to absorb. This is usually true for intuitive insights, as compared to more explicit teachings, the lessons of which can be made one's own in a much shorter time because they rarely touch the core of one's personal problems as an intuitive statement can.

For example, in a flash Johnny had taught me how inclined we are to believe that the wellspring of our action is concern for the other, rather than self-involvement; and how much we can learn about ourselves from others, provided we accept that what they say or do may reveal things not only about them, but also about us. I had learned this from studying the psychoanalytic literature, but had absorbed it as an abstract concept. Only after it became part of this unsettling experience did theory become personal knowledge. This process confirmed for me that only through one's personal experiences can one fully understand what psychoanalytic theory is really all about.

Simultaneously, Johnny taught me the difference between objective and psychological or experiential time. When one's sufferings are unending, and therefore seem eternal, then two years spent trying to escape them are but a moment. Johnny taught me that the magnitude of one's misery alters the meaning of all experiences, including that of time—something which I later experienced during a year spent in German concentration camps.

Johnny's comment about time permitted me to grasp that neither I nor anybody else can put a limit on the amount of time one needs to become able to cope or to change, and that trying to hurry up the process has more to do with one's own anxieties than with anything else. Only people themselves can judge when they are ready to change.

Over the years, through my work at the Sonia Shankman Orthogenic School of the University of Chicago, I learned to understand psychotic children, and I appreciated the importance of this lesson about time even more. Only when given unlimited time did these children come to trust I was on their side, and not against them, as they perceived the rest of the world to be in trying to have them change their ways. Encouraging them to proceed on the basis of their sense of time was demonstration to them that, given their experience of the world, their reactions were taken by us to be as valid for them as were ours for us. When, on occasion, I got restless after having sat silently for hours, trying to reach a catatonic, I had only to recall Johnny's statement. Then time again became totally unimportant, and I was once more in contact with the patient. It worked like a charm. As soon as I stopped worrying that time was passing and nothing was happening, I also stopped making inner demands on myself and on the patient, and stopped wishing his silence would end. In response, eventually the patient did something significant that permitted gaining a better understanding of his experience of the world, and of what it had been in me that had prevented him from relating.

Other parts of the lesson Johnny taught me took much longer to sink in. Off and on I pondered why Johnny had spoken so clearly to me only on this single occasion, and in a complete sentence to boot. After years of working with psychotics I came to understand the crucial difference my motive in relating to them made in their ability to relate, and in their view of themselves. I could elicit no response if my motive was to "help" them. But if I sincerely wanted them to enlighten me about something of great importance about which they possessed knowledge unavailable to me, they could respond. My belief that Johnny could give me information (about the value of psychoanalysis) I did not possess put us on an equal footing that allowed this completely unrelating child to relate to me, at least for the time of this interaction. That something crucial in his experience was also so in mine established a bond of common humanity. While in all other encounters I had never taken Johnny for my equal, this one time I had done so, by accepting that as patients in analysis, we had experiences which were parallel. This is what made significant communication possible. From many experiences with other psychotic individuals, I learned later that it was this kind of relating which permits extension to other experiences and finally the establishment of true personal relations.

Only in this one encounter had I treated Johnny as a person who had superior knowledge on a matter of greatest significance—was psychoanalysis doing much good? At all other times when we met, I had felt superior to him. This time I had unconsciously hoped that this crazy child would solve my most pressing problem. And so he proceeded to do exactly that.

When I had finally realized all this, it hit me how little attention I had paid to the fact that as Johnny spoke, he had taken the cactus leaf out of his mouth, which he did on no other occasion before or afterward when he deigned to reply with some nearly inaudible monosyllable. Not only that, but after he spoke, he had put down the leaf; he had no longer needed to chew it. Had I then and there understood Johnny's behavior, I would have learned that when one truly communicates with the psychotic, he does not need his symptoms. This happens when he is put in control of the interaction, as in this case where he had important knowledge to impart, not about himself—this most therapists believe to be true of their patients—but about what was going on in me. My belief that Johnny had better knowledge than I about a matter of great importance provided, at least for the moment, so much security that for the period of our interaction he did not need his symptom.

That Johnny's original trauma had been an oral one explains the particular choice of pain; hurting his mouth. But this I would not have needed to know, because his choice of this symptom made it clear. I learned later that the origin of his misery had been extreme traumatization at the beginning of his life when he was unable to do anything about it. By inflicting on himself a parallel pain, he tried not only to obliterate through pain the mental images which tortured him, but to convince himself that now he could be in control of a pain over which he had been able to exercise no control whatsoever, when it had destroyed him as a human being. Had I understood this at the time, Johnny would have also taught me all one needs to know about the causes and meaning of self-mutilation.

My study of Freud had taught me that one can truly understand another only from the other's frame of reference, not from one's own. This I had learned well as a theoretical concept. But it was Johnny who taught me how easy it is to believe that one has made such a principle one's own, so long as one's strong emotions are not involved. But once one's emotions are aroused, it becomes extremely difficult not to see things only from one's own frame of reference. All the times I had with an inner shudder observed Johnny's chewing of cactus leaves, I had viewed it as a sign of his craziness—not as the indication of his most pressing needs and of their not-so-symbolic expression. Later experience taught me to be ashamed of my readiness to see such things as strange or even nonsensical when in truth they conveyed deep meaning. This principle is basic to all social sciences: one can understand the behavior of others only from their frame of reference. Making the effort to remember this is increasingly necessary, the more one's own needs tempt one to respond on the basis of one's own reactions to a behavior.

I had believed that I had truly learned—if not from Freud, even earlier from Terence's *Humani nil a me alienum puto*—that to be truly human means not being alienated from anything human. Still, I had permitted myself to be alienated by Johnny's behavior. Realizing my insensitivity to his suffering, which prevented me from understanding why he acted as he did, taught me from then on always to believe that whatever the behavior, it would seem the most natural thing for me to do were I in the other's situation. I believe it was this conviction that permitted me, years later, to understand the behavior of SS guards in the concentration camps, and this understanding helped me greatly to survive being there. Again, later, when I began to work with psychotics, this principle permitted me to understand them and become attuned to what their behavior might signify.

Because Johnny's chewing of cactus leaves had horrified me, I could not realize that when he was doing something so painful, it must be of tremendous importance. Not accepting it as a challenge to my understanding, I had failed to concentrate on discovering the meaning of his behavior. To understand what Johnny did, I had to ask myself what would induce me to do it. As I tried to imagine what would make me inflict such physical pain on myself, I realized that if I lived entirely wrapped up in an endless nightmare of persecutory and destructive fantasies, compared to which Hieronymus Bosch's Hell would be a pleasure garden, then anything that would at least temporarily obliterate these fantasies would be a relief. Severe physical pain makes it practically impossible to think of anything else, enough reason to prefer it to extreme mental anguish.

When pain is self-inflicted, it is limited in degree and time, while the psychotic's mental suffering is unlimited in degree and time. Finally and most important, if my pain is self-inflicted, I am its master, I can start and stop it; but I am entirely at the mercy of mental tortures over which I have no control. It becomes understandable, then, that Johnny wished to replace the most intense sufferings from his delusions, over which he had no power or control, by suffering over which he had complete control, as he had over chewing cactus leaves.

Finally, I eventually came to an understanding of still other significant aspects of Johnny's behavior, those which had to do more directly with psychoanalysis, what it is all about, and what one hopes to gain from it. Firstly, the cacti in the living room were, as Johnny either knew or surmised, of interest to his analyst; typically it is the lady of the house who takes care of the plants in her living room. Thus the cactus leaves were something that came from her, were connected with his analyst. Much more important, Johnny hoped to gain through something received from her—as were the cactus leaves—control over what life did to him. So with his seven short words, Johnny had conveyed to me also the essence of what a patient hopes to achieve for himself through his analysis, and what analysis should do for each patient: permit him to become able to control what goes on in his life.

I wish I could have been able to teach the essentials of psychoanalysis to my students in as short, concise, and impressive a form as Johnny taught them to me. In fact, it took in my case many years before I learned this last simple lesson. It thus may take many years until one understands what psychoanalysis is all about, not just with one's head— that is easy—but with one's innermost being. I learned to be patient with my students and my patients when it took them a long time to comprehend and act upon things it had taken me so many years to comprehend myself.

My experiences with psychoanalysis, of which I have recounted only two early and crucial events, have convinced me that it is not the theoretical mastery of a problem which permits its deepest understanding. It is one's inner experiences that permit gaining a full grasp of what is involved in the inner experiences of others, a knowledge which then can become the basis for theoretical studies.

Two Views of Freud

I

ERNEST JONES'S FREUD:

A DISSENTING OPINION

About the difficulty of writing biographies Freud expressed himself very succinctly:

"Whoever undertakes to write a biography binds himself to lying, to concealment, to hypocrisy, to flummery and even to hiding his own lack of understanding."

So in 1936 the eighty-year-old Sigmund Freud, with his own biography in mind, expressed himself to Arnold Zweig, who had proposed to write it. This quotation, coming after more than twelve hundred pages in Ernest Jones's biography of Freud, impresses us once again with Freud's wisdom and the validity of his view of man and man's efforts.

After reporting Freud's comment Jones adds that he feels sure that "Freud would have been surprised to find that one could get nearer to the truth about himself than he imagined possible." This is but one place out of many in Jones's three-volume biography of Freud where Jones declares that his view has more validity than Freud's. But after having

In this essay two discussions of Jones's biography of Freud are combined, one which appeared in *The American Journal of Sociology* of January 1957 and another which appeared in *The New Leader* of May 19, 1958, with some new additional remarks. It seemed worthwhile to reprint these criticisms of Jones's biography of Freud the man and his exposition of Freud's work, since these three volumes are still considered the most authoritative discussion of Freud's life and of his writings.

read Jones's biography, this reviewer still feels that Freud was right about most things, including his view of the predicament in which his biographer would find himself.

The extremely laudatory response to this biography, particularly to the first and second volumes, was probably due to the curiosity which the founder of psychoanalysis evokes, to the wish to learn more about the early history of psychoanalysis and about the kind of person and experiences it took to invent it. Unfortunately this biography, though voluminous, has many shortcomings in all three respects. For long stretches it belabors the obvious, while failing to tell us what we want most to know about the hero and his creation; there are also many errors of omission and commission. Some of this was to be expected. Doing justice to the extremely complex person who was Freud, while at the same time explaining the intricate personalities of those who surrounded him, and trying to illuminate the ambivalent relationships that existed among them all would be difficult for any biographer, let alone one whose personal participation and obvious partisanship diluted his objectivity.

Jones's taking on the task of this biography fulfilled the public's wish to have the master's work expounded by a man who was close to Freud. Jones was also a central figure in the development of psychoanalysis as an international movement—more reason to want to hear the devoted disciple.

During work on the last volume (or volumes), Jones probably knew that the end of his own life was approaching, and so he worked against time. With the biographer's life so closely interwoven with his hero's, it is not surprising that when the "finis" was written on Freud's biography, Jones's days ended, too. This and much more suggest that a reviewer should be considerate rather than critical of an author who strove hard and put his best into what was certainly a labor of love. But Freud was not just another man, he was the shaper of modern man's thought about man; and this is not just another effort at presenting the life of Freud, it is officially and widely acclaimed as the definitive biography of Freud and of psychoanalysis—more, as one of the greatest biographies of modern times.

The *New York Times* reviewer proclaimed this work one of the outstanding biographies of the age. *Time* magazine, not usually friendly to psychoanalysis and generally quite critical of Freud, similarly called it a masterpiece of contemporary biography. (One wonders whether, given the weekly's bias, it was not secretly pleased that the biography so obviously failed to bring Freud the man to life.) *The New Yorker* called it a "superb drama"; here the reviewer probably confused Jones's pedestrian presentation of Freud's life with the intrinsic drama and fascination of his life.

The critical reader, however, may detect in the tedious repetition, the oversimplified exposition of Freud's theories, and the long stretches of Jones's history of the psychoanalytic movement an uninspired rewrite of the much more exciting history Freud himself wrote and published many years ago. Apparently the reviewers' veneration for the subject blinded them to obvious shortcomings of biographer and biography. Such an extension of hero worship—from the subject of a biography to the biography itself and the person who has written it—is certainly an interesting psychological phenomenon, about which Freud might well have had much to say.

Although this should not be considered the definitive biography of Freud, it is certainly an official biography, presenting that picture of Freud which members of the inner circle of official psychoanalysis desired to have accepted as definitive. With all these pretensions, it must be asked whether these three volumes render a picture of Freud that does justice to him and to psychoanalysis. If not, fealty to Freud and the importance of psychoanalysis must take precedence over respect for the biographer, even if Dr. Jones is unfortunately no longer here to defend himself.

This thought became certainty for me upon reading the official *Journal of the American Sociological Society*, an organ usually devoted to critical judgment, not blind admiration. I found spelled out there what I secretly feared as I read Jones's three volumes and their reviews: that there is danger the future will receive not the teachings of Freud, but the explanations of Jones; that psychoanalysis will not be what Freud hoped for, but what Jones made of it. The journal's review begins as follows:

Great masters need great disciples: it is a prerequisite of greatness among those who found movements. . . . Paul is the greatest example of discipleship in the history of our culture, for it is his Jesus that lives, not the historical one.

That master is fortunate who may not see, among his disciples, the closest fall away. . . . Inevitably, Luther had his Carlstadt. Freud had not merely his Jung but also his Rank and Ferenczi. Fortunately for him, Freud retained his Jones. Of the original "committee"—founded by Jones to create a "bodyguard around Freud" and at the same time to carry his message out into the world—some died and others departed; Ernest Jones remained.

Here they are, the allusions to uncritical belief rather than to the rational mind; to the founding of religion rather than to scientific discovery; to messages carried out into the world rather than verifiable data which can and should be subjected to scientific scrutiny. However, if we want to know Jesus, we go to the historical Jesus, not the Pauline Christ. The man who wrote *The Future of an Illusion* did not found a religion, yet we are told that these apostles' accounts of the master will be more important than the master's real life and that the accounts, not the reality, will live in the world. This is a most unfortunate view, similar to not being able to distinguish between fiction and nonfiction.

In this same review, we are told that "Jones completed the task of reconciliation; he has brought Freud to the world." Yes, as Paul brought Christ rather than Jesus to the world, Jones had now given us his image of Freud and of psychoanalysis. But it is neither the historical Freud nor the true history of psychoanalysis. Jones gave us the Freud he understood, psychoanalysis as he interpreted it, but any student of psychoanalysis knows that the picture a disciple gives of his master tells more about the disciple than the master. Of this principle of psychoanalysis Freud's official biographer remained so unaware that he never even mentioned it as a possibility.

Jones does discuss the problem of disciples vs. master, again and again. But whenever he presents it, he decides matters in his own favor, as against Freud and Freud's other disciples. Repeatedly, we hear how Jones was correct from the beginning and how Freud often erred in his judgment of friends, of ideas, and even of his own writings. Since this is the core of my criticism, I should let Jones speak for himself on at least one of these three issues. Here he is on whether Freud meant what he wrote. Speaking of himself and his collaborators on "the enormous labor of translating Freud's work," Jones writes: "We sent him question after question about slight ambiguities in his expositions, and made various suggestions concerning inner contradictions and the like. This process has continued ever since . . . with the noteworthy result that the English translation of Freud's works . . . [will] be considerably more trustworthy than any German version."

Thus Jones declares the disciple's rendering of his master's writings into a foreign language to be "considerably more trustworthy" than what the master himself wrote in his native language. Jones was terribly proud of eliminating the ambiguities and contradictions, yet these are essential to Freud's view of humanity and to psychoanalysis as a growing and developing science of man's mind. In place of Freud's chosen words, we are told to accept as the only authorized version the "more trustworthy," objective "vulgate," the disciple's translation of Freud's work into a language foreign to his thinking. One may imagine how the skeptical Freud, worn down by the tiring questions of this disciple about supposed contradictions and ambiguities, finally gave in, realizing that it was hopeless to get Jones to understand that being able to accept living, thinking, and working with seeming or real ambiguities forms the essence of psychoanalysis.

What might Freud have thought had he been presented with the idea that a translation into a foreign language was more trustworthy than what he himself had written? The fact is that Freud is recognized as one of the great masters of modern German, and he was very deeply concerned with how he put his ideas into words in the language he loved. So why should we believe that a translation is more trustworthy?*

Let us return to the idea of a definitive biography. What a splendid history of Freud the man could have been written if official psychoanalysis had not sealed the Freud archives, with over 2,500 of his letters, for fifty years when they were deposited in the Library of Congress. The reason for this was that the Freud archives also contain interviews with some of his former patients. To reveal the contents of these interviews before that time might be embarrassing for them and their families. What likeness of Freud would emerge if these letters could be made available in their entirety? All we have is the parsimonious and puritanical selection which Jones has presented in ways that barely allow us to

---

* In 1982, many years after this critique of Jones's biography of Freud was written, I published a small volume showing in some detail how untrue to Freud and his thoughts the English translations often are, so there is no point in demonstrating this here in some detail. Interested readers may wish to consult my *Freud and Man's Soul*.

get a feeling for Freud as a human being. One letter that Freud wrote to his family from Rome (which Jones fortunately reprints), excerpts from others of his letters to be found in the text and in the appendices to Volumes II and III, as well as quotations such as that mentioned at the start of this review reveal far more of Freud than do the many hundreds of pages in which Jones writes about him.

Thus, the truly significant value of these volumes derives from the passages where Freud is quoted and from the anecdotes and facts given about him and the figures who surrounded him. Since much of this was not available before in printed form, we must be grateful for it. But why such meager fare? Why so interlarded with directions about how we must and must not understand the genius of Freud, the life histories of his followers, and their motives for remaining "true" to Freud or parting ways with him? Unfortunately for his readers, Dr. Jones could not make up his mind whether he wanted to give us the story of Freud's life or an exposition of psychoanalysis; whether to give us an objective history of the psychoanalytic movement or a justification for its vagaries. In trying to do all, he failed in each.

The first volume reads much better than the following two, if only because it deals mostly with Freud's life before Jones entered it, so Jones could not, as so often in the later volumes, point to himself as the one who had been correct from the start. By comparison, the second and third volumes suffer seriously from Jones's self-justifications and from being so largely taken up with inadequate expositions of Freud's writings and a biased history of the psychoanalytic movement.

Dr. Jones's original great contribution to the psychoanalytic movement was to make it an international one. Therefore, it is even more regrettable that in writing its history Jones tries so hard to prove that except for himself, only those of Freud's followers who were never critical of anything the master said or did were entirely free of neurosis and were, like Jones himself, motivated only by the highest moral considerations. These true disciples were never touched by ambivalence, and this was more true of his biographer than of anyone else. Those close to Freud, such as Ferenczi, who was the closest of all, were unfortunately terribly neurotic, so we are told. Rank, who was one of Freud's closest collaborators for years, was subject to more-than-neurotic depressions, which, according to Jones, distorted his judgments. Critics of Freud among his early disciples (other than Jones) were never motivated by valid reasoning, but only by their jealousy, if indeed they did not have psychopathic motives.

To a psychoanalyst, it is particularly distressing that a biography of Freud written by a prominent analyst should be so unpsychoanalytic. For example, Freud before his self-analysis is described as a very neurotic individual, which he undoubtedly was. But his self-analysis, which, like the analysis of any other person, formed the crucial psychological event of his adult life, is dealt with in barely nine pages of a life history over fifteen hundred pages long! There is abundant source material on it, readily available in Freud's *Interpretation of Dreams,* but Jones ignores this. Indeed, the book itself, Freud's most important, is disposed of in fourteen pages, most of which are taken up by an enumeration of the many editions in which it appeared and how much Freud was paid in royalties.

How unpsychoanalytic Jones, as biographer, can be is further illustrated by the way he disposes of what may have been one of Freud's most important intimate relations. Speaking of Freud's sister-in-law, who for forty-two years lived as part of the Freud family in the Freuds' apartment, Jones states flatly and authoritatively: "There was no sexual attraction on either side." One must wonder about the man Freud who traveled for long periods alone with this mature woman, roomed in hotels with her, but did not find her sexually attractive; one wonders even more how it was possible for this woman not to become sexually attracted to Freud. What kind of woman was she? What kind of man was Freud that he should choose as the preferred companion of his mature years a woman sexually unattractive to him? And if he was such a man, would it not be the prime task of a psychoanalytic biographer to explain this in some detail?

This particular psychoanalytic biographer seems to have felt that sexual attraction between sister-in-law and brother-in-law need not be considered as a possibility, even when the two shared home, ideas, holidays, rooms—the husband so interested in the woman's company that he left wife and children behind. What of psychoanalysis and what it tries to teach, if this was so? Those who have wondered about this relationship seem to have been more psychoanalytically inclined than the psychoanalytic biographer, who labels (rather than discusses) their speculation as "malicious gossip." Evidence missing, this reviewer is willing to believe that possibly the relationship was a purely platonic one. But then we must be told what this must have meant for the man and the woman.

Most distressing for those who try to understand Freud from this biography is its failure to set Freud within the context of his society and its culture. For example, Jones describes Freud's early years as a boy and later as a student at the University of Vienna as if he had been poverty-stricken but, despite it and by his own strength, managed to work his way to fame and success. In reality, while Freud's parents were not well-to-do, they certainly belonged to the Jewish middle class; they were by no means poor. For a Jewish family of the 1880s to have lived in a flat of six rooms meant that they were quite well off. The conditions of Freud's life may seem deprived by the standards of a good middle-class American family of today. But they were excellent when compared with the near-ghetto existence from which Freud's father escaped by moving to Vienna. Freud's deep attachment to the empire of Franz Joseph and to Vienna, which he shared with most of his Jewish contemporaries, must be understood as part of the tremendous social and economic advancement that his father's generation had experienced. The hardships of anti-Semitism came later and were superimposed on an entirely different basis of gratitude and expectation, built up during Freud's father's lifetime and Freud's own earliest years.

Among European Jews of the early twentieth century, an oft-repeated and much-enjoyed riddle was the question of how to prove that the Jews were the chosen people when they had always been persecuted or in misery. The answer was: "But you forget how good we had it under Franz Joseph!" Because of their experience of ever greater self-realization, the Jews of Vienna, in the last half of the nineteenth century, had no choice but to love their culture dearly. So Freud's supposed "hatred" of Vienna was probably the expression of a deep early love that became frustrated by anti-Semitism in the early twentieth century, a frustration the more keenly felt as the earlier love was never given up.

It is within this social context that Freud's life must be comprehended; yet Jones fails utterly to understand it. Repeatedly he mentions Freud's hatred of Vienna, and strangely enough does not question why, if Freud hated Vienna so much, he could not bring himself to leave it, but remained there after the Nazis came, until it was impossible to stay any longer. Here, as in many other instances, Freud's great discovery of the ambivalence of human emotions seems not to apply to Freud him-self—not, at least, according to his biographer.

Jones also shows himself unfamiliar with a correlative pattern among the intellectual society of Vienna—the pretense of speaking disparagingly of Vienna, which was nothing but a cover-up of an irrational love-attachment to the city and its culture. Instead of recognizing this and explaining its neurotic ambivalent nature to the reader, Jones presents only the negative side of Freud's ambivalence. He never elucidates those positive aspects that were obviously stronger, since they always won out.

For example, we are told that Berlin's relative liberalism aroused the envy of Freud, who "had to live in a city ruled by the anti-Semitic Mayor Lueger, and where anti-Semitism prevailed." But the fact is that Freud did not have to live in Vienna; he chose to live there despite the anti-Semitism. Nor are we told that the leading aristocracy was strongly opposed to the lower-middle-class anti-Semitism of Lueger, which it was. It was actually the lower-class anti-Semitism which, in a strange way, brought the Jewish intelligentsia into close contact with an upper-class aristocracy that would otherwise have remained closed to it. But this is only one of many examples of Jones's total misunderstanding of the Vienna which was so important in shaping the man Freud.

It would be wrong to conclude that there is no value in acquainting oneself with this biography. It contains too many revealing incidents of Freud's history, and too many meaningful glimpses into his daily life which are not available elsewhere. But the reader will have to be careful to draw his own conclusions from what Jones reports, and to reject Jones's many misinterpretations.

Only one of many anecdotes may be quoted to show how revealing of Freud these volumes can be as source material. Jones tells how, during meals, Freud would not talk to his family because he enjoyed his food so much that he concentrated on eating instead. If one of his children was absent, Freud "would point mutely at the vacant chair with his knife or fork and look inquiringly to his wife at the other end of the table. She would explain that the child was not coming in to dinner or that something or other had detained him, whereupon Freud, with his curiosity satisfied, would nod silently and proceed with his meal."

In an excerpt from a letter to Jung, Freud says of his method of therapy that "it is in essence a cure through love." To have this authoritative statement about the nature of psychoanalytic therapy, with its utter refutation of the technicians of the deep interpretations and the artisans of the dynamic dissection of the human psyche, makes one grateful for these volumes. As a collection of anecdotes, they are of very great merit. As a biography of Freud the man and as a statement about psychoanalysis, they have many shortcomings. As a history of the psychoanalytic movement, they do injustice to the personalities and contributions of many who were closest to Freud, and thus are misleading. And as a statement of the society and times out of which Freud (and with him psychoanalysis) grew, they are a failure.

II

FROMM ON FREUD

One cannot escape comparing Fromm's one thin volume on Freud with Ernest Jones's three huge ones, however different in approach and intention they are. Out of Fromm's essay Freud emerges alive and of vital concern to us, and by showing how much still remains to be done, Fromm hands us a challenge. By contrast, Jones has erected a monument to his master, giving the impression that all problems related to Freud and psychoanalysis are solved; that all is said and done. In so doing, Jones turns Freud into a major historic figure, which he is—but of the past, which he is not.

Fromm begins with a psychologically convincing and balanced picture of Freud the man and his background, highlighting the tremendous achievements, but not glossing over Freud's failings, always intent on showing how psychoanalysis flowed from both. This is followed by some startlingly new material; Fromm tells of Freud's need and desire

This review of Erich Fromm's book *Sigmund Freud's Mission* (New York: Harper, 1959) appeared in *The New Leader,* May 11, 1959. It should be read together with the preceding essay on Jones's biography of Freud, since it is a companion piece.

his ideas down to our earth, into the human mind. Certainty lay only in reason, a reason he narrowly defined as intellect.

Freud believed that feelings and emotions were irrational and therefore suspect. Unlike Spinoza, he did not accept the view that emotions, like thoughts, can be both rational and irrational, and that the full development of man requires the rational development of both his thoughts and his emotions. Like many philosophers of the Enlightenment, Freud could not see that if man's thinking is split off from his feeling, both become distorted. So much was Freud dedicated to the absolute power of reason that it took him years to overcome the wishful notion that an intellectual grasp of the causes of neurotic symptoms would automatically cure them. His deep passion for rationality as the only basis for security was matched by an extraordinary courage, kept up even in the face of the heaviest obstacles.

Freud's relations to others have to be understood on the basis of his distrust of emotions and his single-minded pursuit of intellectual certainty. Fromm sketches the difficulties Freud met in his relations to women, and the entirely different ones which marred his relations to men. All this has been described in other biographies, though rarely with such acute psychological understanding.

Most biographers have neglected Freud's relationship to his father. Fromm stresses its importance and shows that first in relation to his father and then in regard to matters general, Freud was a rebel, not a revolutionary. He was a rebel when he defied public opinion and medical authority, but he was not a revolutionary, because he wanted to be, and became, an authority for others to submit to. Freud's rebellion was directed against those in authority who did not acknowledge him, and the first of these was his father.

According to Fromm, a person does not overcome his ambivalence toward authority until he frees himself from the attachment to authority that makes him wish to dominate others; only then can he change from rebel into revolutionary. In this sense Freud was and remained a rebel. While he defied authorities and enjoyed his defiance, he was still deeply impressed by the existing social order and its authorities. Gaining recognition from them was of utmost concern to him.

Fromm finds the root of Freud's authoritarian behavior in his wish to create a political movement and remain its leader. It was this "political" desire, and not a crude authoritarianism, for example, that made Freud

to become a world reformer, and of the consequences this had for psy
choanalysis, which therefore became less a scientific society and more
a semireligious movement.

The Janus-like character of psychoanalysis as both a new science
and a reform movement finds its expression in the nature of those great
men with whom Freud compared himself. Occasionally he likened himself to Columbus, the discoverer of a new continent, just as he himself
had discovered the uncharted world of the unconscious. More frequently he compared himself with Copernicus and Darwin, because
each of them, like Freud, inflicted a heavy blow on the self-love of man,
the first by denying that man's abode is the center of the universe, the
second by depriving man of his uniqueness, making him a link in the
chain of evolution. Yet in spite of his comparisons of himself with these
two great scientists, Freud never studied them psychoanalytically and
did not explore the dynamics which led to their great discoveries. On
the other hand, he devoted two major efforts to a psychoanalytic search
into the life of the great world reformer and prophet Moses. These were,
in a sense, the crowning achievements of his life.

Fromm's demonstration of Freud's desire to change the course of the
world—to create a movement that was political in the sense that it
would change man's morals and with it his life on this earth—not only
explains Freud's fascination with the Moses problem but is crucial for
our understanding of psychoanalysis as a movement. It explains one of
the strangest contradictions in Freud: his assertion that psychoanalysis
was a science, and as such was subject to all those criteria which should
apply to scientific investigation; and his contrary insistence that psychoanalysis must be accepted as formulated by him, that any deviation
or differing opinion was not something that could be expected to resolve
itself as scientific evidence accumulated but was instead a heresy, to be
eradicated by expelling the heretic from the movement.

Freud the man Fromm shows us to be basically very insecure, easily
frightened and vulnerable to feelings of persecution, and with little confidence in others. Convinced of their selfish motives, deep down an isolated and lonely man, Freud did not even believe there could be security
in love. Certainty for him was to be found only in reason, through
knowledge. Therefore, he felt the need to master the world intellectually
if he wanted relief from his doubts and feelings of failure. For Freud, as
for Plato, there was certainty only in ideas, except that Freud brought

advocate purging the Jungians from the London Psychoanalytic Society, one of several expulsions to prevent the spread of "heretical" views. The nature of this movement can best be seen from Freud's identification with Moses, which in his later years became ever more evident. Freud reinterpreted the Moses of Michelangelo to show that instead of breaking the tablets of the law, Moses calmed his wrath out of concern for his people. Thus Freud interpreted Moses as a man struggling successfully against inward passion for the sake of reason, and for a cause to which he had devoted himself. Freud identified closely with this Moses, the prophet not understood by his people and yet able to control his anger and continue the task of leading his people to the promised land.

Freud, who as a boy had aspired to become a great military leader or a cabinet minister, as a man yearned to bring a new and higher "law" to the human race, a new understanding of inner man and the world he lived in, a new covenant with pure reason. Neither nationalism, nor socialism, nor religion could be trusted to provide guidance toward the better life; only a full understanding of man's mind, gained by exposing the irrationality of these other answers, could lead man as far as he was destined to go. Freud envisioned man's sober, skeptical, rational appraisal of his past and his present, and an acceptance of the fundamentally tragic and lonely nature of his existence. Perhaps on this all-important point I should let Fromm speak for himself:

> Freud saw himself as the leader of this intellectual revolution, which made the last step rationalism could make. Only if one understands this aspiration of Freud to bring a new message to mankind, not a happy but a realistic one, can one understand his creation: the psychoanalytic movement.
>
> What a strange phenomenon, this psychoanalytic movement! Psychoanalysis is a therapy, that of neurosis, and it is at the same time a psychological theory, a general theory of human nature and specifically of the existence of the unconscious and its manifestations in dreams, symptoms, in character and in all symbolic productions. Is there any other case of a therapy or a scientific theory transforming itself into a movement, centrally directed by a secret committee, with purges of deviant members, with local organizations in an international superorganization? No therapy in the field of medicine was ever transformed into such a movement. As far as psychoanalysis as a theory is concerned, the nearest comparison would be Darwinism; here is a revolutionary theory,

shedding light on the history of man, and tending to change his picture of the world more fundamentally than any other theory in the 19th century—yet there is no Darwinian "movement," no directorium which leads that movement, no purges which decide who has the right to call himself a Darwinist and who has lost such a privilege.

Why this unique role of the psychoanalytic movement? The answer lies partly in the foregoing analysis of Freud's personality. He was a great scientist indeed; but like Marx, who was a great sociologist and economist, Freud had still another aim, one that a man like Darwin did not have: He wanted to transform the world. Under the disguise of a therapist and a scientist he was one of the great world reformers of the beginning 20th century.

Speaking of the "quasi-political character" of the psychoanalytic movement, Fromm shows that it never was based on the spirit of a scientific society, but was organized from the start on rather dictatorial lines. Within it, Freud agreed that Plato's rule by philosophers would be preferable to a more democratic organization. Some psychoanalytical congresses did have earmarks of political conventions. The idea of a secret committee of seven who were to assure the right direction of the movement suggests not so much a lack of trust in the validity of psychoanalytical findings as a desire for rigid and politically reliable control. Such distrust of the powers of reason and the convincing nature of scientific findings is in clear contrast to Freud's philosophical beliefs; it can be explained only by the wish to create a political movement around his scientific discoveries.

In support of this analysis, Fromm notes how Freud spoke of one congress as a "diet" (Reichstag); of "the motherland" and "the colonies" of psychoanalysis; and of the need "to fortify our dominion against all things and everybody." Even today, after so many years, the psychoanalytical societies and their international organization, with its branches and strictures as to who has a right to consider himself a psychoanalyst, are a spectacle rare among scientific societies. There are few other contemporary examples of attempts to chain the progress of scientific theory and practice to the discoveries of a founder, allowing little freedom to revise certain fundamental theses of the master.

As with Freud the man, there are contradictions. Freud denied that psychoanalysis was a philosophy, and consciously he was dedicated to utter intellectual freedom. The excuse for the rigid organization of the psychoanalytic movement was the existence of its detractors. Against them, strangely enough, only a monolithic organization, not the convincing power of truth, seemed to offer protection. Freud's method of therapy and theories had nothing to do with political movements. Why, then, did Freud view the struggle for the recognition of psychoanalysis, both as a scientific theory and as a medical therapy, as a quasi-political battle?

The answer may be found in his belief that "psychoanalysis is the instrument destined for the progressive conquest of the id." While this is not a religious aim, it is certainly an ethical one: the conquest of passion by reason. Comparing Freud with Marx, Fromm remarks: "Just as Marx believed he had found the scientific basis for socialism, in contrast to what he called utopian socialism, Freud felt that he had found the scientific basis for an old moral aim and thus progressed over the utopian morality presented by religions and philosophies. Since he had no faith in the average man, this new scientific morality was an aim that could be accomplished only by the elite, and the psychoanalytic movement was the active avant-garde, small but well organized to bring about the victory of the moral ideal."

Fromm concludes that Freud might have become the leader of a socialist or an ethical-culture movement or, for other reasons, a Zionist leader, had he not had an all-absorbing interest in the human mind and a courageous commitment to the pursuit of truth as he saw it. Also, Freud was much too conservative and skeptical to become a political leader. But "under the disguise of a scientific school, he realized his old dream, to be the Moses who showed the human race the promised land, the conquest of the Id by the Ego, and the way to this conquest."

One of the most interesting parts of Fromm's analysis is the parallels he draws between Freud's system and nineteenth-century middle-class economic beliefs in the virtue of saving and accumulation of capital:

> By nonsatisfaction of instinctual desires, so Freud thought, by self-deprivation, the elite, in contrast to the mob, "saves" the psychic capital for cultural achievements. The whole mystery of sublimation, which Freud never quite adequately explained, is the mystery of capital forma-

tion according to the myth of the 19th-century middle class. Just as wealth is the product of saving, culture is the product of instinctual frustration.

Another part of the 19th-century picture of man was also fully accepted by Freud and translated into his psychological theory: the picture of man as being basically aggressive and competitive. . . . Man, for Freud, was primarily isolated and self-sufficient. He was a social animal only by the necessity for the mutual satisfaction of needs, not by any primary need or desire to be related to one another. . . . Man is basically a machine, driven by libido and regulating itself by the need to reduce painful tension to a certain minimal threshold. This reduction of tension consititutes the nature of pleasure. In order to arrive at this satisfaction, men and women need each other. They become engaged in mutual satisfaction of their libidinous needs, and this constitutes their interest in each other.

Thus Fromm presents Freud's concept of *Homo sexualis* as a deepened and enlarged version of the economist's concept of *Homo economicus*. Only in one respect did Freud deviate from the traditional picture: he declared that the degree of sexual repression was excessive, and causing neurosis.

Whether or not Freud's aim was to create around psychoanalysis a movement for the ethical liberation of man, a new secular and scientific religion for the elite to guide mankind by, he could not have succeeded without kindred needs within his immediate followers, and later within the vast public which became enthusiastically attracted. While Freud's hopes and those of his first loyal disciples are now a matter of the past, the fact that they are still active concerns us most.

Those who embrace psychoanalysis in the image of Freud today are mostly lonely urban intellectuals with a deep yearning to be committed to an ideal, to a movement, and yet without the ability to make real sacrifices for it—to relinquish status or success for an ideal. They are people without any deep religious, political, or philosophical ideals or convictions. The growing circle of analysts comes from the same background; the great popularity of psychoanalysis in the Western world, particularly in the United States since the 1930s, has this same basis. Here is a middle class for which life has lost meaning. Its members are without political or religious ideals, yet are in search of a meaning, an idea to devote themselves to, an explanation of life that requires neither faith nor sacrifices, and that will enable them to feel part of a movement without any major commitment.

All these needs were fulfilled by the psychoanalytic movement. But as it began to serve this need for passive comfort, the new movement shared the fate of so many others which began with great courage and high resolve. The original enthusiasm, freshness, and spontaneity weakened, and a hierarchy took over which claimed its prestige from the correct interpretation of the dogma and exercised the power to judge who could be counted among the faithful. Eventually dogma, ritual, and idolatry toward the leader replaced that leader's creative daring and imagination.

The result is that many patients who enter therapy are more devoted to the ritual and dogma and care less for the essential search for truth and mastery over their own unconscious. They are attracted because through psychoanalysis they become "part of the movement, experience a sense of solidarity with all others who are analyzed, and a sense of superiority over those who are not. Often, they are much less concerned with being cured than with the exhilarating sensation of having found a spiritual home," not a home that serves as a secure haven from which to sail as yet uncharted seas of human experience, but a home which is a castle safely enclosing their empty lives.

Much in this review has been a paraphrasing of what, to me, seemed most important in Fromm's analysis, not of psychoanalysis, but of the psychoanalytic movement. Fromm sees the greatest weakness of this movement as its failure to extend the understanding of the individual's unconscious to a critical analysis of his society, and as the failure of Freudian psychoanalysis, past or present, to transcend a liberal middle-class attitude toward society. To these, Fromm ascribes its continuing narrowness and an eventual stagnation even in its proper field, the understanding of the individual unconscious. Psychoanalysis thus becomes a substitute satisfaction for a deep human yearning to find meaning in life, to be in genuine touch with reality and achieve closeness to others:

Here, in the Movement, they found everything—dogma, a ritual, a leader, a hierarchy, the feeling of possessing the truth, of being superior to the uninitiated; yet without great effort, without deeper comprehension of the problems of human existence, without insight into and criticism of their own society and its crippling effects on man, without having to change one's character in those aspects which matter, namely, to get rid of one's greed, anger and selfishness; basically without even escaping one's isolation. All they try, often successfully, to get rid of are certain libidinous fixations and their transference. And while this may be significant in relieving individual distress, it is not sufficient for the achievement of that characterological change which is necessary to be in full touch with reality.

And so, from a forward-moving and courageous idea, psychoanalysis became transformed into the safe cradle of those frightened and isolated members of the middle and upper-class who do not find a haven in the more conventional religious and social movements of their times.

From this book Freud emerges not so much a hero as one of the greatest men of this century, and the last to have radically altered human thinking about man and reality. From Fromm's critique of the psychoanalytic *movement*, it would appear that the *science* of psychoanalysis in its growing application to human affairs—quite apart from its sacred traditions as a "movement"—may still offer one of the best hopes for the future of mankind.

A Secret Asymmetry

In the last months of 1977, Aldo Carotenuto, a Jungian psychoanalyst who teaches theory of personality at the University of Rome, by mere chance became the recipient of a collection of either lost or long-forgotten documents. These had been preserved, also by pure chance, in the cellar of a building which, in years past, had been the headquarters of the Geneva Institute of Psychology. The papers had belonged to Dr. Sabina Spielrein, one of the pioneering psychoanalysts who lived and worked in Geneva during the early 1920s. There she analyzed Piaget for a few months, among others. In 1923, Spielrein decided to return to her native Russia, at which time she probably left these papers behind.

Carotenuto recognized immediately the importance of this newly discovered collection of papers, which contained twenty letters from Freud and many more from Jung. Not immediately apparent was the much greater significance of these letters regarding the person to whom they were addressed—Dr. Spielrein herself. In fact, these letters, published under the title *A Secret Symmetry* (New York: Pantheon, 1982),

This essay appeared with the title "Scandal in the Family," in somewhat different form and without the postscript, in the June 30, 1983, issue of *The New York Review of Books*.

demonstrate Sabina Spielrein's unique impact on Jung's life and the development of his thought, the role she played in the development of both Jungian and Freudian psychoanalysis, and her part in the establishment of Jung's relationship with Freud and then in their estrangement. All this becomes clear not so much from Freud's and Jung's letters to her as from the drafts and copies of her letters to them, and additionally from a fragmentary but most revealing diary of hers. These in combination throw startling new light on important aspects of the Freud/Jung correspondence.

Sabina Spielrein was born in Rostov-on-Don in 1885, the first child of intelligent, well-educated, wealthy Jewish parents; her grandfather as well as her great-grandfather were highly respected rabbis. As an adolescent, Spielrein suffered from what was described as either a schizophrenic disturbance or severe hysteria with schizoid features. In August of 1904, her deeply concerned parents took her to Zurich to be treated at the world-famous Burghölzli mental hospital. Jung had been connected since 1900 with this hospital, and in 1905 he became senior physician there. Spielrein was probably the first patient, or at least one of the very first patients, whom Jung tried to treat psychoanalytically; earlier he had concentrated mostly on studying patients' associations and what these revealed about their inner lives—studies in which Spielrein also participated.

We do not know how long Spielrein lived at the hospital as a patient, but in April of 1905 she enrolled at the University of Zurich to study medicine. Either then or soon thereafter, she was well enough to leave the hospital, continuing her treatment with Jung on an outpatient basis. She received her doctoral degree in 1911 on the basis of a dissertation titled "The Psychological Content of a Case of Schizophrenia." The former schizophrenic patient had by then become a student of schizophrenia, a doctor treating mental disturbances, an original thinker who developed ideas which later became of greatest significance in the Freudian system.

Carotenuto titled this book (originally published in Italy) *A Secret Symmetry.* The book reveals more than one symmetry and, in my opinion, one much more important asymmetry. The title of the Italian original, *Diario di una segreta simmetria,* makes it clear that the symmetry referred to in the title is that between Spielrein's and Jung's development, since it is that which is revealed by reading the entries in Spielrein's diary. It becomes clear that Spielrein, through her relation to Jung, exercised a decisive influence on him and on the development of his system. He, for his part, had the greatest impact on her. This was only natural, since as her therapist he had helped her overcome her severe psychological disturbance—but while he was still acting as her therapist, they became lovers. Spielrein loved Jung deeply, as he was her first love; but loved him also as her savior from insanity, and in addition as the brilliant teacher who introduced her to the study of psychopathology, which became her vocation. She never entirely lost her deep affection for Jung even after he betrayed her love, nor later when she married another man and had a child with him. Eventually, however, her feelings for Jung became quite ambivalent, as is understandable, since the person whom she loved so fervently behaved to her not only callously but in a manner which he himself later correctly described as knavery. More about this further on.

To me it is not the symmetries which become apparent as one reads these documents and Carotenuto's discussion of them that hold the most interest, but an asymmetry that formed as Spielrein moved professionally ever closer to Freud while Jung moved ever more toward his break with Freud and his form of psychoanalysis. The book evidences the very important influence Spielrein had on Jung's thoughts, and this in my opinion gives the book its great human and, as far as the development of psychoanalysis is concerned, its unique historical importance.

Both the human and the historical significance of these documents would be much greater if we were also permitted to read the letters Jung wrote to Spielrein, of which we are told forty-six survive. While Freud's heirs gave permission to publish the letters he wrote to Spielrein, Jung's heirs did not. In consequence, we have only a very few short, carefully screened, but nevertheless tantalizing passages from Jung's letters which Carotenuto quotes. They arouse much more curiosity than they satisfy.

It is not difficult to guess why Jung's heirs did not want the public to learn from his own words the details of his relationship with and behavior toward Spielrein, but the loss in this respect is not too great. Her diary, her letters to Jung and Freud, and already published letters between Freud and Jung permit a sufficiently clear picture of the love relationship, and of what Carotenuto correctly calls Jung's betrayal of his lover.

However, the withholding of Jung's letters also prevents us from assessing to what degree and in what respects the ideas and theoretical formulations which we have come to regard as constituting the basis of Jung's system are entirely or in large parts really Spielrein's. His relationship with Spielrein suggests that her influence on him was very far-reaching. She was not only his muse as he formed his system, but also in many respects his collaborator and, at the very least, his assistant in his intellectual development during the years when he formed some of his basic theories. Without having Jung's letters, or other pertinent information, no more can be said with any certainty.

What we are given leaves no doubt that in Sabina Spielrein Jung discovered his anima; and doing so formed his idea about the all-important role a man's anima plays in his life. Sabina Spielrein was thus the person who served as inspiration for the anima concept, if not possibly also the originator. That much we learn from this book. It also highlights Spielrein's great contribution to the mature Freudian system. A few years before Freud incorporated the concept of the death impulse into his system and assigned to it a central role, Spielrein wrote and published in the *Yearbook for Psychoanalytic and Psychopathological Research* for 1912 (*Jarhbuch für Psychoanalyse und Psychopathologische Forschung*) her germinal paper on destruction as the causation of creation. In it she presented for the first time within the framework of psychoanalysis her ideas about the destructive or death impulse and its intricate and inextricable relation to the sexual drive. A year earlier she had presented the ideas which form the essence of this essay to Freud and the Viennese psychoanalytic group.

Given Spielrein's high intelligence, the originality of her thought, and her extraordinary psychological intuition, which permitted her to make such an important contribution to Freudian thought at a time when his system was in many respects fully developed, it seems reasonable to assume that she contributed even more significantly to Jung's system at its inception, at which time he was working closely with her. In fact, the newly discovered papers presented in this book seem to suggest that possibly all of the central Jungian concepts might owe their origin directly or indirectly to Spielrein, disturbing as this idea may be to Jungians.

For example, it seems quite possible that not only the concept of the anima but also that of the shadow either came directly from Spielrein or

was developed around Jung's relationship with her. In a letter to Freud
in which Jung maligns Spielrein in the course of trying to whitewash
his own behavior toward her, Jung says that because of what has happened, he has understood that he has had "a totally inadequate idea of
my polygamous components," and that because of what he has learned,
he now knows "where and how the devil can be laid by the heels." Here,
by speaking about the devil in himself, he uses but another word for the
shadow. We cannot know what he said on these same issues to Spielrein, or what she said to him, but we may assume that they expressed
themselves to each other much more freely than Jung expressed himself to Freud about these matters.

There is no knowing which of the two, Jung or Spielrein, spoke first
about the devil at work in them, or of the shadow. But Carotenuto, while
trying hard to give the impression that all basic concepts of Jungian
psychology are Jung's creation, from his study of Jung's letters to Spielrein which are not open to us still comes quite close to suggesting that
many of Jung's concepts are directly or indirectly owed to Spielrein. He
writes: "It is not hard to imagine that in a curious way the hypotheses of
persona, shadow, and anima represent the distillation of these old experiences," meaning Jung's experiences in his relationship with Spielrein.
And further on: "Any attentive reading of the phenomenological description of the anima and the shadow takes us immediately back to
those early years" of the relation to Spielrein. Finally he quotes from one
of the last-known letters of Jung to Spielrein, dated September 1919:
"The love of S. for J. made the latter aware of something he had previously only vaguely suspected, that is, of the power in the unconscious
that shapes one's destiny, a power which later led him to things of greatest importance." Thus, whatever the specific contributions of Spielrein
to the Jungian system, Jung asserts, and Carotenuto follows him in this
opinion, that it was in their love relationship that the system itself
originated.

The importance of these all too few short quotations from Jung's letters makes one keenly aware of all that has been withheld. At the same
time, and by implication, the refusal of Jung's heirs to permit publication of his letters to Spielrein presents a troublesome problem in regard
to the publication of her diary and letters. From all available evidence it
seems that Spielrein worked in Russia as a psychoanalyst until psychoanalysis was outlawed there in 1936. She probably perished in 1936 or

1937, during Stalin's purges. But she had a daughter and also three younger brothers, and so it is quite possible that some of her heirs are still alive, particularly since we know that at least one of her brothers was living outside of Russia. Nothing we are told in this book suggests that any effort was made to find her heirs and to secure their permission to publish Spielrein's letters and diary. Glad though I am to be able to read and hence to reflect on what her letters and diary reveal, I cannot help being dismayed that a Jungian psychoanalyst, Professor Carotenuto, should show such respect for the sensitivities of Jung's heirs and no commensurate respect for the sensitivity of Spielrein's heirs. It seems unfair, to say the least, that the rules of confidentiality are here so differently applied, especially when the famous psychoanalyst, as the therapist, has in principle less claim to privacy than does his patient.

And what about one of the issues which probably induced Jung's heirs to refuse publication of his letters to Spielrein—their love affair? Carotenuto goes to great pains to convince the reader that Jung's love relationship with Spielrein remained platonic; however, the documents strongly suggest that this was not so. Obviously, a psychoanalyst should not have sexual relations with one of his patients. Unfortunately it has happened from time to time, with uniformly bad results for both patient and therapist, and it may happen again in the future. Some seventy years later, it is of relatively little interest whether or not the great love Jung and Spielrein certainly felt for each other was sexually consummated. What seems more important is whether the analyst behaved toward his patient-lover with respect and human decency, or whether he was concerned only for his public reputation and not at all for the psychological vulnerability of his patient, who, because of the patient-therapist relation, had no defenses against him. In respect to these questions, the evidence is all too clear that Jung behaved toward Spielrein in a scandalous manner.

As for whether the relationship remained platonic or resulted in intercourse, in September of 1910, Spielrein confided to her diary:

> And yet his wife, who, as his diary makes clear [Jung had given Spielrein his diary to read, telling her that no one but his wife and her had ever read it], hesitated for a long time before marrying him . . . is protected by the law, respected by all, and I, who wanted to give him everything I possessed, without the slightest regard for myself, I am called immoral

in the language of society—lover, maybe *maîtresse*! He can appear any-
where in public with his wife, and I have to skulk in dark corners. I
myself would not want our love to be trumpeted through the streets,
partly out of consideration for his wife, partly so that the sacredness of it
not be sullied; but still, it has always pained me that we must conceal
our feelings.—True, he wanted to introduce me in his house, make me
his wife's friend, but understandably his wife wanted no part of this
business. . . .

On the same date she recalls "single moments, when I rested in his
arms, in which I was able to forget everything," In October of 1910,
speaking about herself and Jung, she writes, "At the time our poetry
began, he had two girls. . . ." "Poetry" is the word she uses to refer to
something in their relationship she does not want to mention openly;
the contexts in which she uses this word make clear that it refers to
something most intimate, most likely to sexual intercourse. (Without
quite realizing it, Carotenuto suggests as much in his note explaining
"poetry," in which he says, "For 'poetry' we must surmise a metaphorical
significance known only to Jung and Sabina. A literary analogy can be
found in Proust. Swann and Odette used the metaphor *'faire cattleya'*
to express the physical act of possession." If Carotenuto did not think
that the metaphor "poetry" stood for sexual possession, why would he
have selected this example to explain the use of metaphors? Incidentally, Carotenuto frequently speaks of Spielrein as "Sabina," but never of
Jung as "Carl," a lack of evenhandedness which is not only unfair and
annoying but makes one doubt that his discussion treats these two persons evenly.)

An unbiased reading of the material permits no other conclusion but
that the relation of Spielrein and Jung was of the most loving and intimate nature, while Carotenuto's insistence that it was platonic leaves
one with the feeling that he protests too much. However, the question
of how far they went in their love for each other really pales into insignificance when considering Jung's scoundrelly reaction once their love
became known.

The Jung/Freud letters, in light of what we learn from this new material about the singular importance his relationship with Spielrein had
for Jung, suggest strongly that this relationship was probably the primary cause that induced Jung to relate to Freud, since it was the first

significant problem he presented to Freud, stating explicitly that he was in need of abreacting about it, and also unable to get himself to do so.

According to the Jung/Freud letters, their exchange began when Jung, then a complete stranger to Freud, sent Freud a copy of his word-association studies. The significance of this becomes apparent in the light of what is said below about the importance of the associations to the name "Spielrein." The very first of the letters between Jung and Freud is a note in which Freud thanks Jung for having sent him this book. Freud reciprocated by sending Jung a collection of his short papers, for which Jung thanks him in return. So far the exchange of letters is polite and remains on a professional, though cordial, level. Quite in contrast is Jung's second letter to Freud, dated October 23, 1906, in which Jung suddenly introduces a topic of great personal concern. In it he writes:

> I must abreact my most recent experience. I am currently treating an hysteric with your method. Difficult case, a 20-year-old Russian girl student, ill for 6 years.
>
> First trauma between 3rd and 4th year. Saw her father spanking her older brother on the bare bottom. Powerful impression. Couldn't help thinking afterwards that she had defecated on her father's hand. From the 4th–7th year convulsive attempts to defecate on her own feet, in the following manner: she sat on the floor with one foot beneath her, pressed her heel against her anus and tried to defecate and at the same time to prevent defecation. Often retained the stool for 2 weeks in this way! Has no idea how she hit upon this peculiar business; says it was completely instinctive, and accompanied by blissfully shuddersome feelings. Later this phenomenon was superseded by vigorous masturbation. I should be extremely grateful if you would tell me in a few words what you think of this story.

With this the letter ends. Thus Jung's involvement with Spielrein is the topic that serves for his opening up to Freud in a more personal way for the first time.

There is little remarkable in Jung's asking Freud for comments on the first case he treats with Freud's method, and in general it would not be unusual that he does not mention the patient's name, although patients' names are freely mentioned in succeeding letters; but in the case of Spielrein, Jung's omission of her name poses some special problems, and may be very revealing.

In addition to this omission, there are at least two other aspects of the letter that deserve special attention: Jung's remark that he needs to abreact about *a most recent experience,* and his *failure to do so.* At the time Jung wrote this letter, he had known Spielrein for over two years, so it could not have been the nature of her past history (which he describes) that was the reason for his need to abreact, since it hardly constitutes a recent experience. From what we know about Jung's intimate, probably sexual, involvement with Spielrein, it is reasonable to assume that it found its physical culmination just at the time Jung sought to relate to Freud by beginning his correspondence with him, coinciding with the "recent experience" for which Jung sought abreaction. Since this experience happened during Jung's first effort, or one of his first efforts, to apply Freud's method in the treatment of a patient, it is understandable that Jung sought Freud's help in what he experienced as a most difficult situation. He alludes to this by describing her as a difficult case, when in actuality, compared to most of the patients treated at the Burghölzli, her case was a relatively mild one, since she could not only live by herself in town but, what is much more important in this respect, also successfully pursue the study of medicine. This is something not mentioned in the letter to Freud by Jung, although it would make Spielrein's case appear in a very different light. Thus, she was a most difficult case only because of Jung's erotic involvement with her.

Despite his expressed need for abreacting, Jung failed to do so, nor did he speak about the nature of his involvement with Spielrein in this letter. So from the very beginning of his relationship with Freud, Jung could not get himself to admit the importance of sex in human relations, and in neurosis. This is why I believe Spielrein plays such a significant role in the Freud-Jung relationship: Jung's relationship with her was what forced Jung to first turn for help to Freud, and Jung's inability to face openly that it was a sexual involvement which pressed for abreaction presages the issue over which his final break with Freud occurred. As is so often the case in complex psychological relations, the end was evident in the beginning.

Jung, whose primary interest had been in word associations, ought to have realized that he was withholding from Freud extremely pertinent information about the case he was describing by not revealing

Spielrein's name, which is of significance in a case where the central symptoms are ideas about defecating on her father, soiling herself, and preventing herself from doing so.

Names—especially their names—have a special significance to small children. A name is an important anchor for developing selfhood; it is an obvious tie to one's family. But if it lends itself to such interpretation, then it is also regarded as a special message of fate to the child. The German name Spielrein consists of a combination of two very common words, *spiel* and *rein*. The first of the two can be either a noun, meaning "play," or the imperative of the verb "to play." The second is an adjective or adverb, meaning "clean." In their combination the two words amount to an admonition, most particularly to a child, to play cleanly. Although the Spielrein family lived in Russia, being Jewish and well educated they were certainly familiar with the German meaning of their name, since most families are interested in what their names signify. Moreover, that the Spielreins took their daughter to German Switzerland for treatment and easily corresponded with Jung in German suggests that they were fluent in this language. It is hard to believe that Jung, given his interest at the time in the study of word associations, was unaware of what it must have meant to a little girl to carry a name ordering her to play clean, when for many years her most important symptom, crucially interfering with her living a child's normal life, was a consuming ambivalence about playing cleanly or being clean, an ambivalence that expressed itself in her trying to defecate on herself and in trying to prevent herself from defecating altogether.

Here it should be mentioned that at the time Sabina Spielrein was a little girl sexual matters were never mentioned to children, certainly not by good middle-class people like her parents, but instead some circumlocution was used. When at that time a child touched herself sexually as most children do, the typical critical admonition was "not to do something dirty," with the clear implication that what the child did was not clean. For this reason, carrying the name Spielrein, with its implication that she ought to play cleanly, must have been a particularly difficult burden to bear for a little girl so exceedingly bright and sensitive as was Sabina Spielrein, from all we know about her. This admonition was so prevalent in talking to children in German-speaking countries that it is likely to have also been used in the upbringing of Jung, particularly since his father was a strict country parson. If so, each time he used

Spielrein's name or thought of it, Jung, feeling that he was already, or on the verge of, "playing dirty" with Spielrein, was reminded not to play or do something dirty, as he had been as a child. This, then, may have been a major reason for his failure to tell Freud her name.

We do not know when, exactly, Jung and Spielrein became aware of their deep love for each other, nor when it found open expression, or in what form. Carotenuto concludes from Jung's letters that at the beginning of 1908 he knew how deeply in love he was with Spielrein, but since according to Carotenuto the extant letters of Jung to Spielrein begin only then, we have no information on what Jung's feelings for her had been in 1906, when he wrote his second letter to Freud expressing his need to abreact in respect to her. But even if at that time Jung was not yet overtly sexually involved with Spielrein, he had by then known her intimately for over two years, treated her, and also invited her to participate in his experiments. Is it not reasonable to assume that subconsciously, Jung may have felt how deeply and potentially sexually he was involved with her? About a year later Jung, without naming her, writes Freud that one of his patient's greatest wishes is to have a child by him. As he was her therapist, a married man, and a father, Jung's sexual relationship with Spielrein would have been illicit on several levels, and such situations easily evoke in the subconscious the injunctions which had been given us in our childhood.

Jung does not identify this patient as the "difficult" one about which he had previously written, and again he withholds an important detail—the proposed name of this fervently desired child. However, we learn from Spielrein's diary of her consuming desire to bear Jung a child to be named Siegfried, and her idea that this child would bridge the gap between her Jewishness and Jung's Aryanness. In a later letter to Jung she connects this idea directly with Jung's relation to Freud: "My Siegfried problem, for instance, might just as well yield a real child as a symbolic Aryan-Semitic child—for instance, a child that resulted from the union of your and Freud's theories." Thus in her mind her relation to Jung paralleled that of his to Freud, and she writes about it in a way suggesting that Jung was quite familiar with such ideas.

We do not know how Jung reacted to Spielrein's wish to have a child with him and name it Siegfried, and her idea that this child should symbolize the union between his and Freud's thoughts. But both Spielrein and Jung were deeply absorbed in Wagner and repeatedly discussed the profound meaning his work had for them, so they could not possibly disregard that in the *Ring* cycle Siegfried is the son of Siegmund, whose name is a variant of Freud's first name, Sigmund. Spielrein thus desired a son whose physical father would be Jung, but whose name would symbolize that his spiritual father was Freud. This idea was very pleasing to Spielrein, but probably most obnoxious to Jung—reason enough for Jung not to reveal to Freud that the patient who wished for a child from him was Jewish, nor that she planned to give this child the name Siegfried.

There were other powerful reasons why Spielrein's great desire to bear such a child must have aroused strong negative, or at least ambivalent, feelings in Jung. He was aware that his great value for Freud lay in his presumed ability to achieve, through his person and his influence, the acceptance of Freud's "Jewish" psychoanalysis in the Aryan world. Freud had made no secret of these hopes of his; he expressed them in various conversations with his friends. It was thus understandable, probably predictable, that in reaction against being used in this manner Jung in time developed his own, non-Jewish psychoanalysis, and, still later, embraced some of Hitler's ideas.

But Jung's attitude toward Jewishness was very complicated, because Jewishness also fascinated him, particularly in women. Later Spielrein, in one of her letters to Freud, elaborated on this, relaying information Jung had given her when their relationship was most intimate. Jung told her that his cousin Helene Preiswick, with whom he had conducted some of his first psychological experiments (described in detail in his dissertation, where he refers to her as S.W.) and whom he seems to have loved greatly, although possibly without being fully conscious of it, pretended to be Jewish. Jung connects his infatuation with this girl who pretended Jewishness with his relation to Spielrein in a letter to Freud in which he mentions Spielrein for the first time by name. There he writes: "then the Jewess popped up in another form, in the shape of my patient," meaning Spielrein.

Sometime before March 1909, the love relationship between Jung and Spielrein became known, probably to his wife. Someone, in all likelihood she, wrote to Sabina Spielrein's mother an anonymous letter, warning her that this relationship could undo her daughter, and asking her to put an end to it. All this we learn from Spielrein's diary and her letters to Freud. But before Freud knew anything about it from Spielrein, or that the person involved was the patient about whom Jung had written him twice before, Jung wrote to Freud on March 7, 1909, that "a woman patient whom years ago I pulled out of a very sticky neurosis with unstinting effort has violated my confidence and my friendship in the most mortifying way imaginable. She has kicked up a vile scandal solely because I denied myself the pleasure of giving her a child." And this although it was not Sabina Spielrein who had created the scandal, but the person who wrote to her mother, as Jung was forced to admit a few months later to Freud, because by then Spielrein had informed him of the true facts.

Unfortunately, the very words describing the nature of Jung's relation to this patient are mistranslated, which is particularly regrettable, because Carotenuto uses "Unstinting Effort" as his title of the chapter in which he discusses these matters. Jung actually wrote, *"eine Patientin, die ich vor Jahren mit grösster Hingabe aus schwerster Neurose herausgerissen habe. . . ."* The German words *mit grösster Hingabe* are wrongly translated as "with unstinting effort." While it would not be incorrect to translate the German words Jung used as "with unstinting devotion" or "with greatest devotion," it would not be as close to the German as it should be, since it fails to render the full meaning of the word *Hingabe,* which means "surrender." *Hingabe* is most frequently used in the sense of sexual surrender. Thus the words Jung used, while overtly asserting only the extreme degree of devotion with which he had dedicated himself to the treatment of this patient, covertly suggested or at the least alluded to the sexual nature of his relationship with this patient.

Carotenuto, being Italian, cannot be blamed for this misleading translation, nor for not recognizing the psychological significance of the name Spielrein. "Unstinting effort" is also used in the official English translation of *The Jung/Freud Letters.* But at least in the text of the chapter called "Unstinting Effort" it is noted parenthetically that "Jung speaks of *unstinting effort* [*grösster Hingabe,* literally 'greatest devotion']." Thus either Carotenuto or those who translated his book into English were aware that "unstinting effort" distorts the meaning of the words Jung used in his letter. The translation "greatest devotion" evades the sexual connotations of the word Jung used, but it is at least much closer to the German original than is "effort," which would have been a correct translation only if Jung had spoken of having worked with this patient with *grösster Anstrengung,* an expression signifying a deliberate and conscious process, whereas *Hingabe* denotes a deep emotional involvement and suggests one of a sexual nature.

It is quite interesting to note that Freud did not react to Jung's speaking of denying himself the pleasure of intercourse, after he had described a few sentences before his attitude to the same woman patient as one of greatest surrender. Jung's wording should have been sufficiently revealing to permit Freud to guess the true nature of Jung's relationship with this patient, particularly since, as he related in his reply to Jung's letter, Freud had been told by Muthman, a Swiss psychiatrist, about "a lady who had introduced herself as your [Jung's] mistress." Probably Freud wished to blind himself to something that might jeopardize his relationship with Jung.

Deeply hurt by Jung's behavior, Sabina Spielrein wrote to Freud, asking for an interview. At first Freud refused, in the interests of avoiding anything that might interfere with his relationship with Jung, which, for reasons already described, was so important to him. So Freud was not straightforward either in his dealings with Spielrein, but tried instead to cooperate with Jung's wishes. In his letter to Jung of June 7, 1909, Freud wrote: "I understood your telegram correctly [its content is unknown, but in it Jung must have informed Freud about some aspects of his relationship with Spielrein, because Freud had written for information after he had received Spielrein's letter, and did not know how to react]; your explanation confirmed my guess. Well, after receiving your wire I wrote Miss Spielrein a letter in which I affected ignorance, pretending that her suggestion was that of an overzealous enthusiast. . . ."

But Spielrein did not give up. Since Freud had refused to permit her to state her case in person, she wrote to him on June 11, 1909:

> Four and a half years ago Dr. Jung was my doctor, then he became my
> friend and finally my "poet," i.e., my beloved. Eventually he came to me
> and things went as they usually do with "poetry." He preached polygamy,
> his wife was supposed to have no objection, etc., etc. Now my mother
> receives an anonymous letter that minces no words, saying she should
> rescue her daughter, since otherwise she would be ruined by Dr. Jung.
> The letter could not have been written by one of my friends, since I kept
> absolutely mum and always lived far away from all other students. There
> is reason to suspect his wife. To make a long story short, my mother

writes him a moving letter, saying that he had saved her daughter and should not undo her now, and begging him not to exceed the bounds of friendship.

This was Jung's reply to Spielrein's mother:

I moved from being her doctor to being her friend when I ceased to push my own feelings into the background. I could drop my role as doctor the more easily because I did not feel professionally obligated, for I never charged a fee. The latter clearly establishes the limits imposed upon a doctor. You do understand, of course, that a man and a girl cannot possibly continue indefinitely to have friendly dealings with one another without the likelihood that something more may enter the relationship. For what would restrain the two from drawing the consequences of their love? A *doctor* and his *patient,* on the other hand, can talk the most intimate matters for as long as they like, and the patient may expect her doctor to give her all the love and concern she requires. But the doctor knows his limits and will never cross them for he is *paid* for his trouble. That imposes the necessary restraints on him.

Therefore I would suggest that if you wish me to adhere strictly to my role as doctor, you should pay me a fee as suitable recompense for my trouble. In that way you may be *absolutely certain* that I will respect my duty as a doctor under all *circumstances.*

As a friend of your daughter, on the other hand, one would have to leave matters to Fate. For no one can prevent two friends from doing as they wish. . . . My fee is 10 francs per consultation.

Jung's declaration that he, a physician, did not see his role as therapist as putting any restraints on his behavior unless he was paid for his professional services is inexcusable. Carotenuto says that this passage "almost together eludes one's understanding," which is putting it mildly. (It should be added that according to Spielrein's account, her parents thought that Jung, as an employee of the Burghölzli hospital—in which their daughter had been his patient and where he continued to treat her after she stopped living there—was not permitted to accept private patients and hence had given him gifts all along in lieu of paying him money.)

Although Freud knew from Spielrein's letter about the impossible situation she had been projected into by Jung's behavior, he still refused to meet her, and continued to dissimulate to her, we must assume so as not to permit anything to interfere with his relationship with Jung. This we learn from the letter Freud wrote to Jung on June 18: "My reply [to Spielrein's second letter] was ever so wise and penetrating; I made it appear as though the most tenuous of clues had enabled me, Sherlock Holmes–like, to guess the situation (which of course was none too difficult after your communications) and suggested a more appropriate procedure, something endopsychic, as it were."

In his letter of June 21, 1909, Jung finally admits that he has wronged Spielrein. In it he deplores "the sins I have committed, for I am largely to blame for the high-flying hopes of my former patient," and he confesses, "Caught in my delusion that I was the victim of the sexual wiles of my patient, I wrote to her mother that I was not the gratifier of her daughter's sexual desires. . . . In view of the fact that the patient had shortly before been my friend and enjoyed my full confidence, my action was a piece of knavery which I very reluctantly confess to you as my father. I would now like to ask you a great favor: would you please write a note to Miss Spielrein, telling her that I fully informed you of the matter, and especially of the letter to her parents, which is what I regret most. I would like to give my patient at least this satisfaction: that you and she know of my 'perfect honesty.'"

In one and the same paragraph Jung refers to Spielrein as both his former and his present patient. That is, when talking about their love relationship he calls her his former patient, but when asking Freud to write to her and convince her of Jung's honesty he calls her simply his patient, so that Freud, in order not to interfere with the patient-therapist relation, would abstain from any further communication with her. At the same time, Jung sought to prevent Spielrein from meeting Freud, claiming there would be no reason for it, since Jung had already told everything to Freud. In this way Freud would be prevented from learning that there was much more to the affair than Jung had admitted to him, despite his claim of "perfect honesty," two words he wrote in English and put within quotation marks in a letter which otherwise was written entirely in German. (In this way, Jung's unconscious made him reveal that the statement about "perfect honesty" was a foreign element in this letter.)

Jung's letter contains a variety of dishonesties of omission and possibly of commission. One of them is giving Freud the impression that his letter to Sabina Spielrein's mother was a spontaneous action on his part, whereas it was written only in response to the mother's asking him not to further seduce her daughter. Nor did he reveal that Spielrein's mother had written in response to a letter she had received (Carotenuto and Sabina Spielrein both assume from Jung's wife) asking her to break up Jung's relationship with her daughter. Lastly, Jung did not reveal the most scandalous part of his letter to Spielrein's parents, in which he stated that a sexual relationship with his patient would only be natural as long as he was not paid for treating her, while when he received payment, this could not happen.

While Freud thus at first had tried to cover up for Jung, nevertheless Jung's betrayal of the person whom he had loved, who still loved him, and who had given him no reason whatsoever to turn against her must have worried Freud. In January 1913, when it had become obvious that a break with Jung was unavoidable, Freud wrote to Spielrein, "Since I received that first letter from you, my opinion of him [meaning Jung] has greatly altered," but he gave no indication whether, when, or to what degree this first letter had contributed to his change of opinion.

One more thing might be mentioned in connection with the false accusations Jung had made against Spielrein in his letter to Freud dated March 7, 1909, after he had learned from the letter of Spielrein's mother that his affair was known. Since he had learned from Freud's reply that Muthman had met someone claiming to be his mistress, it was by then clear to Jung that a scandal was brewing. In the same month in which all this happened, Jung resigned his position at the Burghölzli; we do not know why, nor exactly on what date. But since his resignation occurred in March 1909, it seems reasonable to assume that he did so to prevent an even greater scandal which would have resulted if it became known that (in his letter to Spielrein's mother) Jung had declared that his responsibility for having sexual relations with a patient he was treating at the Burghölzli, first as an inpatient and later ambulatorily, depended on whether or not he was paid for his services. So this statement, given the strict morality of the Swiss, would certainly have resulted in Jung's dismissal from the position of trust he held at this famous institution.

The first time Freud and Jung met after Freud had learned about Spielrein was on August 20, 1909, the day before they sailed together for the United States. During a luncheon on this day Freud had one of the two fainting spells he had in Jung's presence, which Freud claimed were due to Jung's relationship to him. On this occasion, Freud said that he had fainted in reaction to the death wishes he felt Jung harbored against him. That Jung, consciously or not, may have had such death wishes is quite possible, since the position into which Freud had forced him, as Freud's successor, heir, and quasi-adoptive eldest son, clashed with Jung's wishes for independence from a father figure. This created an oedipal situation between them, which, according to Freud's theories and convictions, was conducive to the formation of such wishes.

On the other hand, oedipal emotional situations which bring about death wishes are so frequent in everyday life that if the normal reaction to them were fainting, people would be fainting right and left. It seems much more likely that a fainting due to psychological causes is the result of processes going on in the person who faints rather than in the other person, probably the consequence of efforts to prevent oneself from saying or doing something one wishes to do, but feels compelled not to do. When in November 1912, at a time when the Freud-Jung relationship was drawing ever closer to its breaking point, at their meeting in Munich Freud fainted for the second time in Jung's presence, Freud explained that "repressed feelings . . . directed against Jung . . . naturally play the main part" in his fainting. So one may assume that the same emotional constellation accounted also for the first of these two famous fainting spells.

In any case, the explanation Freud put on his fainting the first time the two met after the Spielrein affair was revealed makes it possible to think that this affair had shaken Freud's trust in Jung and evoked conscious or subconscious fears that Jung might betray his pseudo-father, as he had betrayed his lover. Be this as it may, Jung reports that on this same trip, on the boat, he was for the first time repulsed by Freud's authoritarian attitude toward him. Jung writes that Freud told him one of the dreams he had had and Jung tried to interpret it, and in doing so asked Freud to supply some additional details from his private life. "Freud's response to these words was a curious look—a look of utmost suspicion. Then he said, 'But I cannot risk my authority!' At this moment he lost it altogether." Since this was written many years after the events described, and we have only Jung's word for it, one should accept this story with considerable caution, because if Freud indeed lost his authority for Jung entirely at that time, then Jung's many expressions of deep respect in his letters to Freud during the following few years would have been a fraud.

I mention this incident only because according to Jung's account, Freud reacted so strongly when Jung asked him for information about his private life. This query might have reminded Freud how Jung had behaved where *his* most private life had been concerned. Jung, on the other hand, might have been more inclined to continue to respect Freud's authority had Freud been more critical of Jung's behavior to Spielrein and not connived with Jung in dissembling to her, since there seems no question that Jung afterward felt quite guilty about his behavior toward her. But this is, of course, only speculation.

What we do know for sure is that after Jung had realized he had been wrong in his accusations against Spielrein, there were some stormy scenes between them. In a draft of a letter to Freud, Spielrein describes how she, not realizing what she was doing, had hit Jung in the face in a fit of desperation over his defamation of her, and that when she did so, she had been holding a knife in her left hand, not knowing what she intended to do. Jung grabbed her hand and she ended up bleeding, her left hand and forearm covered with blood. Spielrein tells in the draft of her next letter to Freud, dated June 12, that to escape from it all and get a grip on herself, she left Zurich for the country, and that she received there two letters from Jung, one of them letting her know that on the day of their next "rendezvous" he would be leaving town, because he considered it better that they should not see each other that day so, as he writes, "the whole painful business will be more easily laid to rest." In the draft of the same letter to Freud, Spielrein restates that despite everything that had happened, she still loves Jung.

In the meantime Spielrein's mother, in reaction to Jung's letter to her, had rushed to Zurich to talk things over with Jung, who, it seems, at first refused to see her. She seems to have threatened to turn to Professor Bleuler, head of the Burghölzli and thus Jung's boss, but desisted from doing so, in order not to worsen the scandal. Still, a few weeks later it seems that things had settled down; the relation between Jung and Spielrein continued, as she was working on her dissertation, which he supervised, and they seem to have continued their regular meetings.

Next we learn that Spielrein was supposed to present a paper at the Weimar Congress of the Psychoanalytic Association in September of 1911 but, according to Carotenuto, found a "psychosomatic" pretext for not attending the congress. While he claims to know from a letter of Jung to her that this was so, he does not tell what this so-called pretext was.

From a letter of Freud's to Jung, we know that by October 1911, Spielrein was in Vienna, where she remained at the least until March of 1912, when she moved to Berlin. While in Vienna, Spielrein attended the meeting of the group around Freud and became a regular member of Freud's psychoanalytic society. In his letter of November 12, 1911, Freud tells Jung that "at the last meeting Miss Spielrein spoke up for the first time; she was very intelligent and methodical."

Jung's reply to this comment is most interesting. His letter of November 14, 1911, begins: "Many thanks for your very nice letter which I have just received. However, the outlook for me is very gloomy if you too get into the psychology of religion. You are a dangerous rival—if one has to speak of rivalry. Yet I think it has to be this way, for a natural development cannot be halted, nor should one try to halt it. Our personal differences make our work different." This is ostensibly said in regard to their both being interested in the psychology of religion, but given Jung's deep involvement with Spielrein, who, as he learned from Freud's letter, had become a respected member of Freud's group, it may have had as much to do with Freud's being a dangerous rival in regard to Spielrein.

In his reply, Freud once more asserts his respect for Spielrein by stating categorically: "Spielrein's paper certainly belongs in the *Jahrbuch* [which Jung edited] and nowhere else." Two weeks later he writes Jung: "Miss Spielrein read a chapter from her paper yesterday [it was the paper in which she developed her ideas about the death impulse] and it was followed by an illuminating discussion. I have hit on a few objections to your method of dealing with mythology, and I brought them up in the discussion with the little one. I must say she is really nice, and I am beginning to understand." Thus when talking about Spielrein, Freud interjects a remark stating his objection to some of Jung's methods, an aside which was probably not lost on Jung, since in his reply he expresses his ambivalence by saying both critical and positive things about her, as he writes: "I'll gladly take Spielrein's new paper for the first [half of the] *Jahrbuch* 1912. It demands a great deal of revision, but then the little one has always been very demanding of me. However, she is worth it. I am glad you don't think badly of her."

Within a year from the time Jung stated so concisely his rivalry with Freud, Jung had become so rivalrous with his father figure that he finally broke off all relations. There were, of course, many sound psychological causes for this break, such as the unresolved oedipal situation Freud had created by his demanding choice that Jung be his elected son and his heir as leader of psychoanalysis, embracing him in large measure because he was the son of a Swiss pastor and had a position of importance in the famous Burghölzli. Even if Jung had been a less proud man than he was, believing that he was embraced by Freud because he was a gentile would have been reason enough for a break.

Setting aside for a moment the many other psychological reasons which could explain the course and the end of the Jung-Freud friendship, it seems reasonable to think that the vicissitudes of Jung's relation to Spielrein must have played an important role in his break with Freud. Their friendship had begun with Jung turning to Freud requesting help in dealing with his feelings for Spielrein, but doing so in the ambivalent way discussed. Freud and Jung's relationship ended after Spielrein had changed from being Jung's love and disciple to being Freud's follower, also changing her allegiance from gentile to Jew. Here it ought to be recalled that as far as theoretical positions are concerned, both men, each in his own way, agreed that the main issue of contention was Jung's refusal to accept the central role of sexuality in human affairs, on which Freud insisted. It is important to note that for Jung, what had originally been a personal need to deny the importance of sexuality became a theoretical issue. As so often in psychological matters, highly personal matters eventually determined theoretical positions, something the psychoanalyst should be the first to recognize.

Freud was well aware that the gentile-Jewish issue was important, not only in his relationship with Jung—this had been well known all along—but also in that between Spielrein and Jung. Referring to Spielrein's wish for an Aryan-Jewish child named Siegfried, symbolizing both the Freud-Jung and the Jung-Spielrein unity, Freud wrote to her: "I must confess . . . that your fantasy about the birth of a Saviour to a mixed union did not appeal to me at all," and a few months later: "My personal relationship with your Germanic hero has definitely been shattered. His behavior was too bad." Of course, Freud had received the first clear intimation of this bad behavior when he learned of Jung's false accusation of Spielrein, although at that time he had done his best to

disregard it, out of his hope that psychoanalysis would find in Jung a
"Germanic hero."

In August 1913, after Freud had learned first of Spielrein's marriage
to Pavel Scheftel, a Russian Jew, who, like her, was a physician, and
then of her pregnancy, he wrote her:

> I can hardly bear to listen when you continue to enthuse about your old
> love and past dreams, and [I] count on an ally in the marvelous little
> stranger. I am, as you know, cured of the last shred of my predilection for
> the Aryan cause, and would like to take it that if the child turns out to be
> a boy, he will develop into a stalwart Zionist. . . . We are and remain Jews.
> The others will only exploit us and will never understand or appreci-
> ate us.

Here Freud, deeply hurt by Jung's defection, conveniently forgets how
he had wanted to exploit Jung. This Spielrein—because of either her
continuing affection for Jung or her greater objectivity, or both—could
not disregard. Maybe this is why, one month later, after Freud had
learned of the birth of Spielrein's daughter, Renate, he wrote: "Well,
now, my heartiest congratulations. It is far better that the child should
be a 'she'. Now we can think again about the blond Siegfried and perhaps smash that idol before its time comes."

But this Spielrein could not do, nor did she want to. Despite her continuing professional allegiance to Freud's camp, she continued her relationship and correspondence with Jung, certainly well into 1918, and
probably much longer, as he did with her. From her own bitter experience Spielrein knew all too well that the theoretical disagreements between Jung and Freud, and Jung's development of his very own and
different system of psychoanalysis, had much more to do with Jung's
personal difficulties in relating to Freud and to her than with diver-
gences of theoretical convictions. These, she was sure, could have been
readily bridged, or resolved, if personal animosity had not made this impossible.

And so, at least until her return to Russia, Spielrein tried to convince
both Jung and Freud that they had much more in common in theory
than they had opposed. For example, as late as 1918, more than seven
years after she had joined Freud and more than five years after he had
become disillusioned with Jung, she wrote to Jung: "You can under-

stand Freud perfectly well if you wish to, i.e., if your personal affect does not get in the way." Earlier she had written to Freud: "In spite of all his wavering, I like Jung and would like to lead him back into our fold. You, Professor Freud, and he have not the faintest idea that you belong together far more than anyone might suspect. This pious hope is certainly no treachery to our Society! Everyone knows that I declare myself an adherent of the Freudian Society, and Jung cannot forgive me for this." He probably also could not forgive Freud that Spielrein now psychoanalytically belonged to him, although emotionally she was still strongly tied to Jung.

Finally a few last remarks, first about Spielrein's treatment, and then about her.

The most significant event in Spielrein's young life was that whatever happened during her treatment by Jung at the Burghölzli, it cured her. It is possible that separated from her parents, she might have cured herself, given her young age, high intelligence, and the unusual person she was; but in view of the severity of her disturbance and its early onset, this does not seem very likely. It is much more reasonable to assume, as it was assumed by her, by Jung, and by Freud, that it was what she experienced with Jung that cured her. If so, then Jung's behavior and attitude, as conveyed to her in their relationship—call it treatment, seduction, transference relations, love, mutual daydreams, delusions, or whatever else—was instrumental in achieving this cure. It is certainly also possible to think that her behavior toward him, and his toward her, as she tried to rework and master childhood traumata in late adolescence may have had the symbolic meaning of her being encouraged by him to act in ways which the world considered "dirty," despite the injunction not to do so which her name implied to her. In her infancy she had responded to this injunction with an ambivalence that had kept her in thrall; now she resolved it by realizing that the only important matter was that she act in line with her convictions, whatever the world might call her actions.

Whatever may be one's moral evaluation of Jung's behavior toward Spielrein, his first psychoanalytic patient, one must not disregard its most important consequence: he cured her from the disturbance for which she had been entrusted to his care. In retrospect we ought to ask ourselves: what convincing evidence do we have that the same result would have been achieved if Jung had behaved toward her the way we must expect a conscientious therapist to behave toward his patient? However questionable Jung's behavior was from a moral point of view— however unorthodox, even disreputable it may have been—somehow it met the prime obligation of the therapist toward his patient: to cure her. True, Spielrein paid a very high price in unhappiness, confusion, and disillusionment for the particular way in which she was cured, but then this is often true for mental patients who are as sick as she was.

Perhaps Spielrein's story offers us a useful reminder that, contrary to our easy optimism that we know exactly what is necessary in the therapy of psychologically very sick people, in their treatment there are more things in heaven and earth than are dreamt of in our philosophy.

So much for therapy—but what about Spielrein?

From the evidence of her letters and her diary, Sabina Spielrein emerges as one of the great women pioneers of psychoanalysis. She certainly was a most unusual person who courageously dared to live her life in accordance with her convictions, whatever the world may think of her love affair with a married man who had children. She remained true to her first love by not breaking with him despite his betrayal of her, and despite Freud's efforts to make her separate herself intellectually and emotionally from him. Her marriage and her having a child with her husband did not change this.

Not only was Spielrein brilliant and extremely sensitive, but her psychological intuition was extraordinary. She ended her seminal paper in which she was the first to propose the importance of the destructive impulse for our understanding of man by saying that the drive for procreation and with it the preservation of man arises psychologically "out of two antagonistic components, and hence is as much a creative as a destructive drive."

While Freud and Jung permitted their destructive impulses to drive them apart, the woman Spielrein remained to the end true to the creative impulse which, she hoped, would bring Freud and Jung together in a common enterprise for the benefit of mankind. She was sure that in respect to what is most important—the recognition of the significance of the unconscious, and of its being tamed for constructive purposes— they were basically in accord. To this unification of psychoanalysis she continued to devote herself.

One may hope that the idea to which Spielrein devoted herself may finally come to fruition, and the various psychoanalytic movements, which all derive from Freud's great discoveries, may come to realize that what they have in common is far more meaningful than what separates them. As with Freud and Jung, these differences originate more often in the vagaries of complicated personal relations and ambivalence than in sufficiently important valid theoretical differences, although it is these which are stressed in efforts to hide the all too human personal biases that account for them.

POSTSCRIPT

Magnus Ljunggren, Ph.D., motivated by my article, while studying at Moscow University in 1983 got into contact with Sabina Spielrein's niece, Menilche Spielrein, and gathered from her some biographical facts about her aunt which he kindly made available to me. From him I learned that Sabina Spielrein returned in 1923 to Russia. In the same year she joined the Institute of Psychology at Moscow University. While living in Moscow, she headed a psychoanalytic clinic for children, held seminars in child psychoanalysis, and was very active in the psychoanalytic society. In 1925, when psychoanalysis was no longer officially accepted, Spielrein left Moscow for Rostov. There her husband eventually developed a psychotic disturbance which led to his death in 1930. Because of this, or the changes occurring in Russia, Sabina became depressed and seemed to have stopped her psychoanalytic work around 1931.

On June 22, 1941, the day Hitler invaded the Soviet Union, Sabina's daughter, Renate, who had studied music in Moscow, left to join her mother and sister in Rostov. It is not clear what happened to the three of them. It is reported that when the Germans invaded Rostov all Jews were taken to the synagogue and shot. It seems most likely that the three of them died in this way.

Lionel Trilling on Literature and Psychoanalysis

T
he work of Lionel Trilling, the great literary critic, was much influenced by Freud and psychoanalysis. But psychoanalysis also owes a great debt to Trilling, because his writings accurately interpreted Freud's work for American intellectuals, particularly during the 1950s, when many misapprehensions about Freud and psychoanalysis abounded. In this regard, his book *The Liberal Imagination,* which appeared in 1950, was especially important. It was also the book which firmly established Trilling as the foremost literary critic of his generation.

Not only was Trilling's literary criticism informed by the thoughts of Freud, Trilling was also very impressed by Freud the person. He wrote in his 1962 introduction to the shortened version of Jones's biography of Freud: "Freud as a person stands before us with an exceptional distinctness and significance, and it is possible to say of him that there is no great figure of modern times who, seen as a developing mind and temperament, is of such singular interest."

The author is especially grateful to Diana Trilling for her courteous permission to use the extensive quotations from the work of Lionel Trilling that appear in this essay. The essay first appeared in vol. 3 of *Explorations: The Twentieth Century,* published by the University of Southwestern Louisiana, in the fall of 1989.

He continued: "If we ask why this is so, the first answer must of course be the magnitude and nature of his achievement. The effect that psychoanalysis has had upon the life of the West is incalculable. Beginning as a theory of certain illnesses of the mind, it went on to become a radically new and momentous theory of mind itself. Of the intellectual disciplines that have to do with the nature and destiny of mankind, there is none that has not responded to the force of his theory. Its concepts have established themselves in popular thought, though often in crude and sometimes perverted form, making not merely a new vocabulary but a new mode of judgment."

This "new mode of judgment" dominates much of Trilling's mature literary criticism. It is one of the yardsticks by which he measured literary and cultural achievement. Further, Trilling did his best to combat misunderstandings of Freud's ideas. He had nothing but contempt for the dilution and prettification that had been inflicted on Freud's teachings and those of psychoanalysis itself in the United States. He realized that such a dilution deprived Freud's teachings of their tragic implications for our understanding of man and his fate. He rejected strongly the efforts to distort Freud's teachings into an optimistic view of mankind.

As early as September 1942, Trilling wrote an article in *The Nation,* titled "The Progressive Psyche," in which he discussed Karen Horney's writings and severely criticized her deviation from Freud's teachings. He asserted that her views are "symptomatic of one of the great inadequacies of liberal thought, the need for optimism." He contrasted Horney's facile optimism regarding the feasibility of self-analysis, an optimism that denied the strength of the forces of repression and neurotic defenses, with the seriousness of Freud—who "dared to present man with the truth about his own nature." Trilling particularly praised Freud for recognizing "the complex and passionate interplay between biology and nurture." In this article Trilling also strenuously objected to Horney's view that neurosis is due to nothing but the impact on man of culture in general, and of society in particular.

It probably was not easy for Trilling to free himself of that need for optimism, and he shed it not without inner struggle, because it ran counter to the convictions he had held in his earlier days when, in common with so many of the young left intellectuals of his generation, he had embraced Marxism. Thinking back to those earlier years, he wrote in his essay on Isaac Babel: "In those days one still spoke of the 'Russian experiment' and one might still believe that the light of dawn glowed on the test-tubes and crucibles of human destiny. And it was still possible to have very strange expectations of the new culture that would arise from the Revolution. I do not remember what my own particular expectations were, except that they involved a desire for an art that would have as little ambiguity as a proposition in logic. Why I wanted this I don't wholly understand. It was as if I hoped that the literature of the Revolution would realize some simple, inadequate notion of the 'classical' which I had picked up at college; and perhaps I was drawn to this notion of the classical because I was afraid of the literature of modern Europe, because I was scared of its terrible intensities, ironies, and ambiguities."

Even as Trilling wrote this, he seems to have felt still a trace of nostalgia for the days when he could embrace certainties and avoid ambiguities, for he added: "If this is what I really felt, I can't say that I am now wholly ashamed of my cowardice." But he resolutely freed himself of it, as he relinquished the need for optimism and easy certainties and embraced instead the complexities and the ambiguities of the Freudian concept of man.

Writing about Freud's *Civilization and Its Discontents* in his own *Sincerity and Authenticity*, Trilling praises it as "a work of extraordinary power," and asserted that "for social thought [it stands] like a lion in the path of all types of achieving happiness through the radical revision of social life." Thus it was his making the psychoanalytic view of man his own which permitted him to free himself of his earlier belief in Marxism.

Trilling stressed in his writings how important it was that Freud taught us to see the nature of man and his personality as rooted, not in society, but in his biological inheritance. He based this conviction on what is popularly called Freud's "instinct theory," although Freud, in his own writings, seldom referred to instincts per se—rather, he spoke of drives. The term "instinct" in the English editions of Freud's writings is an erroneous translation of the German word *Trieb*, which Freud uses frequently throughout his writings, and which is translated correctly as "drive."

The drives Freud was mostly concerned with are the sex drive, which Freud variously called libido or eros, and the death drive, or thanatos. Eros is generally accepted as being of the greatest importance in man's makeup, since the continuation of our race is based on it. But thanatos, the death drive, was and is still rejected by the American psychoanalytical establishment, an error which is emphatically decried by Trilling. He—in my opinion correctly—thinks that in the United States the death drive is denied because of what he calls "the need for optimism."

While this is certainly so, I believe it is but part of an even more general tendency in the United States to avoid all thoughts of death. Witness that in popular usage people don't die, but "pass on," and that after death, the corpse is arranged by the undertaker to appear most lifelike. One speaks of visiting the corpse, as if to deny the fact that the person has died. Another aspect of this widespread denial of the ineluctability of death is that even nonbelievers wish to think that a return from death is possible, as suggested by the accounts about persons who supposedly "returned from death," while in reality they never stopped living but only seemed to have done so.

So of Freud's theory of drives only one-half, the sex drive, is generally accepted in the United States. But even the libido's tremendous importance in man's makeup is diminished by the liberal establishment, which holds that man is conditioned and shaped mainly by social and economic factors, rather than by his biological inheritance.

One of the essays in which Trilling dealt most exhaustively with the relationship between literature and psychoanalysis as he saw it is titled "Freud: Within and Beyond Culture" and appeared in his book *Beyond Culture*. Here he wrote:

> Whether or not Freud's formulations of the death instinct stand up under scientific inquiry, I of course cannot venture to say. But certainly they confirm our sense of Freud's oneness with the tradition of literature. For literature has always recorded the impulse of the self to find affirmation even in its own extinction, even *by* its own extinction. When we read the great scene of death of Oedipus at Colonus, we have little trouble, I think, in at least suspending our disbelief in Freud's idea. We do so the more willingly because the impulse toward death is in this magnificent moment, expressed and exemplified by the most passionate of men, the man in whom the energy of will and intellect was greatest, the man, too, who at the moment of his desire for death speaks of his extraordinary power of love.

Now Freud may be right or he may be wrong in the place he gives to biology in human fate, but I think we must stop considering whether this emphasis on biology, correct or incorrect, is not so far from being a reactionary idea that it is actually a liberating idea. It proposes that culture is not all-powerful. It suggests that there is a residue of human quality beyond the reach of cultural control, and that this residue of human quality, elemental as it may be, serves to bring culture under criticism and keeps it from being absolute. . . .

Nowadays there is scarcely a humanistic discipline or a social science that has not been touched by Freud's ideas. . . . But of course no other profession has had so long or so intimate a connection with psychoanalysis as the profession of literature. . . . The great contribution he has made to our understanding of literature does not arise from what he says about literature itself but from what he says about the nature of the human mind: he showed us that poetry is indigenous to the very constitution of the mind; he saw the mind as being, in the greater part of its tendency, exactly of the poetry-making faculty. . . .

The first thing that occurs to me to say about literature, as I consider it in the relation in which Freud stands to it, is that literature is dedicated to the conception of the self. . . . At the behest of literature, and with its help [we are] able to imagine the selfhood of others, no doubt through the process of identification. . . . What the *Iliad* conceives in the way of selfhood is far beyond what could be conceived by the culture in which it was written.

Freud in *Civilization and Its Discontents* "had presented a paranoid version of the relation of the self to culture; he conceived of the self submitting to culture and being yet in opposition to it; he conceived of the self as being not wholly continuous with culture, as being not wholly created by culture, as maintaining a standing quarrel with its great benefactor."

The last paragraph of this essay, which contains one of Trilling's most thoroughgoing discussions of Freudian thought, reads:

I need scarcely remind you that in respect of this "paranoia" Freud is quite at one with literature. In its essence literature is concerned with the self; and the particular concern of the literature of the last two centuries has been the self in its standing quarrel with culture. We cannot mention the name of any great writer of the modern period whose work has not in some way, and usually in a passionate and explicit way, insisted on this quarrel, who has not expressed the bitterness of his discontent with civilization, who has not said that the self made greater legitimate demands than any culture can hope to satisfy. This intense conviction of the existence of the self apart from culture is, as culture well knows, its noblest and most generous achievement. At the present moment it must be thought of as a liberating idea without which our developing ideal of community is bound to defeat itself. We can speak no greater praise of Freud than to say that he placed this idea at the very center of his thought.

Undoubtedly one's life history and personal development do greatly affect one's ability to accept the insights of psychoanalysis and live with them. Mark Krupnik, in *Lionel Trilling and the Fate of Cultural Criticism*, points to some of Trilling's inner conflicts as influences on his personal and intellectual development. He mentions in this respect particularly what he calls Trilling's "positive Jewishness" embraced in his youth and early years of adulthood which conflicted with the ideal of the gentleman scholar and literary critic that became characteristic of Trilling's mature years. An equally problematic conflict was that between what Krupnik calls "the downtown world of radical politics," to which Trilling belonged as part of the circle around the *Partisan Review* and the "uptown world" of Columbia University with its particular ambience. Columbia certainly made its demands on Trilling, not least because he was the first Jew to teach in its English department. These inner conflicts, and possibly also others, probably convinced Trilling that only a view of man as torn by inner conflicts can permit a full understanding of him and his nature. That is, only what Freud called the unending battle between eternal eros and eternal thanatos, between id and superego, can provide us with that deeper understanding of man and his artistic creations which Trilling tries to convey to us in his literary criticisms.

There can be no doubt that as Trilling's mind matured, Freud's biologism replaced Marxism as his worldview, or rather the view of man and his nature most congenial to his purposes and insights. From then on, the conflicts within man, rather than those between social classes, became the central concern informing Trilling's understanding and appreciation of literature.

Trilling makes this worldview explicit in many of his mature essays.

For example, speaking of Henry James's fiction, specifically *The Bostonians,* Trilling writes that at the center of the novel is "the conflict of two principles of which one is radical, the other conservative," and that this conflict can be thought of in terms of "energy and inertia . . . or force and form . . . or Libido and Thanatos."

Still, adherences to "the truth of the body, the truth of full sexuality, the truth of open aggressiveness have a high price," as Trilling asserts in his essay on Babel. It is a truth that particularly Jewish intellectuals—like Babel and, by implication, Trilling himself—have often to pay as the price of a true understanding of culture. Trilling mentions in this connection that Babel complained of being an intellectual with spectacles on his nose and autumn in his heart; spectacles, one must assume, that interfere with seeing the truths of the body and of a full sexuality which stand at the center of Freud's system; while the autumn in the heart results from the realization that true happiness is all but unattainable by man. The reason it is unattainable, according to Freud, is that we are torn by inner conflicts and in addition the knowledge of our mortality, the omnipresence of the idea of death even in the midst of life, vitiates against full happiness in it.

I believe that what made the Freudian system so attractive to Trilling was Freud's conviction that the best we can gain out of life is to be able to love well and to work well, despite our inner conflicts and the knowledge that death is life's inescapable end. Witness the fact that in *The Liberal Imagination* he quotes with high approval Scott Fitzgerald's sentence "The test of a first rate intelligence is the ability to hold two opposite ideas in the mind at the same time, and still retain the ability to function." And one may think that the sentence from *Howards End,* "Death destroys a man but the idea of death is what saves him," which Trilling quotes, represents his idea of what makes for the truly moral and artistic life.

Despite these thoughts, Trilling's view of man and his culture is by no means a negative or joyless one. In his essay "William Dean Howells and the Roots of Modern Taste" he does me the honor of quoting me as follows:

> A fight for survival of civilized mankind is actually a fight to restore man
> in a sensitivity toward the joys of life. Only in this way can man be liber-
> ated and the survival of civilized mankind be assured. Maybe a time has

come in which our main efforts need no longer be directed toward modifying the pleasure principle. Maybe it is time we became concerned with restoring pleasure gratification to its dominant role in the reality principle; maybe society needs less modification of the pleasure principle by reality, and more assertion of the pleasure principle against an overpowering pleasure-denying reality.

Trilling thereupon continues: "It cannot be said of Howells's smiling aspects that they represent a very intense kind of pleasure; yet for most men they will at least serve, in Keats's phrase, to bind us to the earth, to prevent our being seduced by the godhead of disintegration." It was Trilling's conviction that we must not permit ourselves to be seduced by "the godhead of disintegration" which accounted for his strong rejection of that anti-intellectualism which became the dominant mood of the sixties.

In the same essay on Howells and the roots of modern taste, Trilling quotes Hannah Arendt: "To yield to the process of disintegration has become irresistible temptation, not only because it has assumed the spurious grandeur of 'historical necessity,' but also because everything outside it has begun to appear lifeless, bloodless, meaningless, and unreal." This fascination with disintegration, with what Trilling calls the charisma of evil, is a danger of which he is keenly aware, perhaps because in his Marxist days he had been so taken with the idea of a historical necessity which determines the fate of man and of society.

It is Trilling's repudiation of this Marxist belief in a historical necessity, and his conviction that the root of man is not in society but in himself, which accounts for the Freudian concept of the self becoming ever more dominant in Trilling's thinking and writing. He chose *The Opposing Self* as the title of his 1955 collection of essays; and he came to see the affirmation of the self as the central theme of all great literature.

In the book *Sincerity and Authenticity,* Trilling is much concerned with the true self, both in literature and in culture. He states right at the beginning that "Sigmund Freud took the first step toward devising a laborious discipline where it [i.e., one's own self] might be found." Looking back at the beginning of psychoanalysis, Trilling comments: "When Freud's thought was first presented to a scandalized world, the recognition of unconditioned instinctual impulse which lies at the core was erroneously taken to mean that Freud wished to establish the dominion of impulse, with all that this implies of the negation of the socialized self. But then of course it became understood that the bias of psycho-analysis so far from being Dionysian, is wholly in the service of the Apollonian principle, seeking to strengthen the 'honest soul' in the selfhood which is characterized by purposiveness and a clear recognition of limits."

What seemed to have interested Trilling most in Freud and psychoanalysis was the parallel which he saw between their teachings and view of man and his world, and what great literature conveys to us in different but analogous form. In his essay "Freud's Last Book," which he published in *A Gathering of Fugitives,* he discusses Freud's *An Outline of Psychoanalysis.* There Trilling writes: "If we look for an analogue to Freud's vision of life, we find it, I think, in certain great literary minds. Say what we will about Freud's dealings with Shakespeare, his is the Shakespearean vision. And it is no mere accident that he levied upon Sophocles for the name of his central concept." Elaborating on this analogy, he continues: "No doubt the thing we respond to in great tragedy is the implication of some meaningful relation between free will and necessity, and it is what we respond to in Freud. One of the common objections to Freud is that he grants too much to necessity, and that, in doing so, he limits the scope of man's possible development. There is irony in this accusation, in view of the whole intention of psychoanalysis, which is to free the soul from bondage to necessities that do not actually exist so that it may effectually confront those that do exist. Like any tragic poet, like any true moralist, Freud took it as one of his tasks to define the border of necessity in order to establish the realm of freedom."

After discussing how Freud sees man as being limited by his own nature, Trilling continues: "Man as Freud conceives him makes his own limiting necessity by being man. This stern but never hopeless knowledge is precisely the vision of reality that we respond to in tragic art. . . . The tragic vision requires the full awareness of the limits which necessity imposes. But it deteriorates if it does not match this awareness with an idea of freedom. Freud undertook to provide such an idea—it was his life work." It is for these reasons, and in recognition of Freud's style, that Trilling says that this last work of Freud is "the occasion of an aesthetic experience."

Earlier, in his essay "Freud and Literature," which appeared in *The*

Liberal Imagination, Trilling had expressed his conviction that the Freudian system is the one most congenial to poetry because "of all mental systems, the Freudian psychology is the one which makes poetry indigenous to the very constitution of the mind. Indeed the mind as Freud sees it, is in greater part of its tendency exactly a poetry-making organ. . . . Freud has not merely naturalized poetry; he has discovered its status as a pioneer settler, and he sees it as a method of thought." Also, "the idea of the reality principle and the idea of the death instinct form the crown of Freud's broader speculation on the life of man. Their quality of grim poetry is characteristic of Freud's system and the ideas it generates for him."

Elsewhere in this same essay, Trilling writes: "The Freudian psychology is the only systematic account of the human mind which, in point of subtlety and complexity, of interest and tragic power, deserves to stand beside the chaotic mass of psychological insight which literature has accumulated through the centuries. To pass from reading a great literary work to a treatise of academic psychology is to pass from one order of perception to another, but the nature of Freudian psychology is exactly the stuff upon which the poet has always exercised his art. It is therefore not surprising that psychoanalytic theory has a great effect upon literature. Yet the relationship is reciprocal, and the effect of Freud upon literature has been no greater than the effect of literature upon Freud." This great effect that literature had on his thinking Freud always freely and gratefully acknowledged, as Trilling likewise acknowledged the effect of Freud's thinking and teaching on his literary criticism.

Trilling sees psychoanalysis as one of the culminations of Romantic literature, because it was passionately devoted to research into the self. His prime example is Diderot's *Rameau's Nephew,* written in 1762, from which he quotes: "If the little savage," meaning the little child, "were left to himself, if he preserved all his foolishness and combined the violent passions of a man of thirty with the lack of reason of a child in the cradle, he'd wring his father's neck and go to bed with his mother." Here, well over a century before Freud, the essence of the boy's oedipal wishes are spelled out and taken for granted by a great writer, insights which Freud attained only through laborious study of himself and of his patients. These are ideas which even now, despite Freud's teachings, are by no means generally accepted. It is also one illustration of the truth of Freud's claim, which he stated repeatedly, that he did not discover anything about the human psyche that the great poets and artists of past times had not known.

Trilling continues in the same essay, "What, then, is the difference between, on the one hand, the dream and the neurosis, and, on the other hand, art? That they have certain common elements is of course clear; that unconscious processes are at work in both would be denied by no poet or critic; they share too, although in different degrees, the element of fantasy. But there is a vital difference between them which Charles Lamb saw so clearly in his defense of the sanity of genius: 'The poet dreams being awake. He is not possessed by his subject but he has dominion over it.' This is the whole difference: the poet is in command of his fantasy, while it is exactly the mark of the neurotic that he is possessed by his fantasy."

Despite this crucial difference, literature and psychoanalysis do have much in common. As Trilling points out in *Sincerity and Authenticity,* "I need scarcely say [that] psychoanalysis is a science which is based upon narrations, upon telling. Its principle of explanation consists in getting the story told—somehow, anyhow—in order to discover how it begins. It presumes that the tale which is told will yield counsel."

In *Beyond Culture,* Trilling moves to consider the importance of the suspension of disbelief in literature and in psychoanalysis:

> One of the best-known tags of literary criticism is Coleridge's phrase "the willing suspension of disbelief." Coleridge says that the willing suspension of disbelief constitutes "poetic faith." . . . This Freud was able to do in a most extraordinary way, and not by the mere impulse of his temperament, but systematically, as an element of his science. . . . [When his patients told him stories they invented,] he did not blame them, he did not say they were lying—he willingly suspended his disbelief in their fantasies, which they themselves believed, and taught himself how to find the truth that was really in them.
>
> From it followed the willing suspension of disbelief in the semantic value of dreams, and the willing suspension of disbelief in the concept of mind, which all well-trained neurologists and psychiatrists of Vienna knew to be a chimera. Freud's acceptance of the fantasies of his early patients, his conclusion that their untruths had a meaning, a pur-

pose, and even a value, was the suspension of disbelief in the selfhood of these patients. Its analogue is not, I think, the religious virtue of charity, but something in which the intelligence plays a greater part. We must be reminded of that particular kind of understanding, that particular exercise of the literary intelligence by which we judge adversely the deeds of Achilles, but not Achilles himself, by which we do not blame Macbeth. . . .

If we go on with our gross summary comparison of literature and psychoanalysis, we can say that they are also similar in this respect: that it is of the essence of both to represent the opposition between two principles, that which Freud called the reality principle and the pleasure principle. . . . Freud is scarcely unique in conceiving of literature in terms of the opposition between reality and pleasure. This conception is endemic in literary criticism itself since at least the time of Plato. . . . Wordsworth speaks of the principle of pleasure—the phrase is his—as constituting the "naked and native dignity of man." He says, moreover, that it is the principle by which man not only "feels, and lives, and moves," but also "knows": the principle of pleasure was for Wordsworth the very ground of the principle of reality, and so of course it is for Freud, even though he seems to maintain the irreconcilability of the two principles. And the mature Yeats, in that famous sentence of his, which is as Freudian in its tendency as it is Wordsworthian, tells us, "In dreams begins responsibility." He bases the developed moral life on the autonomy of the youthful hedonistic fantasies.

"Beauty is truth, truth beauty," said Keats. . . . When Keats said that beauty is truth, he was saying that the pleasure principle is at the root of existence, and of knowledge, and of the moral life. When he said that truth is beauty, he was putting in two words his enormous complex belief that the self can so develop that it may, in the intensity of art or meditation, perceive even very painful facts with a kind of pleasure, for it is one of the striking things about Keats that he represents so boldly and accurately the development of the self, and that, when he speaks of pleasure, he may mean—to use a language not his—sometimes the pleasure of the id, sometimes of the ego, and sometimes of the superego.

In "Freud and the Crisis of our Culture," Trilling writes about Freud that "we cannot fail to pronounce him one of the greatest humanist minds." In this respect Trilling was his equal, and in many other respects, too, as noted here, theirs were kindred minds. From Trilling's writings one can gain a better comprehension of Freud and psychoanalysis than from most other books written about them. Freud could not have wished for a better spokesman to tell about his contributions to our understanding of culture in general, and of literature in particular.

PART II

On Children and Myself

Essential Books of One's Life

I f we enjoy reading, books enrich our lives as nothing else can do. Some throw new light on vexing problems, others open up new vistas on the world or on man in general and—most important of all—on ourselves. Although many books can enlarge our horizons, and some may influence aspects of our life, only a very few will change its course.

At least so it was with me: while many books made a strong impression on my thinking, only a few changed my very being. On reading these books, I experienced what Edmund Wilson so aptly described as a "shock of recognition," because they enlightened me about what were (at the time) my most pressing problems in finding my way in life. And they did so despite the fact that I knew not all of them were great books while I was reading them, powerfully impressed by them as I was. Some were great books, but others were not, neither as works of literature, nor by virtue of their content. As it happened, becoming acquainted with these books at particular moments in my life took on the features of revelation—of new vision that put my inner world into some order,

This essay appeared in the French Swiss magazine *Le Temps Stratégique*, Nos. 23 and 24 (1987–88). It is here for the first time published in English.

where before there had been great uncertainty and confusion, if not outright chaos.

The reading of a book could bring about this "shock of recognition" only because something had been going on in myself which, unbeknownst to me, had made me ready for and even needful of the message. Some inner process had been at work, something vague which suddenly attained form and concrete content through reading a book. Thus some books have made it possible for me to recognize what has been germinating in me, usually for quite some time, with no awareness on my part beyond a feeling that something was not quite right with me and my life, that something needed rectifying—and this without my having any idea what was wrong, or what needed to be done about it. In a different form, I encountered this experience in my own psychoanalysis, when a significant unconscious process suddenly became clear to me, and I realized, with a shock of recognition, "This is it!"—the "it" being something with which I had been struggling, perhaps even to the point of obsession, without knowing that this was going on in my mind. Years later, as a practitioner of psychoanalysis, I met with this shock of recognition again in my patients, when suddenly things fell into place for them and confusion was replaced by clarity.

Books that do this for the reader provide quite a different experience from that provided by other books which also make a strong impression. Luckily there are many books that can move one deeply, even though they do not produce the shock of recognition and do not reveal something of greatest personal significance.

At the time that I read books that helped me change my life, permitted it to attain greater meaning and some new direction, I also read many other books which were "great literature," masterpieces that I admired. But the world of these books, while fascinating, was too alien for me to feel that the books were in some ways also about me and my life. An example that comes to mind is the novels of Dostoevsky. They moved me deeply and opened up a world very different from my own. I could not put them down, and I read one after another, entranced by the world they showed me. But they were not about me and my pressing problems. While they added much to my life, they brought about no change in it. Perhaps the Russian ambience was too alien for that; but I think it was rather the deeply felt Russian religiosity permeating these novels which prevented me from feeling that they carried a personal message.

However, it cannot only have been that the Russian "soul" was too strange to my experience, because the same was true for other novels that impressed me very much while depicting a world more familiar to me. For instance, I was very taken by Romain Rolland's *Jean Christophe.* I loved reading it, but I did not find myself in it. I can only conclude that nothing in me had prepared me for making significant changes sparked by the experience of reading these books.

For a book to change one's life, processes—as mentioned before— must have been going on within oneself to make one ready and eager to change. Other books may have an impact that carried one away for a time, without actually influencing one's life. For example, when I read Sinclair Lewis's *Arrowsmith,* and for a few days afterward, I was convinced that only becoming a medical researcher could fulfill my hopes in life. However, this did not last long, because even while reading *Arrowsmith* I felt that it was not quite up to my own literary standards as a great book; and although I was tempted for a time to think of myself as a future medical researcher, deep down I knew that this was not the right profession for me. Clearly, nothing in me had prepared me to respond to this reading with the lightning shock of recognition which would say, "This book answers questions, solves problems, that have deeply disturbed me, that I have been struggling with without my knowing that this was so; and through reading it, suddenly everything has fallen into place, all my unasked questions have been answered by it."

Whether or not a book will influence us depends on our mental state at the time we are reading it. The more finally our personality has been formed, the more set in our ways of thinking and living we are, the less will books be able to change us; also, the more our personality will determine both our choice of books and what we get out of reading them. Then we are likely to read those books which are in accordance with our values and preferences. Witness the fact that most people read chiefly those books and periodicals whose values conform to their own, thus reinforcing their point of view. A magazine or book or newspaper likely to present views opposite to those we cherish will have little appeal, if any. And even when we read them, our minds will be closed to their message. Hence most books are denied the chance to alter opinions already firmly held.

All through life we may read books for enjoyment and for the information we gain, arousing and at the same time satisfying our curiosity; but only at certain periods in our lives will we read books in the hope that they will influence it, give it direction, solve pressing problems. This is especially true when we find ourselves in a crisis of life or when we are undergoing obscure inner developments. Then a book can influence our whole being, while the same book read at another, more settled period of life may impress us very little. Thus all depends on when in our development as persons we read a book. Very few books can be read with pleasure all our lives, and even when one can, the pleasure we experience is different at different ages.

One of the best ways to see how much we have changed and, we hope, grown over the years is to reread books that at one time were very meaningful to us. This experience was so valuable in understanding my own development that, in teaching psychology to university students, I encouraged them to reread books they had loved at one time. Their task was to try to understand why this had been so, and why it often no longer was, or not to the same degree. They were usually amazed that in this way they were able to recognize change in themselves and to speculate about its causes. Thus how we react to what we read is always a function more of what is going on in us at the time than of a book's content.

I learned to love the theater when I was quite young. In adolescence I saw three, four, or even five serious plays a week, which was easy to do in Vienna, a city that was then and still is devoted to the theater. I was so infatuated with the theater that when I entered the university I decided to study drama and the history of the theater. But after two years of these studies the theater stopped being a central preoccupation for me. While I have continued to enjoy good theater all my life, it lost much of its luster as I aged. Other forms of literature became more important to me, and as far as the theater is concerned, I began to be touched deeply by plays that had not affected me in my youth. Typically, classical Greek drama became even more significant to me.

While I was young, the first part of Goethe's *Faust* entranced me; and this not just because, like *Faust*, I had tried by then to study a variety of disciplines without finding through them the answers I was seeking; and not because, like him, I was thirsting for the ideal love. At that time, when the tragedy's first part filled me with admiration and had so much to offer me, the second part of *Faust,* while intellectually stimulating, had little personal meaning. The end of the second part was disappointing when it turned out that Faust's great effort to improve the fate of mankind was an abysmal failure, even destroying lovely Philemon and Baucis, as Gretchen was destroyed at the end of the first part. But there Faust had tried to save Gretchen, whereas he made no attempt to save Philemon and Baucis. It seemed pitiful to me that the old and blind Faust could be so easily deceived about what he regarded as the crowning achievement of his life. I had little sympathy for him, perhaps because I had to silence my fear that I might be similarly fooled about the merits of my life's work. So I protected myself against this danger by believing that nobody could fool me like that.

However, in old age I was deeply touched by this scene and the end of the tragedy of *Faust.* By then the desire to feel that one has not labored in vain, that one has accomplished something in life which will benefit future generations, was so familiar that I understood from personal experience how wishing might blind one to what was really going on. Faust's blindness at the end of his life, which in my younger years I had taken for simply one of the infirmities of old age, I then recognized as a symbol of how hard it is, even for the wisest of men, to see reality when the wish and hope that one has lived a meaningful life becomes overwhelming. As a young man I was convinced that one had to create something worthwhile to believe that one's life had not been wasted; but as an old man I knew that the best one can hope for in one's life, and what is sufficient for one's salvation, is contained in the statement justifying Faust's apotheosis, as the angels sing: *"Wer immer strebend sich bemüht, den können wir erlösen"* ("He who always strains and strives with all his power, him we are able to redeem").

This was not an isolated experience for me in respect to a masterpiece created in old age. Whether these were works of literature or art or music, they became accessible to me to the fullest extent only after I had reached old age. Still, while it took old age to attune me to the second part of *Faust,* and to the works created in old age by Rembrandt, Titian, Michelangelo, and others, my greater and more complete appreciation of them was not so much because in a long life I had become ever more familiar with them—which may have helped—but much more because my own development permitted me to find much deeper meaning in them. This development led me beyond admiration, which I had felt all along for these works, to feel finally that they were, in some no longer so mysterious ways, also about me. Thus it was my own development over my own course of life which permitted a much more refined appreciation of these works; they had not influenced or brought about this development in me.

There seem to exist—at least for me—affinities between one's own age and that of the creator of great works of art and literature, affinities that clear the way to one's understanding so that these works become much more meaningful on a very personal level, and not mainly in an artistic way. This is the reason I have no doubt that one's own development allows some books to become more meaningful than they had been before a particular stage in one's life. Books lie in wait for our readiness, and this is probably true in any civilization that has books.

B y contrast, there are also other books that strongly influence personal development, that make development possible and shape it in large measure, if not entirely. In my own experience, this is more likely to occur at a time when one seeks to find oneself, particularly in periods when one strives to form an identity; typically, this occurs during adolescence. Then books can and do work powerfully to shape one's views of oneself and the world.

Freud's work and writings eventually made me become a psychoanalyst, but this dominant influence was exercised on my development long before I made a professional choice. Becoming acquainted with his writings was the single most liberating experience of my early adolescence, despite the fact that I planned for a very different career at that time.

As I try to sort out which were the books most influential in making me become the person I am, I recall that Freud, in his autobiographical writings, reports that his professional choice (and with it his creation of psychoanalysis!) was due to his reading an essay of Goethe's. Goethe's great essay on nature made Freud abandon an earlier desire to become a political leader who would change the course of the world for the better, and decide to become a natural scientist. Thus, the course of Freud's life was in part determined by a work of literature.

In my case, no such sudden revelation due to my becoming aware of a work of literature led to a radical transformation. But there were some books which, read at the right time, made me become the person I am. Without drastically changing my life, they gave it new direction and content.

Probably the earliest works of literature that strongly influenced me were fairy tales, as first told by my mother, and then read by myself; but I do not consciously recall that these tales exercised a formative impact on me. However, they must have done so, because otherwise I would not, late in life, have spent years trying to understand their psychological meaning for children, an undertaking which I found most rewarding, not least because it entailed a careful rereading and contemplation of many fairy tales of various lands. Just why and how fairy tales became so important to me I can no longer fathom, although I am pretty sure that the reason is that they were mainly told to me by my mother. Thus we see that how and by whom works of literature are mediated to us can account for the depth of meaning they acquire. As I have written elsewhere, parents who want to deepen their relationship with their child can do so by reading to the child, but of course their interest in this activity must be genuine. We also see that poems read aloud by the poet often make a much deeper impression than when read silently to oneself. Similarly, fiction read aloud can become much more meaningful to the listener than when read silently.

It makes a great deal of difference whether a work of literature is experienced also as an event between people, for instance between parent and child; also, there is a difference in the impact of a drama seen on the stage and that of one read silently. Some of the books which influenced me most deeply were read and appreciated at the same time by close friends with whom I discussed them at great length. Thus, whether or not reading a book is an interpersonal experience can become decisive for the impact it makes.

Like most people, I read a great deal that was somehow useful to me, without such reading influencing my life in a particular way. Even during my childhood I was a voracious reader, but then mostly of escapist literature. Historical novels permitted me to escape into the distant past, while other books, such as those of Karl May, gave me a chance to escape into the faraway Wild West; some utopian literature, the science fiction of those days, allowed escape into the distant future. All these books helped me to escape the distressing reality of the years of the First

World War, from 1914 to 1918. For a Viennese boy who up to the beginning of the war had lived a very sheltered existence and a life of greatest ease and comfort, the war came as a very rude awakening to the hardships of life, for which nothing had prepared me. Escapist literature permitted me to forget for long periods of time how difficult life had become for me, so I learned at an early age what great relief books can provide.

All this rather suddenly changed in 1917 when, at the age of fourteen, I reached adolescence. By then the ravages of the war made it much harder to blind oneself to them by escaping into fantasies fed by reading. While before I had taken the world of my parents more or less for granted, growing up and gaining a different awareness made me angry and critical of a world which permitted such a terrible slaughter to take place and even to continue unabated. This made me reach out to books that would help me form my own judgments and achieve an independent personality, instead of merely following the guidelines of my background and education; I wanted books which would suggest how the horrors of the world at large could be rectified, rather than merely provide escape from such horrors, as had been sufficient for me up to this time.

This wider world touched me and infringed upon my freedom in the school—in my case, that of the Real Gymnasium. Its authoritarian nature offended me very much, while at the same time I came to cherish—for the rest of my life—the humanities taught there. So the first books that I found truly liberating were those which were critical of the existing educational system and thus supported my conviction that there must be better ways to educate the young. At this moment I no longer recall whether my joining the leftist youth movement of Vienna, the Jung Wandervogel, preceded or closely followed my becoming aware of the Freie Schulgemeinde (Free School Community) which Gustav Wyneken had created at Wickersdorf in Germany. The slogan of the Jung Wandervogel was ADEA, which stood for *Abboniere den Anfang,* meaning "subscribe to the *Anfang*" ("Beginning"), the publication of this movement for school reform.

And subscribe to it I did. I was enthusiastic about the educational methods advocated there. Having been forced to study what my teachers decided I should learn, as well as learning it in the way they insisted, I was delighted by the idea that children should have a say in what they learned and how they learned it. That all learning should be an activity in which teachers and students participate more or less as equals, that much learning ought to occur around projects which required study for its completion—these were all entirely new ideas to me, who had up to that time known only an education in which students were the passive objects of the educational enterprise. That children could decide how the school would operate, or at least have an important influence on it, was so contrary to what I had known in home and school that these ideas truly opened up to me a new world of thinking and being.

What I learned and gained from reading the *Anfang* was truly a new beginning for me. It formed the basis of my educational convictions, which, many years later, I was fortunate enough to be able to set into practice in the United States when I became head of a pioneering educational institution. Thus, this reading was crucial for my personal, my intellectual, and my vocational development. At the same time, publications opposing the war, foremost Karl Kraus's *Die Fackel,* provided much-desired spiritual guidance, both for my pacifist and my intellectual and literary leanings. With my close friends in the Wandervogel youth movement I discussed both the pacifist ideas derived from Karl Kraus and the thoughts about school reform, and this was another experience that taught me how one's reading can attain much more meaning, with correspondingly deeper inpressions, when close personal relations are brought to bear.

Participation in this youth movement also happened to introduce me to Freud and psychoanalysis. That sex need not be a taboo area and that sexual anxiety can be relieved and sexual repression undone were terribly liberating notions for a middle-class adolescent in Vienna at that time. This was personal liberation, but the writings of the free school movement represented social liberation, since it offered an alternative to the regime under which I chafed. It offered a freer, better, and more humane way to educate the young—like me. Freud seemed to offer freedom from the sexual restraints and anxieties from which I, a typically inhibited middle-class adolescent, suffered; and the combination of sexual liberation and educational reform became a revelation, since both suggested that I need not suffer from what severely oppressed me. What greater service can books give us than to free us from anger and anxiety about possible school failure and the nightmares of sexual fear?

The impact of these readings never weakened and even still continues to shape my life. From the age of fourteen, I read everything that

Freud had written and devoured whatever he published from that time on. In my university years, I tried to read more systematically about educational reform, Dewey most of all, but also early writings by Rousseau, Pestalozzi, and others. Little did I know that the seeds then planted would lead to my life's work in which I tried to combine the insights of psychoanalysis with techniques of education that would liberate both the mind and the emotions.

During the years of my adolescence, which I now calculate to be from the age of about fourteen to my twenties, other books were very important in my personal and intellectual development. These were the times of the end of the First World War, the collapse of the Hapsburg Empire, the terrible inflation, and other catastrophic events which, in their combination, forced on me a reevaluation of all my values. I had been brought up with the words of the song which asserted that Austria would last eternally, "Österreich wird ewig stehen," and had firmly believed it in my childhood. So events forced me to acquire a new understanding of history. Circumstances led me to give up cherished beliefs which had made life comfortable and secure, and to acquire new ones truer to reality. In such a time of upheaval in one's inner world, and in the outer world in which one lives, the right books—that is, those which meet one's needs for understanding and clarification—will make a deeper impression than they might make at any other time in one's life.

Personal experiences within my family and my adolescent turmoil combined with a terrible war to make me feel deeply pessimistic about life and myself. The belief in progress which my parents had instilled in me and which the teachings of history in school had solidified could not be maintained in view of what was now happening in the world. From my reading of Freud I had learned how great a role in man's life is played by the irrational element of his mind. So it was a revelation when in reading Theodore Lessing's *Geschichte als Sinngebung des Sinnlosen* ("History as Projecting Meaning into the Meaningless") I learned that history is not an account of man's progress over time, but that this progress and the meaning of historical events are only projections of man's wishful thinking. Lessing's stress on the irrational elements in history and historical writings made excellent sense to a youngster who had found Freud's emphasis on the irrational in man such a liberating experience.

Through Lessing I became acquainted with F. A. Lange's remark

"Man needs to supplement reality by an ideal world," an idea I needed very badly to make life bearable for me. This quotation induced me to read Lange's *History of Materialism,* which also changed my view of history. But Lange's writings, while very enlightening, did not alter the course of my life, did not help me to cope with the immediate problems which my depressive tendencies posed to me and which stymied my actions. However, Lessing's encouragement to believe in fiction as a way to make life bearable actually helped me greatly in making a go of things despite my deep-seated pessimism. Lessing's book convinced me that to proceed on the fiction that the cosmos is an orderly place is a great convenience. Lessing led me to read Hans Vaihinger, whose *The Philosophy of "As If"* demonstrated the need and usefulness of acting on the basis of fictions that are known to be false. His remark that mankind was a species of monkey suffering from megalomania impressed me very much, because it seemed to explain the behavior of my schoolmasters and of many other persons in authority without seeming to apply to myself. Vaihinger's view was that pessimism can give one the moral strength that enables one to endure life, at the same time helping one develop a more objective sense of the world; this seemed to justify my pessimism and, more important, permitted me to think of it as constructive, whereas before I had been convinced that my pessimism was only destructive, though since it was my honest view I could do nothing about it. Together these two authors provided the guidance I needed most of all: how one may manage to live a meaningful life despite one's inner doubts. This lesson has proved its value all through my life.

Despite my philosophical conviction that we must live by fictions—not just to find meaning in life but to make it bearable, which was such a revelation to me and shaped my underlying attitudes to life—I failed to apply this idea to my understanding of the second part of *Faust.* This I did only after I was over eighty years old. Only then did I realize Goethe's great wisdom in having the old Faust believe in the fiction that he had done great things for the betterment of mankind. At the time Lessing and Vaihinger made such an impression on me, I could not yet apply their insights (which I had found so liberating in my personal life) to my culture heroes, who I still wished to believe were able to reach their greatness without recourse to a belief in fictions.

Reading about the philosophy of history opened up a world to me that also made me receptive to Spengler's *Untergang des Abendlandes*

(*The Decline of the West*), which added to my pessimism about man's fate and provided even more reason to proceed on the basis of fictions one knew were false in order to be able to live a meaningful life.

These books that so strongly influenced my intellectual—and indirectly also my psychological—development led me to change my studies in my third year at the university from literature to philosophy. But somehow, while I studied philosophy I found it too abstract to fill my life. I needed something more positive, not only something I could admire for the quality of its thought but something that would warm my soul, as philosophy did not. So after having concentrated during the next two years on philosophy, I once more changed my major concentration, this time to the history of art, as I shall describe later on.

But before or while I thus altered the course of my studies, several other quite different books changed my life.

As I tried to fight free of the world of my parents, more haphazardly than by design, I encountered books by Martin Buber which told about the world of the Hasidim, a world as strange and exotic as those in the utopian novels I read during my efforts to escape reality. But this was a world of my ancestors, and yet not even a glimmer of it was left in the life of my parents, although they were barely two generations away from the world about which Buber was writing. Because of the assimilated life of my entire family, all I knew about being a Jew was that I and my closest friends, most of whom were also Jewish, had to suffer from the taunts, the rejection, and occasionally the open aggression of some of our gentile schoolmates and even some of our teachers. Now, suddenly, my Jewishness had a positive content. Although in the classes on religion I had learned about the ancient history of the Jews, it had not taken on any personal meaning for me. But the mysticism that permeated the Jewish world of the *shtetl* according to Buber fascinated me; it seemed a good correlative to the rationalistic and somewhat pedantic view of the world in which I had been brought up. It was this reading, much more than any anti-Semitic persecution, that made me deeply aware I was a Jew. While it did not turn me into either a religious Jew or a Zionist, my reading of Buber, and later of Gershom Scholem's books on Jewish mysticism, helped stir in me feelings of pride in being thus heir to a venerable tradition, heir of a group that had given so much to the world.

This new positive consciousness of myself as a Jew was another bond between myself and Freud, and it meant a great deal to me that his last great completed work was *Moses and Monotheism*. My affirmative sense of Jewish identity became especially important to me, and possibly even life-preserving, in the face of the abuse and mistreatment I suffered in German concentration camps because I was a Jew.

Despite my opposition to the authoritarian educational establishment and my rejection of its methods of teaching, I remained beholden to the cultural values that I was exposed to in my parental home, and those which I considered best in my schooling. This is why the liberating books just mentioned were not the only ones shaping me as a person. Goethe and Schiller were the culture heroes of my parents, and were also those of the few teachers I respected. But these were mainly inherited values, values bred into me. To become the independent person I wished to be, I had also to find my very own culture heroes.

During the early years after the end of the First World War, the new movement in art and literature was Expressionism. Its opposition to traditional values was very seductive to an adolescent who wanted to be sure that he did not simply follow the directions that his elders wanted. It was an artistic movement that seemed as liberating in the arts as Freud had been in the sexual area, and as school reform had been in the world of education. But as I thus embraced an anticlassical movement, I also felt a need to gain a deeper understanding of the more classical approach to the cultural achievements of the past. With all my fervor for reform, I had not lost my commitment to the humanities. And I consider it fortunate that at this juncture in my development I discovered Jacob Burckhardt. His *Die Kultur der Renaissance in Italien* and the spirit which colored it throughout impressed me greatly, and because of this book and his other writings I decided to make the study of the art of the Renaissance my avocation. Burckhardt regarded the state itself as a work of art, and this fitted in well with my notion that states and their governments must become very different from the nations that were devouring each other during the First World War.

The second part of this book, which was devoted to the development of the individual, met my need to develop my own personality in ways I could approve. And as Burckhardt described how the discovery of the world and that of man himself as an individual went hand in hand, I found this reflected in myself: I saw that my own life/self-discovery and my growing understanding of the real world were integrated with each other, of necessity.

As part of the new freedom I had gained, and because the peace in Europe finally permitted travel, I set out to become acquainted with a wider world than that of my parental home and of school. My abiturium trip (a trip which customarily was the reward for having passed the final examination which permitted university studies) had still been restricted to Germany and had been directed toward making myself more familiar with the achievements of German Gothic art and architecture. But the following year, at the end of my first year at the university, I traveled to Italy, motivated largely by my reading of Burckhardt's writings. His *Der Cicerone* was my vademecum; it is no exaggeration to say that for more than a decade it became my bible. I tried to make every year at least one and sometimes two prolonged trips to Italy, the *Cicerone* at all times in my hand. It was this experience that helped me to switch my major from German language and literature to art history, and finally to aesthetics, in which I took my degree. In my dissertation I tried to integrate a psychoanalytically informed approach to the psychology of art with a philosophical understanding of beauty (based mostly on Kant) and with the history of art. During my study of philosophy I came to realize how relatively trite the educational reform philosophy of Wyneken was when compared with the much more penetrating one of Dewey.

With this tracing of my development, it should be clear which have been the essential books of my life. First, Freud's writings, too numerous to list in full; but foremost among them were less his clinical books and more those dealing with man and his culture. To name some of them: *Civilization and Its Discontents, The Future of an Illusion, Moses and Monotheism.* Second, Jacob Burckhardt's *Die Kultur der Renaissance, Der Cicerone,* and *Weltgeschichtliche Betrachtungen.* Third, Martin Buber's *The Tales of Rabbi Nachman,* and later *Die Legenden des Baalshem,* and Gershom Scholem's writings on Jewish mysticism.

Last but certainly not least, casting its light on all the other books named and unnamed, serving as a model always to be striven for but never to be fully attained, was Goethe's life and works. But who is the educated German-speaking person who has not been deeply influenced by Goethe, this paramount preceptor of all Germans, and much of the rest of the world to boot? That he was also Freud's culture hero made him, in both his life and his works, all that much more meaningful to me. The writings that influenced me most, besides both parts of *Faust*, were both parts of *Wilhelm Meister*, which, as *Bildungsroman*, induced me always to strive to improve my own *Bildung*. And as Burkhardt's *Die Kultur der Renaissance in Italien* had opened my eyes to the meaning of Renaissance history and art for European culture and had led to my own discovery of what art and the history of culture could (and did) mean to me, so Goethe's *Italienische Reise* served as my model for how to go about finding myself on the voyage through life.

The Art of Motion Pictures

The moving image, whether it is in the form of film or videotape, is the only art truly contemporary with the twentieth century. The motion picture is our universal art which comprises all others: literature and acting, stage design and music, dance and the beauty of nature, the use of light and color. It is always about us, because the medium is truly part of the message and the medium of the moving image is uniquely modern. Everybody can understand it, as everyone once understood religious art in church. And as people used to go to church on Sundays (and still do), so many today go to the movies on weekends. But while in the past most people attended church only on some days, they now watch moving images every day.

All age groups in most countries watch moving pictures, and they watch them for many more hours than ordinary people have ever spent in churches. Children and adults watch them separately or together; in many ways and for many people, it is the only experience common to parents and children. It is the only art today that appeals to all social and

This essay is based on an article of the same title which appeared in *Harper's* in October 1981, and on the first Patricia Wise Lecture of the American Film Institute, delivered on February 3, 1981, in Washington, D.C.

economic classes, as did religious art in times past. The motion picture is thus by far the most popular art of our time.

During the short span of one lifetime, this new and most modern art grew from uncertain and fumbling beginnings into maturity. Because of the chance of my birthdate, I witnessed the truly fantastic development of the moving picture from the magic lantern of my early childhood, to the great silent films I saw during my later childhood, to the talking pictures of my adolescence, to the TV shows of my adulthood. I can still vividly recall how exciting it was to see *and* to hear the first sound movie. I do not believe that with any other art so much has been accomplished in so short a time. In its rapid growth, the art of the moving picture is very much a child of the twentieth century.

Despite my assertion that the art of the moving image is the most authentically American art, it was not as such that I first experienced it. Going to the movies was an important and exciting part of my growing up in Vienna, much as going to the movies and watching TV are to young people of today.

As adolescents, I and my friends went to the movies as often as we could, and for much the same reasons this age group does today: we needed images we could emulate in forming our personalities, and we were eager to learn about those aspects of life and adulthood which were still hidden from us. Moving pictures give the illusion that it is permissible to spy upon the lives of others, which is exactly what children and adolescents love to do, to discover how adults manage their desires.

Another primary motive for attending motion pictures was our wish to escape from reality into daydreams, for which the movies provided content. Waiting for the next installment of *The Perils of Pauline* gave us something exciting to look forward to and to fantasize about in class, instead of listening to our teachers. The movie houses to which I went as a youth were created to be true pleasure domes, very different from those of today, which are characterized by a cold functionality. As soon as one entered these old dream palaces, one felt transposed to another world. Inside, there were nooks and crannies and boxes with heavy curtains, which suggested privacy and intimacy. Here one could escape the watchful scrutiny of one's parents and all other adults, and do nothing constructive whatsoever—just daydream.

The movie houses also provided unique opportunities for letting down one's defenses, even to experimenting with being in love, seduced into doing so by the love scenes one was watching on the screen. The unreality of the setting, its attractiveness, and most of all the enveloping darkness added to the dreamlike quality of the experience. All this encouraged uninhibited reactions to what was seen on the screen, including sexual experimentation. But such lowering of inhibitions was by no means restricted to the sexual area. I do not recall ever having laughed as heartily and unrestrainedly as I did when watching funny scenes in these pleasure palaces. In fact, it was such hilarity much more than the lowering of sexual inhibitions which made me view these theaters as pleasure domes.

Watching the movies, one can be carried away to the degree that one feels part of the world of the moving picture. It is an experience that lifts one out of oneself into a world where one is not beholden to ordinary reality, at least for the length of the films. So it seems that what one feels and does while in the movies does not really count.

But as soon as the lights are turned on, the spell is abruptly broken; one is again in the ordinary world. One does not feel responsible for the time spent under the spell of the film, and further, this unreality prevents one from devoting much serious attention to what was considered in my boyhood not an art, but "mere" entertainment. This was how some of the generation of our parents, and most of our teachers, disparaged the movies. Like most people, they liked to be entertained, but they did not consider the movies to be an art.

Our attitude to what we considered the classic arts was very different, and not just because these were venerated by our parents and teachers, although that probably had something to do with it. Yet the difference went deeper and was due to the inner experience of these other arts. Reading great literature, seeing good plays, listening to good music, appreciating painting and sculpture seemed to be experiences very different from going to the movies. Only listening to operas seemed to have some slight similarity, because these, too, carried one away in some manner.

These other art experiences, when deeply felt, made a significant difference in my view of myself, the world, and my place in it. The culmination of such experiences was a sort of "shock of recognition" which was an experience simultaneously of the work of art and of myself. It was an experience that heightened my feeling of self as it made me glad that I was part of the greatness of man and of his culture. They opened up new vistas on what it meant to be human.

Highly enjoyable as watching some films was, moving pictures hardly ever led to parallel experiences, although many films were very exciting to watch, many illuminated strange and unknown cultures and shed new light on human behavior. So these films were by no means lacking in human interest, and were meaningful on a wide variety of levels. Yet most movies fail to give one the deeper understanding of oneself or of man's place in the world which helps make sense of life.

It is not that some films do not grip one, or shake one up—sometimes quite violently. Seeing Eisenstein's *Potemkin* when it was first released was for me such an experience, but afterward I felt manipulated by it, as though it had played on my emotions without leaving me time to make up my own mind. In contrast, an ancient Greek drama, in which the troubles and issues were so much more distant from my world and my experiences, could touch me on a deeper and more personal level.

The important distinction was that in connection with the experience of great art, my personal concerns were replaced by a feeling of being in communication with something bigger than I, as if I were in the presence of, and participating in, greatness. This experience evoked in me something akin to what Freud described as an oceanic feeling: a feeling of being in tune with the universe, of all personal concerns being lifted, all needs satisfied. It felt as though I were in touch—in communication with man's past and connected with his future. I had a glimpse of it, and I felt reassured by it. In the art experience I was always present and active, but in the experience of an absorbing movie, I simply existed while I saw and heard. In art experiences which were deeply meaningful, my experience was that of being at the height of selfhood. In the movies, there was no self-awareness, no selfhood, just the experience of events happening on the screen.

This tremendous and nearly unique power of the movies, to lift the spectator out of his selfhood, is what makes them so fascinating. Not without reason has the experience of watching a moving picture been compared with dreaming. Movies have the same elasticity of time and space, the same sense of immediacy, and the same haunting vividness as dreams. As in a dream, what happens on the screen can move forward and backward in time and in space. The dream mode and that of the movies are an endless *now.*

When we watch a film, we regress and lose our critical faculties. The darkness of the room suggests a return into the womb, but our regression is much more than the result of the fact that we have become entirely passive. By identifying with the viewpoint of the camera, we experience pure perception. We lose awareness of our body position, we no longer orient ourselves within the world of our experience—we are being oriented by the camera, forced now to look this way and now that way. Experiences are inflicted on us, and short of shutting our eyes or looking away from the screen, we are powerless to condition what we experience, just as when we were in the womb, or when we were very small children. We are easily seduced into the regression, because we know that what we are about to experience cannot really harm us, and that the people on the screen who draw us into their magic circle cannot really influence our lives. The regression experienced either in dreaming or in watching a movie will not lead to a meaningful progression in the development of our personalities. Once we are back in reality after the movie has ended, we are exactly the same person as before this experience.

This, then, has been the differential between my experience of moving pictures and that of other art forms. The more significant my experience with some other arts has been, the more I responded to a work of art, the deeper it carried me into myself. The more I responded to a movie, the more it carried me away into its world, and the less of myself was left in the experience.

Surely the moving image is an ideal medium for escape, for escaping what oppresses us so much that we wish to forget. But escape, to do us some good, must not be only an escape *from* something; it must also be a guide *to* something better, more meaningful. To be truly an art, the moving image must help us to find ourselves, not just to escape from ourselves.

While I have been thinking about the art of moving pictures, I have tried to inform myself about what others have written about it. Some of what I read was instructive, occasionally even enlightening, but unfortunately the literature dealt mainly with technical matters, occasionally with some minor aspects of the experience of the viewer, never with what I considered the essence of art. I learned quite a bit about such things as the method by which the cameraman or the director gains and holds our attention. What I did not learn was why our attention should be held to keep us watching the film, and what we have to gain from the experience.

With the exception of some rare references to the cathartic experience, which is the result of watching dramas and moving pictures alike, nothing was said concerning any humanly desirable contribution of this particular art to our lives. Now catharsis, as the discharge of emotions and not their refinement, at best provides temporary relief. It doesn't lead to a solution of what oppresses us. In fact, catharsis leaves the problem unchanged, soon pressing for the next discharge.

It is not catharsis that does anything of significance for us, but being confronted with the causes of those pressing emotions that need cleansing. When we are confronted with them in such form that we can comprehend what they are all about, then we can free ourselves of them permanently. Only on the basis of such comprehension can we solve the impasse into which these emotions project us. When I speak here of emotional problems which press for discharge, I do not refer to those caused by psychological illness; on the contrary, art cannot cure emotional disturbance. Otherwise, artists would be psychologically the healthiest of people, which they are not.

The emotional problems to which I refer are the existential ones, the most important problems of man, and these are the legitimate subject of art. These are questions such as "Who is Man?" and "Has life a purpose?" and "If so, what is it?" In religious times, the supreme question was that of the relation of God and man. Today when religion has become less the center of our lives, it is "How can we cope with the adversities and contradictions which life endlessly seems to present to us?" The task of art is to give us answers to all the important existential questions in an appropriate form. A work of art must touch our conscious and our unconscious mind alike. To be effective, it must speak to universal human concerns, which are also of considerable individual importance at the moment.

Given the dominance of the visual image in the moving picture, its answers to the existential questions have to be in the form of visions of man. These visions, at their best, are to give us not answers, but ideas which convey where we come from, why we are here, how we ought to live, what our future may be or ought to be. Beyond these existential questions hides always a doubt about the meaning of life. Great art answers this doubt, and this is what makes it great. It is my conviction that one cannot truly experience art and also put the meaning of life into question, because art is the embodiment of beauty and beauty is always meaningful.

My thesis it that like all great art, the art of the moving image ought to concern itself with the problem of what it means to be human. It must affirm, even celebrate, being human, explore all levels of existence, all kinds of human experiences and relationships, but always in ways appropriate to its particular medium. It ought to provide us with a deeper appreciation of the meaning of heroism, even of crime; of sex and of death; of what it means to grow up and find oneself or to prove oneself through courage and suffering. It ought to tell us, in its own way, where we came from, where we ought to be, and where we ought to be going. We need to be connected with our past as individuals and as part of society, as part of our race. We need to have convictions about the future, our own and that of our planet. For all this, for an understanding of our past and for a perspective on the future, we need myths.

Because the facts available about our past are insufficient, because the future is inscrutable and the present too confusing, man needs the assurance that myths, and predominantly religion, used to offer: the conviction that his society will survive him and his work, thus transcending his all too limited existence, and extending it beyond his days, so that he will not have lived in vain. With such a conviction, we will not have to tremble in fear of death, because it is not the end of everything.

Myths and religion, and their embodiment in art, have long sought and found the answers to the existential questions. It was a long time before art began to exist independent of religion, and even then, the visual arts such as painting and sculpture continued to give concrete expression to the religious and mythical experience.

But art is more. Greek sculpture, for example, by concentrating on the human body and its beauty, celebrated man himself. Greek drama, by telling the story of the origins of Greek culture, at the same time refined it. Its themes were the relation of God to man and how man can achieve greatness despite what the gods or fate have ordained as his destiny. *The Iliad,* the poem with which the history of Western culture begins, provided a vision of what it meant to be Greek, and in what true humanity ought to consist. Homer's vision imbued the various Greek tribes or petty barbaric kingdoms with the idea of a common, heroic culture which could give meaning to the life of the individual. It illuminated Western life for thousands of years.

The mythical story of the Jews' slavery in Egypt, and of how God delivered them from Egypt to freedom, is a second great source of Western culture. This myth rejects the notion that the workings of society have to be based on slavery. It is a vision of the dignity of the ordinary man and has inspired many generations of men to strive for freedom from bondage.

Even greater than our concern with our origins is the problem of how to bring order into an existence that remains chaotic, without purpose and thus without meaning. The overarching problem of art is how to bring order into this chaos that otherwise will swallow us in a maelstrom and carry us away, without our lives leaving any trace that we existed.

Shakespeare's plays tell what it means to be English, as Homer tells what it meant to be Greek, and both deal with what it means to be a man. All Shakespeare's plays—his histories and tragedies as well as his comedies—celebrate humanity and its greatness, despite all frailties, errors, and failures. *Hamlet* deals with the problem of how to establish and maintain social order, such as by assuring the rightful succession to the throne. Another concern is the idea of kingship, what it means, how it is attained, and its function in combating the chaos men are apt to suffer from. But the real topic is the celebration of man *and* of kings, how human dignity may be achieved, and how it may be maintained despite all the vicissitudes of life into which men are continually projected. Laertes and Claudius, Polonius, Rosencrantz and Guildenstern, are all guilty of sins of commission, whereas Hamlet's is a sin of omission—by not living up to the son's obligation to avenge the murder of his father, by not meeting the crown prince's obligation to assume the throne and to punish the usurper. Because he is unable to restore order to his inner confusion and fears or to the realm, Hamlet destroys Ophelia and himself.

The tragedy concludes when chaos is rooted out and order has been reestablished in Denmark by Fortinbras, as he assumes the kingship. But first, dignity and greatness have to be restored to Hamlet: Fortinbras orders a royal funeral for him. If Hamlet was unable to live as a king, in death he was appropriately celebrated. As the play ends, order reigns again in the lives of individual man and of society. Man's ability to think well of himself and to live the good life are reestablished.

Only after the right order of succession has assured the continuity of society, only after man's ability to maintain his dignity even in the most tragic circumstances has been celebrated, can he relax and decide the time is right for comedy. After we have become convinced of the potential greatness of man, we can afford to laugh at the weaknesses and foibles to which we are all also heir, because these then add to our humanity rather than diminish it.

This is the eternal aim of art: to give expression to the myths we need to live by, and to affirm life, both in tragedy and comedy. The task of art is the celebration of man and his destiny, to help us accept our mortality by convincing us that what gives meaning to man's life transcends our individual existence. Art gives dignity to our lives by showing us how ancient our history is and what its deeper meaning is, and by telling us about our future, as guaranteed by the law of succession, according to which the child takes the parent's place in an uninterrupted chain of being and ever new becoming.

The central artistic achievements of a period are composed of all the arts which now we think of as separate. The setting for the Greek drama was a theater that was an unsurpassed architectural masterpiece. It was enhanced by the beauty of nature, and so nature became an essential part of the theater. A performance was a religious, an artistic, a social, but most of all a human event, to which an artistically used nature and all the arts made their contributions: architecture, poetry, acting, dance, music.

Until recently, the church was the recognized place for man's spiritual experiences. There the various arts combined to provide a setting appropriate to evoking a vision of life's true meaning, a vision through which man transcended his petty worries and was lifted beyond his ordinary existence. Many arts were combined to achieve this end: architecture, sculpture, painting, oration, music, drama. No single art could have come close to achieving the same effect. The story of Christ and the tree of life depicted in light filtering through the stained-glass windows was yet another important visual element helping to transport man from his ordinary existence into a world where he could experience the sublime. Thus nature in the form of integral light was again an element in this total work of art.

Since religion in its organized form has lost its hold on many of us, there is more reason why we look to the arts to lift us onto a higher plane. We desperately need a vision of who we are and of what life ought to be that is powerful enough to sustain us in the worst of times. Since in even the most religious periods all the arts were needed to give man a vision that could sustain him, so today only an art form in which all other arts participate can do this for us. It must be an artistic achievement that can captivate all of us, because it is germane to our times and to our place.

When I speak here of the moving picture as the authentic American art of our time, I do not think of art with a capital A, nor of "high" art. Putting art on a pedestal robs it of its vitality. When the great medieval and Renaissance cathedrals were erected, and decorated outside and inside with art, these were popular works that meant something to everybody. Some were great works of art, others not, but every piece was significant and everyone took pride in each of them. Some gain their spiritual experience from the masterpiece, but many more gain it from the mediocre works that express the same vision as the masterpiece but in a more accessible form. This is as true for the church music or the church itself as for paintings and sculptures. This diversity of art objects achieves a unity, and differences in quality are important, provided they all represent, each in its own way, the overarching vision and experiences of a larger, important cosmos.

So among the worst detriments to the healthy development of the art of the moving image are efforts by aesthetes and critics to isolate the "art film" from popular movies and television. Nothing could be more contrary to the true spirit of art. Whenever art is vital, it is always equally popular with the ordinary man and the most refined person. Had Greek drama and comedy not appealed to the majority, they would not have sat entranced on hard stone all day long, watching the events on stage; nor would the entire population have conferred prizes on the winning dramatist. The medieval pageants and mystery plays out of which modern drama grew were popular entertainments, as were the plays of Shakespeare.

Michelangelo's *David* stood at the most public place in Florence, embodying the people's vision that tyranny must be overthrown, while it also related to the religious vision as it represented the myth of David and Goliath. Everybody admired the statue; it was simultaneously popular and great art, only nobody thought of it in this way. Nor should we. To live well, we need both: visions which lift us up, and entertainment that is down-to-earth. There is not just a place for entertainment, there is also a need for it. The drearier our lives, the more leisure time we have, the greater is our desire to be entertained. Entertainment, too, ought to be an affirmation of life, part of the vision which makes our lives worth living.

In the past, the great occasions for entertainment and affirming man and life were the religious holidays, or the feast days of beloved saints or kings, or days celebrating the changing of the seasons, such as Christmas or May Day. Thus entertainment, although occasionally coarse, was connected in significant ways with that which gives deeper meaning to man's existence, and the arts served to enhance these entertainments.

Art and entertainment, each in its different form and way, are embodiments of the same vision of man. If art does not speak to all of us, common men and elites alike, it fails to address itself to the true humanity which is common to all of us. A different art for the elites and another one for average man tear society apart; separate arts offend what we most need: visions that bind us together in common experiences affirming life and man. Such affirmations are not to be found in the presentation of fake images of life as wonderfully pleasant. Life is best celebrated in the form of battles against its inequities, of struggles, of dignity in defeat, of the greatness of discovering oneself and the other.

Quite a few moving pictures have conveyed such visions. In Kurosawa's *Kagemusha,* the great beauty of the historical costumes, the cloak-and-dagger story with its beguiling Oriental settings, the stately proceedings, the pageantry of marching and fighting armies, the magnificent rendering of nature, the consummate acting—all these entrance us and convince us of the correctness of the vision here: the greatness of the most ordinary of men. The hero, a petty thief who turns impostor, grows before our eyes into greatness, although it costs him his life. The story takes place in sixteenth-century Japan, but the hero is of all times and places: he accepts a destiny into which he is projected by chance and turns a false existence into a real one. At the end, only out of a wish to be true to his new self he sacrifices his life and thus achieves the acme of suffering and human greatness. No one asks him to do so; no one but him will ever know that he did it. He does it only for himself;

his action has no consequences whatsoever for others. He does it out of conviction; this is his greatness. A life that permits the lowest of men to achieve such dignity is a life worth living, even if in the end it defeats him, as it will defeat all who are mortal.

Two other films, very different, render parallel visions that celebrate life, a celebration in which we, as viewers, vicariously participate although we are saddened by the hero's defeat. The first was known in the United States by its English name, *The Last Laugh,* although its original title, *The Last Man,* was more appropriate. It is the story of a hotel doorman who is demoted to cleaning washrooms. The other movie is *Patton.* In one of these films the hero stands on the lowest rung of society and existence; in the other, he is on society's highest level. In both pictures we are led to admire a man's struggle to discover who he really is, for, in doing so, he achieves tragic greatness. These three films, chosen arbitrarily from among many others, affirm man and life, and so inspire in us visions that can sustain us.

What our society suffers from most today is that absence of consensus about what it and life in it ought to be. Such consensus cannot be gained from society's present stage, or from fantasies about what it ought to be. A consensus in the present can be achieved only through a shared understanding of the past, as Homer's epics informed those who lived centuries later what it meant to be Greek, and by what images and ideals they were to live their lives and organize their societies.

Most societies derive consensus from a long history, a language all their own, a common religion, common ancestry. The myths by which they live are based on all of these. But the United States is a country of immigrant peoples, coming from a great variety of nations. Lately it has been posited that an asocial, narcissistic personality has become characteristic of Americans, and that this prevents us from achieving a consensus that would counteract a tendency to withdraw into private worlds. In his study of narcissism, Christopher Lasch says that modern man, "tortured by self-consciousness, turns to new cults and therapies not to free himself of his personal obsessions but to find meaning and purpose in life, to find something to live for." There is widespread distress because national morale has declined, and we have lost an earlier sense of national vision and purpose.

Contrary to rigid religious or political beliefs, such as are found in totalitarian societies, our culture is one of great individual differences, at least in principle and in theory. But this leads to disunity, even chaos. Americans believe in the value of diversity, but just because ours is a society based on individual diversity, it needs some consensus about some overarching ideas more than societies based on the uniform origin of their citizens. Hence, if we are to have consensus, it must be based on a myth—a vision about a common experience, a conquest that made us Americans, as the myth about the conquest of Troy formed the Greeks.

Only a common myth can offer relief from the fear that life is without meaning or purpose. Myths permit us to examine our place in the world by comparing it to a shared idea. Myths are shared fantasies that form the tie that binds the individual to other members of his group. Such myths help to ward off feelings of isolation, guilt, anxiety, and purposelessness—in short, they combat isolation and anomie.

We used to have a myth that bound us together. In *The American Adam*, R. W. B. Lewis summarizes the myth by which Americans used to live: "God decided to give man another chance by opening up a new world across the sea. Practically vacant, this glorious land had almost inexhaustible natural resources. Many people came to this new world. They were people of special energy, self-reliance, intuitive intelligence, and purity of heart. . . . This nation's special mission in the world would be to serve as the moral guide for all other nations."

The movies used to transmit this myth. American westerns, particularly, presented the challenge of bringing civilization to places where before there was none. The same movies also suggested the danger of that chaos; the wagon train symbolized the community men must form on such a perilous journey into the untamed wilderness, which in turn became a symbol for all that is untamed within ourselves. Thus the western gave us a vision of the need for cooperation and civilization, because without it man would perish. Another symbol often used in these westerns was the railroad, which formed the link between wilderness and civilization. The railroad was the symbol of man's role as civilizer.

Robert Warshow delineates in *The Immediate Experience* how the hero of the western—the gunfighter—symbolizes man's potential to become either an outlaw or a sheriff. In the latter role, the gunfighter was the hero of the past, and his opening of the West was our mythos, our equivalent of the Trojan War. Like all such heroes, the sheriff experienced victories and defeats, but through these experiences he grew wiser and learned to accept the limitations that civilization imposes.

This was a wonderful vision of man, or the United States in the New World; it was a myth by which one could live and grow, and it served as a consensus about what it meant to be an American. But although most of us continue to enjoy this myth, by now it has lost most of its vitality. We have become too aware that the reality of the opening of the West involved the destruction of nature and the American Indian. Just as important, that myth was based on an open frontier that no longer exists. But the nostalgic infatuation with the western suggests how much we are in need of a myth about the past that cannot be invalidated by the realities of today. We want to share a vision, one that would enlighten us about what it means to be an American today, so that we can be proud not only of our heritage, but also of the world we are building together.

Science fiction movies can serve as myths about the future and thus give us some assurance about it. Whether the film is *2001* or *Star Wars*, such movies tell about progress that will expand man's powers and his experiences beyond anything now believed possible, while they assure us that all these advances will not obliterate man or life as we now know it. Thus one great anxiety about the future—that it will have no place for us as we are now—is allayed by such myths. They also promise that even in the most distant future, and despite the progress that will have occurred in the material world, man's basic concerns will be the same: the struggle of good against evil, the central moral problem of our time, will not have lost its importance.

Past and future are the lasting dimensions of our lives; the present is but a fleeting moment. So these visions about the future also contain our past; in George Lucas's *Star Wars* and its sequels, battles are fought around issues that also motivated man in the past. There is good reason for Yoda's appearance in the first sequel, *The Empire Strikes Back*: he is but a reincarnation of the teddy bear of infancy, to which we turn for solace; and the Jedi Knight is the wise old man, or the helpful animal, of the fairy tale, the promise from our distant past that we shall be able to rise to meet the most difficult tasks life can present us with. Thus, any vision about the future is really based on visions of the past, because that is all we can know for certain.

As our religious myths about the future never went beyond Judgment Day, so our modern myths about the future cannot go beyond the search for life's deeper meaning. The reason is that only as long as the choice between good and evil remains man's paramount moral problem does life retain that special dignity that derives from our ability to choose between the two. A world in which this conflict has been permanently resolved would eliminate man as we know him. It might be a universe peopled by angels, but it would have no place for man.

What Americans need most is a consensus that includes the idea of individual freedom, as well as acceptance of the plurality of ethnic backgrounds and religious beliefs inherent in the population. Such consensus must rest on convictions about moral values and the validity of overarching ideas. A basic ingredient of the aesthetic experience is that it binds together such diverse elements. But only the ruling art of a period is apt to provide such unity. For the Greeks, it was classical art; for the British, Elizabethan art; for the many petty German states, it was their classical art. Today, for the United States, it has to be the moving picture, the central art of our time, because no other art experience is so open and accessible to everyone.

The moving picture is a visual art, based on sight. Speaking to our vision, it ought to provide us with the visions enabling us to live the good life; it ought to give us insight into ourselves. About a hundred years ago, Tolstoy wrote, "Art is a human activity having for its purpose the transmission to others of the highest and best feelings to which men have risen." Later, Robert Frost defined poetry as "beginning in delight and ending in wisdom." Thus it might be said that the state of the art of the moving image can be assessed by the degree to which it meets the mythopoetic task, giving us myths suitable to live by in our time, visions that transmit to us the highest and best feelings to which men have risen. Let us hope that the art of the moving image, this most authentic American art, will soon meet the challenge of becoming truly the great art of our age.

The Child's Perception
of the City

The manner in which we respond to living in a city, our urban experience, is conditioned by the ideas we develop about it in and around our home, long before we have much direct experience with the city. These early impressions, vague, disconnected, and highly idiosyncratic, nevertheless are decisive for the impact the urban experience makes on the child, and with it how the person will experience the city and life in it during later years.

There are many influences on the child's experience of the world and his place in it: the people who form the child's human environment, the relations they establish between them and him, what takes place between parent and child in the home and also when together they go out into the city. These experiences are decisive for whether the child will open himself gladly to the urban experience or shrink away from it. Much depends on how his parents mediate his experiences, and this, in turn, is determined by what they themselves make of the city: whether they feel it enriches their lives or threatens their existence. Whether

This essay is a much revised and enlarged version of a lecture given at a conference on Literature and the Urban Experience at Rutgers, the State University of New Jersey, in April 1980. It was published in its original form in *Literature and the Urban Experience* (New Brunswick, N.J.: Rutgers University Press, 1981).

and how they see and use, or avoid and reject, the urban experience creates the framework within which the child views the city and what he encounters in it.

It is people who therefore condition the urban experience, not buildings, streets, public places, parks, monuments, institutions, or means of transportation, although all enter into our image of the city and our vision of what it means to live in one. The urban existence generally involves a large number and wide variety of people living closely together, each of them enjoying meaningful contacts with a few, and anonymity as far as the multitude is concerned. Within this large agglomeration of people, what counts for us is a very limited number of them. To the young child these are his family, a few neighbors and friends, and some other persons with whom he has frequent contact. Later, teachers and schoolmates will join these. From an early age, what is read to us and what we read and see on TV also influences our view of what a city is all about. But it is always people who at base determine what city life means to us, because people in large numbers constitute the urban experience.

It makes a great difference to the people who live in a city whether they are housed comfortably or poorly, whether or not the city provides for the amenities of life, where the city is located, and how it is governed. These factors determine whether living in a city is pleasant or difficult, whether the life of the inhabitants will be secure or brutish. But even the citizens of the most tyrannically ruled city, living in the most unhealthy conditions, will live an urban existence as long as there are many of them, living closely together.

Literary sources suggest the same. They assert that the essential features of the urban experience are the unique human opportunities it offers and the easy access to them it permits. However much an author may prefer to live secluded out in the country, away from the bustle and the pressure of the large city, the metropolis is the setting which makes high culture, and with it his literary creations, possible. Shakespeare wrote his plays not in Stratford but in London, one of the largest cities of the Western world. Only with the creation of a large city and a permanent capital in Kyoto in the eighth century did Japanese literature begin to bloom. At the beginning of the present technological civilization, after having spent most of his long life in a small town, Goethe said that Germany's cultural life was mediocre because men of culture and talent were scattered, rather than living in one large city, such as Paris, "where the highest talents of a great kingdom are all assembled on one spot and, by daily intercourse, strife, and emulation mutually instruct and emulate each other," conditions which permit or at the least greatly facilitate the creation of high literature. Goethe himself and his talent were not formed in the country town of Weimar, where he made this remark, but in Frankfurt, which then was one of the most important cities of Germany.

Nearly two and a half millennia before Goethe's time, Aristides the Just expressed the same idea: "Not houses finely roofed or the stones of walls well built, nor canals or dockyards make the city, but men able to use their opportunity." Thucydides said it more concisely: "It is men who make the city, not walls or ships." Shakespeare, as one might expect, put it most tersely: "The people are the city."

According to Euripides, "The first requisite to happiness is that a man be born in a famous city." All through the Middle Ages, and well into modern times, the conviction was that only city air makes us free, for in many places the law decreed that a serf who reached a city, or managed to live in it for at least one year, automatically became a free man. Further, in the city, an average man had relatively ample opportunities to develop his mind and some freedom to live according to his beliefs, to be truly himself. The high city walls provided safety, compared to the arbitrary domination of a feudal landlord and the frequent periods of famine, not to mention destructive wars, which ravaged the unprotected countryside.

Today many people think that living in cities pollutes our lungs, crowds us so closely together that we have no space to ourselves, and cripples our lives. Of course, the cities of the past were incredibly more polluted than those of today, and the inhabitants were crowded into what to us seem unlivably narrow confines. As far as the urban experience is concerned, objective facts count for little when compared to our image of them; and these are largely derived from literary sources.

Life is with people, and nowhere more so than in cities, as the authors I have quoted firmly assert. What life is like, what people are like, what life with people is like—this we learn first at our mother's knee, often from the books she chooses to read to us. Our parents' views of the city and life within it depend mainly on how they experience it, and today this is influenced to a large degree by what they learn about urban life by reading and watching TV.

Since we so often gain our initial impressions of urban life from our mothers, it is not surprising that in our unconscious we often experience the city as a woman. The Greek goddess Pallas Athena was the symbol, the protectress, the embodiment of the spirit of the city in which great literature first flourished. But in real life, and much more in our unconscious, there are also evil mothers, destructive ones. Thus the city can be experienced in the image of a good or of a bad mother.

Mothers are experienced as both good and bad; depending on the individual experience, one of these opposite images will dominate, although rarely to the total exclusion of the other. Since we all carry within ourselves these two contrary primordial perceptions or archetypal images, much depends on whether we relate a specific part of our experience, such as the urban experience, to our image of the good or of the bad mother.

Here the literary interpretation of the urban experience can make all the difference. Not without reason have I quoted three famous Athenians in praise of city life. Although life was often vile in Athens, the interpretation of the urban experience we owe to these ancient authors spreads a glow over the Athens of their time which still captivates our imagination two and a half thousand years later.

What is true for so many experiences is also true in regard to the urban experience, that beauty and ugliness reside more often than not in the eye of the beholder. Much would depend, for example, on whether we are guided in forming our views of, say, Paris, through its praise by Goethe or its vilification by Céline, as embodied in his *Voyage to the End of Night*. And this although it is impossible to imagine that Céline could have become a writer of his stature had his talent not been nurtured by his living in a city such as Paris.

The literary images of the urban experience we encounter are grafted onto much earlier ones formed in childhood. So let us return to considering how a sense of the urban experience is first acquired. As mentioned at first, the child tends to think of the city in the same terms as do those with whom he lives. On his own, he begins to develop his view of the urban experience on the basis of what he knows about life in the very limited part of the city in which he dwells. A few blocks are all most children know of the city in which they live, and this will form the matrix of their view.

A matrix is a womb, and not only etymologically speaking; it is unconsciously experienced as such. The womb can be experienced as the safest, most comfortable and satisfying of all dwelling places, where one lived in perfect bliss. But it can also be experienced in the opposite way: as something denying and frustrating that tried to get rid of one, that nastily pushed one out into an inimical world to suffer, if not to perish. In which of these two ways the womb will be experienced depends not on what happened while one grew in it, but on one's early experiences after one left it—that is, on how one was treated by one's mother after birth. Likewise, the feelings the child has about his first dwelling place are those he is apt to project onto all later ones.

If all goes well, the child comes to think that this matrix of his life, his neighborhood, like the womb from which he entered it, is protective and offers mainly positive experiences. The only vaguely known or entirely unknown rest of the city is experienced as an extension of this. When the part of town in which he lives is the safe abode where he finds whatever happiness he knows, then he is convinced that his city is the best place in the world, never mind whatever shortcomings it has, of which the child cannot help becoming aware as he grows up. Such deficiencies will then seem relatively unimportant, because of the child's earlier conviction of the city's perfection, which was based on the unconscious identification of this city with the good mother, an identification which continues to color all later, more mature evaluations.

This was my personal experience regarding my native city of Vienna. My conviction of the desirability of an urban experience was derived from the security I knew in my home and was reinforced by what my parents and grandparents told me about it. My image of the urban existence came from three major sources: an impressive story my mother told me, another she read to me, and a billboard sign. As far as my conscious recollections go, it was the last which made it most explicitly clear what was good about living in my native city. But the message of this advertisement would not have reached me, or made a strong impression, if it had not reinforced in simple, down-to-earth words the message my parents and relatives had already conveyed to me.

Vienna, where I was born and grew up, was also where both my parents had been born; to me it was thus part of my heritage. My view of urban life was but a reflection of my parents' view; while other people lived out in the country or in other cities, such life was not for me. I took our urban existence for granted; no other seemed possible, thinkable, or desirable. I did not reflect on what an urban existence offered or demanded, did not wonder what made for Vienna's particular culture or beauty nor question it; that came only much later. As the child is convinced that his mother is beautiful, although he does not know why and how, so was I convinced of the unique merits of my hometown. I did not ponder what particular opportunities my urban existence provided me with; whatever opportunities the city permitted were all the opportunities there were or could be. Nor did I worry about any damage the city might inflict on me—and there were risks and liabilities to life in Vienna then and later, as there are in any environment—just as the child does not worry about the damage life within his family may do to him, great though it may be.

The tale my mother told me, and one other my father told, were significant parts of our family's oral history. I am sure they made such a deep impression on me at an early age because they contained so many elements of another literary tradition with which I was quite familiar: that of fairy tales. The traditional fairy-tale elements were the evil stepmother who, to advance her own children, cast out the child of her husband's previous marriage; an ineffectual father who could not stand up to his second wife nor protect the child of his first wife; and a boy abused by his stepmother and then pushed out of his home at an early age, forced to seek his fortune in a strange and unknown world, or perish. Then this boy overcame great hardships and through his courage and determination made a marvelous success of his life.

This was actually the life experience of both my grandfathers. For me as a child, it was not their true stories which lent veracity to the many fairy tales I knew but the fairy tales that convinced me of the truth of my grandfathers' stories. Although the life history of my paternal grandfather was in many ways even more remarkable than that of my maternal grandfather, as a child I was less impressed with it, since he died before I was born and thus I never knew him. So let me begin with the story of my maternal grandfather, whom I knew well.

The mother of my maternal grandfather died in childbirth, after bearing my great-grandfather a son. He soon remarried, and there were several more children. The family, living in a small Czech village, was quite poor. My maternal great-grandfather made his living as a peddler. He spent all week driving from village to village, trying to sell the few goods he had loaded on his horse-drawn carriage. Being a devout Jew, he returned home only for the Sabbath, which he spent in the local synagogue. Thus he was hardly ever at home, and so was unable to control what went on there during the week.

His second wife resented the oldest son, since she and her own children had to share the very little they had with him. She also felt that he was favored by his father and feared that he would be favored by him over her own children. Spurred by such feelings, she mistreated the boy during the week when the father was not around. As the boy grew older, she pestered her husband until he agreed that after the boy had had his bar mitzvah—that is, according to Jewish religious belief, had reached manhood—he would have to leave home.

So, soon after his thirteenth birthday, my grandfather, who had never left the small village in which he had been born, was sent out into the world. All he had was the good suit of clothing he had received as his coming-of-age present and a silver piece of five guilders, worth about two and a half dollars, which his father had given him surreptitiously upon his departure. To protect his only pair of shoes, the boy walked barefoot the hundred miles from his village to the big city, Vienna. There, in a very hard struggle, he eventually managed to make a great fortune.

In my grandfather's mind and in that of his daughter, my mother, and hence in my mind, it was Vienna, our hometown, which had rescued him by giving him his opportunity. It was this city which miraculously changed his life from one of dejection to one of success. Nowhere else but in Vienna, or in a fairy-tale place, would a cast-out child make his fortune, or so it seemed to me. Obviously, I had not yet heard that the streets of New York were paved with gold.

The story of my paternal grandfather was similar. He never talked about his parents, either because he was orphaned at such an early age that he knew nothing about them or because he was born out of wedlock and deserted by his mother to cover her shame. Whatever the true story of his birth, he was raised from infancy in a Jewish orphanage. It was soon discovered that he was very bright, and he was educated to become a rabbi.

When my paternal grandfather was still quite young, the richest man of the realm, Baron Rothschild of Vienna, engaged in a search for the best man to become the tutor of his sons. My paternal grandfather was chosen, and so he was removed from the small provincial town where he had been trained to become a rabbi and went from living in desperate poverty into the grand palace of the Rothschilds in Vienna. There he educated his charges, who grew so fond of him and were so impressed by his brilliance that when they became leaders of the Rothschild bank, they put him in charge of many of its operations. In consequence, he not only became very rich but exercised great influence over the social life of the Jewish community of Vienna. Thus again, it had been my paternal grandfather's move to Vienna which had miraculously changed his life. Such things—or so it seemed to me when I was a child—could happen only in Vienna, were possible only because of the unique character of my native city.

The stories of my two grandfathers making their fortunes in Vienna were supported by other stories my mother told me or read to me. For example, Peter Rosegger, a highly esteemed regional author of the time, related in his autobiography, entitled *When I Was Still a Poor Peasant Boy in the Mountains*, the story of the marvelous change in his life which was the consequence of his move to Vienna. The only part I still remember, and the one which was meaningful in shaping my views of the great merit of living in Vienna, was his story of how on finishing school around thirteen—like my grandfather—he had walked barefoot to Vienna, attracted by its glamour. Particularly moving was his account of how happiness overwhelmed him when he finally reached the top of a hill from which he could make out Vienna in the distance. This place was already famous in folklore because, according to tradition, there the wives of the Crusaders had sat spinning while anxiously waiting and looking out for the return of their husbands from the Holy Land. The hill was marked by an ancient cross with which I was familiar. There, Rosegger said, he felt anxious about his future, but also extremely lucky that he had made it to Vienna and would be able to live there. And there he indeed rose to great fame.

In my mind, these three stories merged and seemed incontrovertible proof that my hometown was the place where everybody desired to live, and where it was possible to achieve what one most desired: my grandfather's riches, the author's fame.

As an adolescent, on an excursion into the mountains I once visited the poor village in which Rosegger had been born and from where he had set out for Vienna. Seeing this place confirmed for me how lucky he had been to escape to Vienna. I never visited the places where my grandfathers were born, but I was certain they were just like the writer's village.

Even in those distant days, long before radio or TV, advertising made its impact felt. The messages of advertisements are part of the literature to which the child is exposed earliest; they are usually among the first printed words he is able to read, and form some of his earliest literary experiences. During my childhood, the most impressive ads in Vienna were huge billboard signs proclaiming that the Viennese cherish most Vienna's water—much praised for its purity and freshness since the time it was first piped into the city from faraway mountainous areas— and Anchor Bread, the product of the largest bread factory in the city and the brand eaten in most homes, including mine. These ads cleverly and effectively created a close association between the city, bread, and water—these basic foods being since most ancient times the symbol of sustenance. To me it was a most convincing association: like my mother, like my home, this larger home in which we all lived, the city, nurtured me well.

Like most Viennese children, I loved the hot Anchor rolls, products of the same bakery, which I ate for breakfast and many between-meals snacks. When many years later Proust's masterwork was published, I was not at all surprised that the taste of the madeleine brought back memories of his childhood, including events and the places where they had taken place. I was familiar with such associations because of my love for the hot Anchor rolls. They were delicious, but the intimate connection established through the billboard signs between these rolls and Vienna was what made them much more significant: a symbol signifying both hometown and favorite food.

Even at the early age I am talking about, the child does not uncritically accept all literary statements about urban existence. At that time— and still today—two songs were extremely popular which conveyed a most attractive, although oversentimental, image of Vienna. I heard them sung by people close to me, who liked them a lot. One song praises the beauty of the blue Danube; the other asserts that Vienna will always be the city of one's dreams. Despite my deep commitment to living in Vienna I rejected both songs. It wasn't so much that I thought them hackneyed, for my aesthetic sensitivities were not sufficiently developed for that. I rejected the one song for extolling the blue Danube because I knew that the river's color was really a muddy gray. No strong positive emotions tied me to the river, so there was no reason to envision it in a glorified way, contrary to the evidence of my eyes. Thus literary statements which run counter to the child's experience usually will be rejected.

Vienna did figure in my dreams, sometimes pleasantly, but often also in nightmares, during which I got lost in the streets. This was enough reason to reject a song asserting that Vienna would always be the city of my dreams. I wanted my hometown to be the city not of dreams, but of their realization. Thus there are limitations to literature's shaping the child's conceptions of his urban existence, even at an early age.

As I outgrew a naïve concept of my urban experience, it became modified under the impact of more sophisticated literature. Then, for example, the influences of Karl Kraus's extremely critical views of Viennese culture became merged with the sharp but nevertheless loving irony with which Robert Musil described life in Vienna in his *Man Without Qualities,* and with the romantic nostalgia of Strauss and Hoffmannsthal's *Rosenkavalier.* These were but a few of my more mature choices from a vast literature devoted to Vienna which I permitted to alter my earlier uncritical images of an urban existence.

Further, literary images vastly influenced my attitudes toward other cities which I first experienced through literary sources and only later put to the test of reality. My perspective on Paris was shaped mainly by Balzac, Zola, and Proust. However much time I spent in a Paris very different from the one these and other authors described, I continued to see much of it as I had learned to do from my reading of these authors.

In my thirties, I had to adjust to an urban existence very different from that I had known before. It is hard to imagine two cities more different than Vienna and Chicago. But my adjustment was based on my attitude, ingrained in childhood, that an urban existence is what suits best my needs and aspirations. All that was needed was to free my inner image of the city as the only appropriate matrix for my life from its specific Viennese traits and to modify it in line with my perceptions of Chicago, externally so different.

Here, too, images derived from literature helped me to form a picture of Chicago which had both negative and positive aspects, but which permitted me to feel that the city was not an unknown entity with which I did not know how to cope. The strongest impression of Chicago I had received before going there was derived from reading Upton Sinclair's *The Jungle*. But once I began to live there, James Farrell's *Studs Lonigan*, and his other novels set in Chicago, permitted me to form a much more positive image of life in that city. Just a few years after I read Farrell's books, I was fortunate enough to become good friends with him. Walking with him through the streets of the South Side of Chicago, where he grew up and where I then lived and worked, was a unique experience that made me feel much more at home in Chicago. It taught me how differently a novelist sees and experiences his native city, compared to the way, for example, a politician or a social scientist might view it. Such latter views I obtained from Paul Douglas, then an Illinois senator, and Louis Wirth, the sociologist, both of whom were friends and colleagues of mine as professors at the University of Chicago.

It was a true eye-opener for me to compare how these three distinguished persons, all three of them authors, responded both as persons and as writers to their hometown. They helped me to appreciate Chicago's particular merits, as earlier I had been made aware of the particular merits of Vienna by the authors who wrote about it. Thus in the experience of both cities which were for so many years my home I was greatly helped by the vision of them which I had derived from literary sources. Chicago's writers helped me, for example, to replace enjoyable excursions into the Vienna Woods and swimming in the Danube with very different, but equally enjoyable, visits to the lakefront and swimming in Lake Michigan. Vienna had its ancient history and buildings, but Chicago had its exciting vitality and modern architecture.

As I had made my own images of Vienna gained from literature and rejected others, the same was true for Chicago. While still in Vienna, I had accepted uncritically that Chicago was a city of gangsters and slaughterhouses, the latter notion picked up from my reading of Upton Sinclair. When I settled in Chicago, I realized that my life there had nothing to do with gangsters or slaughterhouses, nor would the ambience of the stockyard area become the matrix for my life. So the images of Chicago which I had carried in my mind for years dropped away within weeks under the reality of the city, to be replaced by images owed to a very different literature and in line with my experiences of the city. But that I could transfer to Chicago a past commitment to an urban existence as the best setting for my life helped me very much in acquiring an image of Chicago eminently suitable to living happily there. It is one example of how the images of urban life gained in childhood can and do determine one's later attitudes to the urban experience.

So far I have tried to suggest how important my early childhood experiences of city life were in the shaping of my urban experience; how my basic positive view of the city as the most desirable matrix for my life was to a large degree based on oral and written literature; and how my convictions about urban life could be easily transferred to another city, even one in many ways very different from my native city.

With this is mind, let us consider the images of urban life to which our children are exposed at an early age, when ideas are formed which are basic to their experience of living in a big city, where many of them will spend their lives.

Since children's early, most decisive experiences within their families are too diverse to permit generalizations, I shall concentrate on those literary sources to which American children are exposed: the textbooks used to teach them reading, which in many cases are their first experience with literature. Although the vast majority of American children live in cities, one could not guess this fact from the contents of the books they read during their first three or four years of school, when they are at a most impressionable age. The readers designed for kindergarten and the early grades depict life as universally pleasurable. However, the settings in which this pleasant life unfolds are not citified but rural or suburban. Consequently it is impressed on the child that to have an enjoyable life requires living in a nonurban setting. Even in a book entitled *City Days, City Ways* the children in the stories live only on tree-lined streets in detached single-family homes. While the reality of urban life is not explicitly described here as undesirable, it is denied importance through complete neglect, which suggests to the child that it is not worthy of attention.

All the various pleasant activities in which the children described in these primers engage take place in settings which convey nothing of urban life, although some of them are located in a playground. When outdoors, the children chase rabbits and squirrels, swim in pools, go on picnics, take motorboat rides on lakes, and ride on ponies; they even travel on trains and airplanes. While a visit to a zoo may suggest a city facility, it indicates more a desire to escape a city's confinements than to make a go of an urban existence. When children do enter a more urban setting, they do so only temporarily, to shop in stores. A great deal is thus said about the pleasures one can enjoy out in the country, but, aside from the fact that one can buy such things as jackets or shoes in the city, nothing good is told about it.

The story titles in the first reader of a widely used series of basic texts may illustrate the emphasis on rural life: "In the Meadow," "Too Much Clover," "In the Green Woods," "Faraway Farm," to name just a few. Not one single title suggests a city setting, and none of the forty-seven stories in this book is placed in an urban environment.

In all the first five books in this series, urban life is directly mentioned only once—in the second-grade reader, in a story where a dog compares his previous life in the country to his present one in the city. Since the dog is the hero of an entire thirty-page section of this reader, the child is clearly expected to identify in a positive way with the dog, particularly also in his view of the undesirability of city life, since nothing in the story contradicts it. Typical of the underlying attitudes toward city life which these readers convey are the following lines: "Before we came here, we lived in a little town called Hillside. We lived at the edge of town. Out there we had enough space to run and play and have fun. It was not my fault that we came to live in the city. Do you know what a city is? A city is houses and garages, cars and people. There is no room for anything else. A city is where everyone keeps on saying 'Don't play in the street.' 'Don't run in front of cars.' 'Don't ride on a bicycle.' 'Keep off the grass.' 'Stop, look and listen before you cross the street.' . . . When I first moved to the city I *hated* it." Can anyone wonder why?

Let us consider the images of an urban existence conveyed to the child in readers which were specially designed for use with minority children who live in metropolitan areas. One of the readers of this series is titled *Uptown, Downtown,* promising to reflect in its stories an urban existence. A story titled "What Do You Think?" reads as follows: "The little girl came out of her new house, and what do you think she saw? Just a corner. She went around the corner, and what do you think she saw? Just another corner. She went around that corner, and what do you think she saw? Still another corner. So she went around it, and then what do you think she saw?" The emptiness and purposelessness of a city existence here projected is not an isolated instance in the content of this new series of readers, designed for city children.

The primer of this series is entitled *Around the City*. It promises that by reading the stories the child will learn about life in the city. However, these stories project without relief a depressing image of an empty, boring urban existence. A typical story reads: "All around the city, all around the town, boys and girls run up the street. Boys and girls run down. Boys come out into the sun. Boys come out to play and run. Girls come out to run and play. Around the city, all the day. All around the city, all around the town, boys and girls run up the street, boys and girls run down."

Thus we are telling our children, most of whom live in cities, that city life has nothing positive to offer. It is little wonder that they have small love for an urban existence, the existence most of them will have to live. Being forced to read that the matrix of their lives is bleak and disappointing does not encourage them to read, either, particularly when no suggestions are offered concerning how things could be improved. Such reading tends to discourage both interest in literature and living in cities.

I have concentrated on the literary impressions I received in my childhood because these left me with an attitude toward living in cities which permitted me even in difficult moments to be very satisfied with an urban existence and encouraged me to engage in efforts to improve those of its aspects I felt it was in my power to improve. I wish the impression our children gain from their classroom reading would do the same for them. If it did, maybe the urban existence of the next generation would be a vast improvement over that of the present one.

Children and Museums

M ost people go to museums for mixed reasons, of which they are by no means conscious. Some seek interesting and enjoyable entertainment which is at the same time instructive, but I believe that many seek something more that might be likened to a semireligious experience. For example, many people visit museums on Sundays, and the traditional spirit of Sunday is not totally absent from that which one hopes to find in museums. Most visitors wish to find there something that transcends the narrow confines within which the rest of their lives unfolds. The museum building, which often looks like or even sometimes once was a royal palace, or else reminds one of a temple, helps to create the mood they seek.

Today's museum has ancient origins. The Greek—and earlier the Egyptian—temple precincts included treasurehouses in which all kinds of valuable objects were kept: works of art, articles of gold, jewelry, and other rarities. Churches, too, were simultaneously places of worship

This essay is an outgrowth of a presentation given at the International Symposium on Children in Museums held at the National Gallery of Art in October 1979. It was published in the proceedings of this conference by the Smithsonian Institution in 1982. I had been asked to speak on the topic "Curiosity—Its Application in a Museum Setting." It is here reprinted with alterations and additions.

and works of art, and repositories of all types of wondrous, rare, precious, curious, valuable objects. They housed not only sculptures and paintings, but also jewels and technical masterpieces, such as incredibly complicated astrological clocks, and wonders of nature and objects of historical significance. For example, in the nave of the cathedral of Seville, a stuffed alligator hangs from the ceiling next to an elephant tusk, right alongside the images of saints and other objects of artistic and historical interest.

However, while temples and churches all over the world were and still are places of worship in which one is invited to marvel at the rare, the beautiful, the historically interesting, and the otherwise significant, the modern museum is more directly linked to palaces, such as the Vatican. Most great museums of the Western world had their origins in princely collections of treasures and rarities.

The purpose of these princely collections was to satisfy the taste and curiosity of those who assembled them. But these collections served also to demonstrate the wealth, power, and grandeur of the prince; to impress viewers with a greatness these objects reflected, as they, in turn, added to it. In most of the princely collections, the rare, the costly, and the beautiful were inextricably combined with the religious, the magical, and the supernatural, such as when the relic of a saint was housed in a reliquary that was both a great work of art and a priceless object, because of the gold and jewels worked into it. Most of the early paintings were of religious subjects. In addition, these same collections of treasures and rarities contained many natural wonders: ostrich eggs, tusks of animals thought to be unicorns. There were rare or strangely formed minerals right beside such things as the headdress of Montezuma, and objects which were wondrous because of their sheer technical perfection: fancy clocks, astrolabes, automatons. Beautiful and wondrous objects were made specifically for these collections, called in German *Kunst und Wunderkammern,* because what they contained aroused curiosity, wonder, and marvel.

Francis Bacon said long ago that "wonder is a seed out of which knowledge grows." It is a statement that does not permit reversal: rational knowledge does not spawn wonder, which is an emotion. All too many of today's museums try to convey knowledge to children, out of which no wonder will grow. I believe that the best we can do is to instill in children the awe, the wonder, out of which alone meaningful knowledge grows. Such knowledge truly enriches our lives by permitting us to transcend the limits of our everyday life, an experience we badly need if we are to grow into the fullness of our humanity. Curiosity is not the source of seeking learning and knowledge; in fact, much of curiosity is very easily satisfied. It is wonder, I believe, which presses one toward an ever deeper penetration of the mysteries of the world, and to a true appreciation of the achievements of man.

There were and are many museums in Vienna, where I grew up. Of these, three were most important to me: the museums of the history of art and of natural history, and the technical museum. Let me concentrate on the first two, which are housed in very impressive identical buildings that look like huge palaces, standing opposite each other, so that they mirror each other. As a child, it did not make sense to me that these two museums, showing such radically different objects, serving such entirely different purposes, should be housed in identical buildings. It occurred to me only much later that those who were responsible for the design of these two museums were primarily motivated by the fact that they were both museums, no matter what their differences in content and purpose. To those who had built these museums and housed the two so different collections in them, it must have seemed more important to give appropriate body to the *idea* of the museum, and to its purpose of enlarging our horizons, than to any specific content. They emphasized what might be called the platonic idea of the museum, rather than any specific and with it relatively ephemeral embodiment of this idea, of which the individual museum is but a pale reflection.

These possibilities occurred to me when I began to wonder not only why the two buildings were alike in their exteriors but also why, as one entered them, one was purposely overawed by the grandiosity of the identical entrance halls and magnificent stairways. Was it an important part of the realization of the platonic idea of the museum that the visitor, on entering, should be filled with awe? In regard to these two Viennese museums, it would be easy to ascribe it all to the desire of the Hapsburg emperors to convey how magnificent it was of them to donate a large part of their imperial collections to the public, and to a nineteenth-century tendency to show it off. Other collections, such as that of the Louvre, could be explained along the same lines. But when visiting such twentieth-century creations as the Guggenheim Museum or the

National Museum of Art, erected only a few decades ago, and its East Wing, which is one of the newest museum buildings, one is equally impressed by the grandiosity of the buildings and entrance halls, which neither display important objects nor communicate anything but their own grandeur.

Maybe these grandiose buildings and entrances, which are apt to evoke feelings of smallness and awe, are designed to transport us out of the bustle of the city in which the museum is located into what appears to be a hallowed place. If so, they serve an important purpose: to put us in a mood to admire and to wonder, to prepare us for enchantment by giving us a feeling that in these buildings, amazing things are waiting for us. Maybe this is what permits thinking about museums in general: that despite their immense variety, they all have in common the ability to make us marvel and wonder, where we haven't before; and if we happen to be so inclined, they can arouse a curiosity that is not easily satisfied but leads to lifelong veneration for the particular wonders of the world this particular museum offers to us.

It was easy to be turned off by the ballyhoo and the commercialization surrounding the showing of the "Treasures of Tutankhamen." But the exhibits were objects of a religious nature. It was that, combined with their great age and extreme rarity, the abundance of gold, and the legends woven around the finding of the tomb, which attracted the masses. The masses came to be impressed, eager to have a chance to venerate, happy to be expected and thus permitted for once in their lifetime to be astounded, despite the rationality that is usually expected of them in other situations. Maybe, then, this is what museums are for, particularly for children—to enchant them, to give them a chance to marvel, an experience which they are badly in need of, because everyday life has become deprived of all the miracles which a religious age saw everywhere.

If so, the museum's task might be to make people more ready to wonder, to be enchanted, so that their ability to experience wonder will not be restricted to so few objects, so few occasions. Maybe too much explanation of these marvels reduces them to more or less everyday experiences, and with it deprives them of what most people are desirous of finding in museums. Many of today's well-organized, rationally and systematically arranged exhibits, which are mainly intended to be instructive, are less apt to arouse marvel for that reason. For the unsophisticated person, such as the child, there is apt to be a trade-off between the wondrous and the instructive: the more of one, the less of the other.

At the Smithsonian Institution, for example, there is a truly amazing show of Pacific Islands artifacts. It's one of the most beautifully arranged and displayed expositions I have ever seen; but it makes me wonder what it may mean to most children who are lucky enough to visit it. Each label tells very well what the object is, and such facts as that it was used in some secret ritual, was forbidden to women, served to establish mysterious links to ancestors, or had an enigmatic connection with the origins of the tribe. However, these labels tell little or nothing about the spiritual properties of each of these objects, which alone gave them great meaning to their originators; nor do they explain that the characteristics that we are tempted to view as decorative elements are what invested them with magic properties.

The occult and the magical are curious ideas to a modern American child, who is brought up to think rationally. Most children do not know at first hand what mythic or transcendental experiences are, and often parents require the child to free himself—the sooner the better—of his childish beliefs in magic. The information that an object was part of a secret ritual which alone gave higher meaning to life means nothing to a child if he himself has not had some mystical experience. If the child does not believe in the supernatural, has no feelings for it, does not live in awe of it, he will at best be impressed only by the most external aspects of these objects and will miss the essentials: their use to this particular culture. If sex has been explained to the child in rational terms, as it's now done in schools, it has lost much of its mystery and its secrets. If so, he cannot have empathy with the enigmatic aspects of sex which find expression in the delicate figures with both male and female sexual characteristics.

If we have not felt awed that we are part of an unending chain of generations which originated with a god or totem animal; if our place in this chain is not a source of unending wonder; if it does not determine our own place in life and in society; if procreation is not a miracle for us, then we shall fail to comprehend what these objects in the Smithsonian exhibit are all about, and seeing them with our own eyes will not be of much help.

Some may think that such exhibits give viewers an understanding of another culture, but unfortunately, we are taught to find understanding only in our own terms, which are alien to most other cultures. To understand another culture, one has to step outside one's own cultural frame of reference and into the other. But the very manner in which objects in our museums are so beautifully displayed, puts them within the framework of our culture and not their own. How will a child, brought up to think of objects in terms of their practical use, be able to appreciate that the figures on this flywhisk are not just pretty decoration, or that the carving on the post of a house has the purpose of investing this object with magical properties of deepest meaning and supernatural power?

And concerning this matter of bringing awareness of other cultures to our children, I think that we should not try to ask our children to understand what we ourselves, as adults, do not. I doubt that most museums are really equipped to truly communicate other cultures, and I believe from my knowledge of children that children need, most of all, first to grow strong roots in their own culture, before they can branch out to understanding others.

Robert Herrick reminded us that "thou prizest things that are curious and unfamiliar." Children in particular have a strong tendency to take the familiar for granted. It takes quite some sophistication to admire what we are most familiar with. But when, in museums, we are able to marvel at these wondrous objects—natural objects, pieces of machinery, works of art—we eventually begin to marvel at man, at what we are. The awe we feel for these wonderful creations of nature and those of man's talent and ingenuity eventually extends backward to ourselves. This is an experience which I believe all children need very much. Yet if these objects are to instill wonder and enchantment, the viewer needs not rational information, but patience and quiet perseverance, until at last he is brought to a genuine confrontation with the object of his contemplation, and with it a confrontation of himself.

Let us consider some findings about what makes people become regular museum visitors, specifically of art museums. According to these findings, only 3 percent of regular visitors to art museums credit school or educational trips with stimulating their interest, while 60 percent attribute their interest to the fact that somebody in their family, usually their parents, influenced them when they were young. And 77 percent were influenced by a combination of parents, friends, and teachers who instilled this interest in them.* Thus, a lifetime interest in museum-going is created and sustained by highly personal experiences, and not by the relatively light sprinkling of interest which seems to be all that educational programs can provide.

This certainly was true in my case. My mother took me to museums, and her delight at what was to be found there impressed me so much that I tried to discover for myself what enchanted her so much. Later, this interest was reinforced by friends, but it became a lifelong interest only when it grew beyond the seeds these people had planted.

I believe that as a child I never tired of visits to museums and never found them disappointing because I was never told how to look at things or what to see in them, or had their intrinsic meaning explained to me. These things I had to discover all for myself. I simply wandered around all by myself and picked out for contemplation what was in line with my mood of the day, my preoccupations of the moment, as I had seen my mother do. Since I was not instructed in what was important about what I was looking at, on different days I saw very different things in the same object. This aroused my curiosity, and made the object much more fascinating than it would have been had I seen in it each time the same things some expert had pointed out. Because nobody helped me to find something worthwhile in this or that work, I had to find it in my own way. Therefore I was free to reject many things in the museums, and nobody made me feel bad about my lack of judgment by telling me that what I had no use for was really very important or great. Without knowing it, at that time in my life, despite great insecurities, I was trying to form my own judgments about things important to me. If somebody in authority had asked me to appreciate things as he thought I should, this would not have made me secure in my appreciation, and the experience would have lost most of its meaning for me. If a guide had asked me to stand in front of something that he and everybody else considered significant but that had not by itself touched a responsive chord in me, I would have closed my mind and probably also my eyes, so that I would not have to agree to a response which was not really my own.

In this manner, without my receiving any specific guidance, visiting

---

*Barbara Y. Newsome and Adele Z. Silver, eds., *Art Museum as Educator* (Berkeley: University of California, 1977).

museums became a lifelong activity for me. Many years later I discovered that Schopenhauer could have been my mentor. He wrote: "You must treat a work of art like a great man: stand before it and wait patiently till it deigns to speak." This is exactly what I did. I decided all on my own what I considered, often for very spurious reasons, a great work, and then I waited until it spoke to me. At other times, suddenly a shock of recognition would strike me in my innermost being. This would not have happened had it all been explained to me, for then it would not have been my very own discovery, my very own moment of truth. Somehow I must have known what I eventually found Ruskin saying: "No one can explain how the notes of a Mozart melody, or the folds of a piece of Titian's drapery, produce essential effects. If you do not feel it, no one can by reasoning make you feel it."

Some might think that appreciation can be fostered by firsthand efforts at drawing or painting, but I can refute this, since I was taught drawing and painting for several years. This only demonstrated to me the abyss which separated my own efforts from those I admired in the museum. Mastering the technique of etching does not open any avenue to a meaningful understanding of Rembrandt. It stresses the accidental and ephemeral to the neglect of the essential. And so do romanticized stories, such as about Rembrandt's life or his bankruptcy. I believe Erwin Panofsky is right when he says in *Meaning in the Visual Arts*, "I do not believe that a child or adolescent should be taught only that which he can fully understand. It is, on the contrary, the half-digested phrase, the half-placed proper name, the half-understood verse, remembered for sound and rhythm rather than meaning, which persists in the memory, and captures the imagination. . . ."

This, then, I believe to be the museum's greatest value to the child, irrespective of what a museum's content may be: to stimulate—and even more important, to captivate—his imagination; to arouse his curiosity so that he wishes to penetrate ever more deeply the meaning of what he is exposed to in the museum; to give him a chance to admire, in his own good time, things which are way beyond his ken; and most important of all, to give him a feeling of awe for the wonders of the world. It is hardly worth the effort to try to grow up into—and live fully within—a world that is not full of wonder.

Children and Television

If we look at history, it is hardly surprising that parents, educators, and other moral overseers of our own day should be greatly worried about the damage television is doing to all of us, and particularly to our children. Moralists, by nature, have always had a tendency to worry about and decry the newest dominant form of popular entertainment. In Plato's ideal state, all imaginative literature was to be banned because of the bad influence it supposedly exercised, although this same literature has been admired ever since its creation as one of the proudest achievements of man.

Smoking, congregating in coffeehouses, dancing—each in its turn was thought to corrupt the young. Neither operas nor music halls escaped severe censure. Even such a masterpiece as Goethe's *Werther* was blamed for causing a wave of suicides (although at that time no records were kept from which one could have ascertained whether suicides had indeed increased).

Any new form of mass entertainment is viewed with considerable suspicion until it has been around for some time. It usually becomes accepted once people realize that life goes on in the same haphazard

This article appeared in the September/October 1985 issue of *Channels Magazine*.

way as before. Then a newer entertainment medium becomes the focus of the same concerns. When I was a child, all kinds of evil influences were ascribed to the movies; today these are blamed on television. When I was a young man, the comics were denounced because they supposedly incited the innocents to violence.

Even then, however, it was acknowledged that children were not all that innocent. It was known that they harbor angry, violent, destructive, and even sexual fantasies that are far from innocent. Today as well, those who evaluate the impact of television on children ought to truly understand what children are all about, and not maintain Victorian images of how perfect children would be if only they were not exposed to bad influences, or condemn as evil anything that children greatly enjoy.

New forms of entertainment are particularly suspect to adults who had no chance to enjoy them in childhood. Most parents who are young enough to have thoroughly enjoyed watching television in their childhood worry less about its detrimental effects. They know that their own youthful hours watching television did not prevent them from getting educated or from living useful lives. If they feel uneasy, it is about using television as a baby-sitter for their own children.

Despite all the concern and the innumerable articles about what television does to our children, hard facts are few and difficult to come by. We know as little about the topic as my parents' generation knew about what movies did to us. My parents worried about children spending so much time in the dark movie palaces—castles where we lost ourselves in dreams as often as our meager finances permitted. At least television does not require the child to leave home or spend most of his allowance on tickets.

One of the attractions of the movies, though we were unaware of it, was that they helped us escape our parents' watchful eyes at home, and other children's competition at play. Watching films, we daydreamed of being as successful in life and love as their heroes or heroines. We participated in exciting fantasies that made our humdrum (if not outright unpleasant) existence more bearable. We returned to everyday life restored by having seen the movie—often not just once, but a second or even third time when ushers permitted it.

Our children manage to do the same thing, right in their homes, and no usher prevents them from watching what is essentially the same program over and over again. They are neither bored nor stultified; all of us need to dream the same daydream until we have had our fill of it. In the public debate on the effects of television on children, the fact that TV programs provide material for daydreams is so much taken for granted that it is hardly discussed. There seems little doubt that most of us need to engage in daydreams—and the more frustrating reality is for us, the greater is our need.

Although we like to think of young children's lives as free of troubles, they are in fact filled with disappointment and frustration. Children wish for so much, but can arrange so little of their own lives, which are so often dominated by adults without sympathy for the children's priorities. That is why children have a much greater need for daydreams than adults do. And because their lives have been relatively limited they have a greater need for material from which to form daydreams. In the past, children saturated their imaginations with folk tales, myths, and Bible stories. Of course, they would have much preferred to *see* as well as hear the tales, to have them acted out in front of their eyes, had that been possible.

There is plenty of violence and crime in Old Testament stories, as well as in fairy tales. There is a lot of cruelty, enmity within the family, homicide, and even patricide and incest in Greek drama, as there is in Shakespeare's plays. This suggests that people have always needed a fare of violent fantasies as an integral part of popular entertainment. Aristotle said that such fare is required for catharsis—for the relief of our emotional tensions. Children need as much of that relief as adults do—perhaps more—and they always will.

Among the concerns about television's effects on our children, none is greater than that it may induce them to commit violence. Probably no concern has been more thoroughly investigated. As much as I personally dislike watching violence on the screen, I cannot deny that as long as it is not vicious or cruel—which it very often is—it holds a certain fascination.

Many children not only enjoy aggressive fantasies, but also need them. They need material for aggressive and retaliatory daydreams in which they can vicariously act out their hostile feelings without hurting close relatives. While the very young child may beat up a doll (thinking all the while of the new baby who stands in his way) or lash out at a parent, the slightly older child can no longer afford to express his aggression so directly. In healthy development, the child soon moves to daydreams in which not he but some imaginary stand-in discharges his anger against another distant and imaginary figure. That is why it is so gratifying when a cartoon shows a helpless little animal, such as a mouse, making a fool of much bigger and more powerful animals.

As part of a study on violence and television published in 1976, in an experiment, violent cartoons were shown to both normal and emotionally impaired children. The latter, being unstable, were expected to be more vulnerable to the cartoons' influence. But after watching the violent scenes, children in both groups were less chaotic in expressing their aggressiveness, and did so in less random fashion. Having acted out aggressive feelings vicariously in fantasy as they watched the cartoon, most of these children had less need to act aggressively in reality.

On the other hand, some of the seriously disturbed children did become more violent after watching the cartoons. Some youngsters *do* get ideas about how to act aggressively from what they see on the screen, which they then attempt to carry out in real life. The decisive factors are not the type of events shown on the screen but the child's own personality (which is formed in the home under the parents' influence) and, though to a much smaller degree, the child's present situation.

For normal children as well, television offers children a wide variety of models to fantasize about and try out, as if for size. Children tend to dress, stand, walk, and talk like TV characters they admire. Whether this helps or hurts a particular youngster seems to depend on which television figure he identifies with. And this is determined much more by his personality and the problems he faces at the moment than by what is shown on the screen.

As Wilbur Schramm and other researchers recognized more than two decades ago, "The chief part television plays in the lives of children depends at least as much on what the child brings to television as on what television brings to the child." And the younger the child is, the more this is so.

In an experiment reported in 1978 in *Child Development*, second-graders were made to view a program and then were asked to retell its story so that "someone who has not seen it would know what happened." In response, the children strung together random events. They showed no recognition or recall of relationships among the events. But children several years older, such as fifth-graders, were able to recall fairly well what they had seen. Thus the younger the child, the less responsive he is to the actual content of the program; he responds to it in terms of his inner life. Only the child whose emotional life is very barren or whose conditions of life are extremely destructive will "live" in the world of television programs. In his case, doing so may be preferable to facing his actual life, which could lead him to give up all hope, or to explode into violence against those who make his life miserable.

In fact, most children seek refuge at times in television-fed fantasy, although they usually do not permit it to engulf more than a very limited part of their lives. Television is truly an ideal medium for the purpose, because it permits the child to return immediately from the fantasy world to real life, and also to escape as quickly into the television world when reality becomes too much to handle. All it takes is turning a switch.

We ought to remember how restricted children's lives have become. It used to be possible to let children roam all by themselves for much of the day, or in the chance company of other children. They used to play somewhere in the neighborhood, or in an empty shack, or wander the woods and fields. There they could dream their own daydreams, without parents nearby demanding that they use their time more constructively.

Today, for our children's security, we cannot permit them to fend for themselves in that way. Yet, to grow up well, every child needs time and space to be himself. Watching television gives him this chance. Being able to choose the program with which he wishes to dream off has become a way for the modern child to exercise his self-determination, an important experience in growing up.

Oddly enough, in the dizzyingly active world of TV fiction, one kind of movement is in short supply: personal growth. The child's greatest need is to learn from his experiences and to grow because of them. This is why the child is best served by programs that show how characters' experiences change them—in personality, in outlook on life, in relations to others, in the ability to cope better with future events. Not only children's programs but also adult programs watched by children should avoid using stock characters who remain predictably the same.

Even such an exceptional program as *All in the Family* was centered around main characters who never changed and never learned, no matter how obvious the lessons of past episodes. In this, as in many other programs of less merit, the good guys learn as little from their experiences as do the bad guys. Even after the most incredible events, characters remain the same as before. But growth and development, and images of such growth, are what the child needs if he is to believe that he himself can grow. He needs to fantasize about how he will change, learn, and become a better person because of what life has taught him.

Not only do television characters fail to learn from their experiences, but no matter how severe their difficulties, the writers always provide them with simple, easy, instantaneous solutions, as simple as those promised by commercials. Using some particular brand of hair spray guarantees success in life and love; ingesting some pills does away with all our worries. Programs and commercials alike mislead the child by making it appear that there is, or ought to be, an easy solution for every problem he encounters, and that there must be something wrong with him, his parents, and society if these so readily available answers are withheld from him.

In this respect even public television's educational programs are misleading. Whether *Sesame Street* or *Nova,* they create the illusion that one will easily and immediately become well educated. And whether the child is promised popularity by toothpaste commercials or knowledge by PBS, he is encouraged to believe that success will come effortlessly. It doesn't, of course, and he becomes dissatisfied with himself and society.

A large part of the problem is inherent in the medium. To hold viewers' attention, television programs have to simplify matters and cannot follow the arduous process required for a person to gain knowledge. Some programs do *tell* how slow and difficult progress is, but hearing that said on television makes little impression on the child when characters on the same program can usually solve the greatest difficulties within thirty or sixty minutes.

Television is, after all, a medium best suited for entertainment; it does not readily lend itself to the balanced judgment, to consideration of all the pros and cons of an issue. We should not expect of this medium what is contrary to its nature. The information received from television programs will always tend to be one-sided, slanted, and simplified. That is why a young child will not truly learn by watching even the best programs—even those designed for his age; his life experience is too limited. Adults or late adolescents can bring their accumulated life experience to watching TV, which permits them to adopt the proper perspective. The child needs adult help to do so.

There is hardly a program from which a child could not learn a great deal, provided some responsible adult does the necessary teaching. Even violent programs are no exception, provided the child is not so anxious or angry that he is completely overwhelmed by what he watches. It is very important for children to develop the right attitudes toward violence, and closing one's eyes to the existence of violence can hardly be considered the most constructive attitude to have. Every child needs to learn what is wrong with violence, and why; why violence occurs, and how one ought to deal with it in oneself and others.

What is necessary is for parents to explore with the child what he, all on his own, made of what he saw and heard. We must let the child tell us what he got from the program, and start from there in helping him sort out which impressions came from within himself and which from the program, which were good and which were not, and why.

This requires, of course, that the adult watch along with the child. Doing so, the parent can no longer use television as an excuse for not spending time with his child. That, I believe, is the real danger of television—a human limitation, not one inherent in the medium. We should blame neither our children nor television if the reason they watch it is that we, their parents, are not very interested in spending time with them. We ought to consider that the more time we spend with them, the less time they will be watching the tube. The more time we devote to talking with them about what they have watched, the more intelligent and discriminating will their viewing become. The fact remains that our personalities and values will have much more effect than television in shaping our children and their outlook on life.

Master Teacher and
Prodigious Pupil

The story of how Anne Sullivan was able to restore Helen Keller's mind was of particular interest to me because, to my knowledge, it is the first time a method of therapy was invented that was so unique it had no name, but was viewed as miraculous. When, in the early 1940s, I introduced milieu therapy as a treatment for severely disturbed children at the Sonia Shankman Orthogenic School in Chicago, I had no knowledge of Sullivan's invention, which was substantially the same type of treatment. While writing about it in 1948, I gave it the name "milieu therapy." All essentials of this new method of trying to reach the most isolated, withdrawn, and angry children had already been used by Anne Sullivan in her efforts to return the young Helen Keller to humanity. To achieve a complete rapport with Helen, Anne had to remove her from her family and force her to live day and night only in her company. Anne accepted, and tried to understand, the most outrageous and violent behavior of her charge. She attempted to satisfy all Helen's needs in the most caring manner, and eventually was able to induce Helen to relate to her on a one-to-one basis. The results

This essay appeared with the title "Miracles" in *The New Yorker*, August 4, 1980. It is based on Joseph B. Lash's book *Helen and Teacher: The Story of Helen Keller and Anne Sullivan Macy* (New York: Delacorte, 1980).

of such extraordinary efforts to reach children who seem unreachable may indeed appear miraculous to outsiders. Actually, they are the results of extremely difficult labor, of great devotion, and of an acceptance of what seems like incomprehensible behavior derived from empathy based on one's own difficult and very painful experiences.

We are fascinated by the miracle that Helen Keller was and—thanks to William Gibson's play *The Miracle Worker*—by Anne Sullivan, who brought it about. As long as both lived, they were an inseparable two-some, deservedly world-famous. Helen Keller wrote a great deal about their lives, and so did others. The two women gave us images of themselves which we wish to believe and which they, for their own reasons, did not wish to disturb. Our great desire to give credence to the possibility of miracles blinds us to much of the hidden, and painful, reality of this story. However, Lash's book, *Helen and Teacher: The Story of Helen Keller and Anne Sullivan Macy*, opens our eyes to the discrepancy between the carefully maintained image of Helen and Anne and the difficult reality forced on them by the extreme disabilities Helen had suffered since infancy.

To get at this reality is no easy task. We would like to believe that it is possible to transcend completely the most severe physical handicaps—even complete blindness and deafness aggravated by partial mutism—when there is a will and a devoted helper. Indeed, most of Lash's book is given over to rendering the public image known and loved by millions of ordinary people and the very great alike. All who saw and listened to Helen or met her in person were moved by her courage and show of cheerfulness despite the greatest adversity. But Lash often also let the two women speak for themselves, sometimes making for repetitious and tedious reading, but revealing the true Helen and Anne come to life.

Who was the miracle and who the miracle worker? In a lifelong symbiotic relationship, this is difficult to ascertain, and it may be unimportant—even the wrong question to ask. An ancient Chinese saying asserts that whoever saves a life from then on remains beholden to the person he saved; it does not mention, as too obvious, the fact that the person saved owes his life to his savior. Anne's and Helen's lives were so intertwined that one is hard-pressed to say which of them gained more from their relationship. Anne turned a blind, deaf, dumb, savage little girl into the most marvelous human being; the Helen Keller we know was her creation. In forming Helen, Anne changed from a very bright and spunky but limited, angrily defiant adolescent into one of the most outstanding educators of all time. In this process, two essentially ordinary human beings, who until then had been unusual only in the deprivations they had suffered, made themselves, and simultaneously each other, into geniuses.

Gibson's play ends when Helen says her first word and, much more important, comprehends for the first time the power of words; that only through words can one make the world comprehensible to oneself and communicate with others. But this is merely the most dramatic moment in Anne's creation of Helen; Anne had started creating Helen the moment she met her. Helen was a reflection of what Anne wanted her to be, although Anne, who was much more down-to-earth, was often skeptical of Helen's idealistic notions, which came to her from lack of experience with everyday reality. Occasionally, Helen and Anne made feeble attempts to become separate selves, but none of these was serious. In 1905, John Macy married Anne, but he married into a twosome who were determined that this marriage would make no difference to them. After nine years, the marriage broke up, although Anne loved John Macy very deeply. She continued to love him long after he deserted her, and even after he died. Yet all along Anne knew that she could not leave Helen. The creator cannot free herself of her creation, and does not want to.

Anne Sullivan knew well that the good teacher, much as she may wish to hold on to prize students, has the obligation of helping them free themselves of their teacher and go out into the world. On Helen Keller Day at the 1915 Panama-Pacific Exposition, in San Francisco, when Anne was awarded the fair's Teacher's Medal, she said in her acceptance speech, "For years I have known the teacher's one supreme reward, that of seeing the child she has taught grow into a living force." From her own experience, Anne also knew the inescapable difficulty that the prize student must undergo to become free of the teacher. Anne herself had been nearly blind, as a result of a childhood illness. At the age of fourteen, she entered the Perkins Institution for the Blind in Boston, and there she became the prize student of the director, Michael Anagnos. He loved her like a daughter and wished to hold on to her; the break between them, which she provoked, was a tragedy for him.

Anne had been deeply attached to Anagnos and knew what she owed to her mentor; it was extremely painful for her to free herself of his possessive influence. But Anne could not let go of Helen, because Helen, with her handicaps, could not live independently without Anne. So Anne had to remain Helen's teacher for life. In the speech from which I have just quoted, Anne also said, "You see before you a teacher whose mature years have been passed wholly in the performance of one task, the training of one human being."

Helen was no student whom the teacher could with confidence send out into the world, because Helen could not cope with the world without a teacher who at all times literally held her hand. For being that teacher, Anne paid a high price. Even when she was awarded the Teacher's Medal, the event took place not on "Anne Sullivan Day" but on "Helen Keller Day." When Helen got a B.A. from Radcliffe, Anne, who had sat beside Helen in all her classes, spelling into her hand what the professors said, and who had read many required books to Helen, received no recognition. The creator was neglected in favor of her creation.

Helen, who deeply loved Anne and could not live without her, knew that Anne's greatest distinction was not that she was the most devoted friend, the infinitely loved companion, but that she was "Teacher." Helen always referred to Anne in that way; it was the highest praise Helen could confer on her, who alone made life possible and bearable. And so Anne remained all her life the teacher of only one pupil. But what a teaching and learning experience it was for both.

The more jealously Anne held on to her creation, the more she became enslaved by the demands this made on her. She became the vehicle for Helen's growth. All knowledge passed through Anne as she spelled the accumulated wisdom of the ages into Helen's hand, but it was Helen who profited from it and enlarged upon it. Since Helen was Anne's life, it is understandable that she wished to keep Helen under her control. For example, when it was suggested that Helen should be taught to talk, Anne's immediate reply was "I do not want her to speak." Helen did learn to speak, yet she hardly ever spoke with her own voice; she wrote, thought, and eventually spoke the words that Anne had first given her. As Helen had direct contact with the world only through touch, taste, and smell, she could use these words to think abstractly, and even poetically, but hardly ever concretely, with one exception: her insistence that blind and deaf persons be given a chance to become self-supporting, so that they might be able to respect themselves.

So strange is the relationship between creator and creation that

Helen, into whom Anne poured only what was best in herself, ended up the better person of the two, although somewhat unreal. Helen, because of her handicaps, always remained somewhat one-dimensional, goodness incarnate, as much as this is possible in a living being. Anne, who created this goodness and made it possible, never really aspired to it for herself. She could recognize and accept her shortcomings, and feel remorse because of them. Helen could not permit herself such luxury, and felt obliged always to be only loving and accepting—except in her fight for the deaf-blind, and against those whose politics she rejected, in her often biased and naïve opinion, as not being loving enough of mankind.

How did Anne, a poorly educated, inexperienced girl of twenty, find within herself the knowledge of what was needed to change the wild little animal that Helen was into a creative, sensitive, much better educated person than she herself? What Anne did in treating Helen was based in part on the work of those who came before her—mainly Dr. Samuel Gridley Howe, of the Perkins Institution, who was the first to teach language to a blind deaf-mute, Laura Bridgman, by spelling into her hand. His work was continued by Michael Anagnos, who accepted Anne into the Perkins Institution, and who was so important to her development and her life. It was he who arranged that she become Helen's tutor. While Anne learned much from these men, her approach to Helen was her own; nobody could have taught her how to get a hold on Helen so that she would become reachable, because nobody knew how to do it.

To say that Anne Sullivan drew her inspiration from within herself is true but explains very little. If we understand the inner resources she drew upon to enable her to approach Helen, we may also understand whence comes the inspiration of a truly great and innovative teacher. Like so many other great discoveries, Anne's had simple sources. She had not closed herself off from early childhood experiences, as most people do, in a process that has been called the development of childhood amnesia. Anne knew and never forgot what it felt like to be a desperately lonely, utterly deprived, nearly blind child, barely able to vegetate under the most miserable conditions in a nineteenth-century poorhouse. Worse, she had lost there to death the only person for whom she deeply cared and felt responsible: her little brother. She never forgot what she had then wished for most: that somebody would care infinitely for her, as she had cared for her brother—somebody who would not only

love her but hold on to her firmly and with determination, and not permit anybody to interfere with this relationship, which would be her entire world.

Anne kept this experience of childhood as her most private possession. Not until late in life did she tell Helen about it, and even then only
reluctantly. Further, Anne never permitted what others taught her
about educating the deaf-blind to obliterate what she knew from her
own experience. This was the source of her genius: in order to bring
Helen to life as a human being, Anne had to become her entire world—
what she had wished for, and wished to be for her little brother. She was
determined not to lose again. This is the secret underlying the "miracle"
she worked.

On the day that Anne met Helen, she spelled into her hand the
words "doll" and "cake"—the two things she had brought Helen for
their first meeting. Little Anne must have longed for such things when
she had neither toys nor decent food during her years in the poorhouse.
So from the very beginning of their relationship, Anne wanted Helen to
have what she had wanted most for herself. But Anne also knew that if
we want a child to understand words, to read them and, most important,
love them, we must give the child words that signify our love for him,
our wish to give him what he wants most. To give the child the signifier
without giving him also what it signifies is a very poor way to teach. It
is, in fact, how we teach reading in our schools, with the unfavorable
consequences that are well known. We still have not learned what Anne
knew when she first met Helen: that food and toys symbolize love and
care to the child, and that on these symbols and on what they symbolize
relationships can be built that truly humanize the child.

At the age of nineteen months, Helen had become blind, deaf, and
soon also mute, and had reverted to an animal-like existence. Five years
later, her life as a human being began anew when all her needs, like an
infant's, were taken care of by only one mothering person: Anne. Anne
knew—or, what is probably more accurate, felt empathetically—that
only such complete mothering could restore Helen. So she insisted that
at least for a few weeks at the beginning, nobody else was to enter the
little house in which the two of them spent their days and nights. There,
for a month, Anne took care of all Helen's needs; and there Helen permitted Anne to take her on her lap, to fondle her, and to sleep with her
in the same bed. The result was that Helen could take up where she had

left off when she fell ill: she began once more to get a feeling for what another human being could mean to her, could give to her, and so she tried to communicate with Anne.

It was pure chance that the first word Helen understood and tried to say was "water." By this I do not mean that it could have been any word. It had to be a word of great emotional significance—or, rather, what it signified had to be of great importance to her: a cherished toy, an essential food, a beloved person. (For the same reason, the first word of most children is "Mom" or "Dad.") Helen did not know that all life began in water, that life is not possible without water. Yet she began her efforts to comprehend the world by responding to the symbol for the most important nutrient, and she could do so only when the symbol for it was spelled into one of her hands while the other touched what the symbol signified—the sense of touch being what permitted Helen to be "in touch" with reality. Anne's genius was to recognize all this, however dimly or subconsciously, from her own experience. That she herself had been nearly blind for stretches of time and had then to rely on her sense of touch must certainly have aided her in reaching Helen.

If being "in touch" with her own childhood experiences and applying them in first reaching and then teaching Helen was Anne's genius, Helen's genius was her great eagerness to learn, her excitement about learning words once she had begun to discover the universe of signifiers, and her determination even without sight and hearing to build a semblance of the world out of signifiers. Helen could not get enough of learning and seemed addicted to it. The world of words, concepts, ideas suddenly opened up to her as if it were a miracle. She learned many hundreds of words in a few weeks—learned to read them when they were spelled into her hand, and to spell them back into Anne's hand.

It takes us years to teach an average child to read and spell a limited number of words, all much simpler than those Helen so eagerly and quickly mastered. Maybe there is a lesson here for the education of all children. Maybe, where academic learning is concerned, we should let the child follow his own inclinations for a few years; his intellect might be much more ready to engage in abstract thought after he has had his fill of self-chosen concrete experiences. Anne certainly thought this is so. "Every child begins life as an eager, active little creature," she said, "always doing something, always trying to get something that he wants very much. . . . Our educational system spoils this fine enthusiasm. . . .

Our schools . . . kill imagination in the bud. They uproot the creative ideals of childhood and plant in their place worthless ideals. . . . The fine soil of the child is of far greater importance than high marks, yet the system causes pupils to prize high grades above knowledge."

Helen learned extremely quickly after the world of words was made accessible to her; she continued all her life to learn, and she read voraciously whatever was available to her in Braille. This happened although no intellectual learning had been possible for Helen from the age of nineteen months until she was nearly seven years old. Her eagerness to learn got her through Radcliffe and way beyond; and her use of words and of her intelligence, despite her limitations—her intelligence and even her sense of touch were found to be only about average—made her a marvel of the world.

Helen Keller devoted her life to working for the deaf-blind. Although much of her work was done for the American Foundation for the Blind and under its auspices, she was most concerned for those who were so isolated from the world that they had to rely entirely upon others to be fed knowledge, as she had been. That Helen could accomplish so much was made possible first and foremost by Anne, but also by the adoration of the world. Helen needed that response; that is why she traveled incessantly all over the world, could never meet enough people, and did work so exhausting that it would have been beyond practically anybody else's strength. She continued to do all this into old age. Why did she receive this extraordinary adoration? Why did everybody love her, rave about her? Yet, of all these millions, why did hardly anyone try to be her close friend? In fact, those who so admired her, arranged things for her—and there were many of these—shrank away when it came to taking care of her, to spending time with this splendid person, to spelling the world into her hand. Only Teacher did this, and no one else. After Anne's death, Polly Thomson, who tried to take Teacher's place, could never do nearly so much for Helen, which only made Polly the more possessive of Helen, much to Helen's grief.

The world raved about Helen because she permitted us the illusion that one can have a complete, happy life although one is blind and deaf. It is our wish to delude ourselves that those who are severely handicapped are not excluded from living, that we therefore do not owe them a compassion much deeper than words, which should express itself in deeds. It was Anne's wish that Helen should have a full life through her, and she tried to fulfill this wish at the expense of her own life. Anne gave Helen the strength to pretend to have a full life of her own, and this pretense freed us, the public, of our obligation to be our handicapped brother's keeper. Because of this, Helen was admired and loved—from a distance. Her public performances, her clever repartee, her sense of humor—all permitted us to forget how terribly she suffered.

Since Helen was never truly able to be a person in her own right, much as she pretended to be one for our benefit, even Anne always remained "Teacher" to her. Helen could never outgrow the pupil stage. By pretending to have a full life, by pretending that through touch she knew what a piece of sculpture, what flowers, what trees were like, that through the words of others she knew what the sky or clouds looked like, by pretending that she could hear music by feeling the vibrations of musical instruments, she fooled neither her teacher nor herself. But we loved her for making it possible for us to fool ourselves that those who are so terribly handicapped are not really suffering deeply every moment of their lives. And we fool ourselves about it out of our anxiety that we might lose the ability to hear or see. Helen's pretenses reassured us that this would not be so horrible. For this she was given love, in addition to the admiration she so well deserved for her courage and her determination to carve out a most useful life for herself.

Not everyone was thus deceived. Some recognized the terrible loneliness in which Helen lived. Will Cressy, who wrote a column on celebrities for the *New York Star,* said:

> I never met one who attracted me and fascinated me as does Helen Keller. . . . Whatever she is doing I watch her. And some way I never get over the feeling of her sitting there in that steel cell, alone, in total silence and absolute darkness, stretching out her hands to get into touch with the world that must seem so far away to her.
>
> I have sat in her room and watched her waiting so patiently and yet so eagerly to be told what is going on; what is being said and done. Her hands are continually seeking Miss Sullivan's lips to know if she is speaking. Or her hands are flying to Miss Sullivan's hands to spell out some question.
>
> There she sits, in that invisible steel cell of hers.

When Helen was seventy-seven years old, she finally permitted herself to say it publicly: "No one knows—no one can know—the bitter denials of limitation better than I do. I am not deceived about my situation. It is not true that I am not sad or rebellious; but long ago I determined not to complain. The mortally wounded must strive to live out their days cheerfully for the sake of others."

I am not sure that Helen rendered us a service by not letting us see the misery that lurked behind her masterful show of cheerfulness. Joseph Lash's book could help us avoid forcing such a life of deception on the severely handicapped, and permit them instead to scream out the truth of their suffering. For what this book helps us to accept is that although there may be miracle workers, there are no miracles, and that the world is full of suffering human beings who desperately need our recognition and help.

Feral Children and
Autistic Children

In science, more than in other fields of human endeavor, the correction of a widely held error often contributes more to the solution of a thorny problem than some new discovery or theory, for erroneous ideas can prevent the valid knowledge we already have from making its influence fully felt. This is amply demonstrated by Professor Ogburn's "The Wolf Boy of Agra," which disproves the supposedly feral origin of the boy Parasram. For years, on the basis of much experience with severely autistic children, I had been convinced that most of the so-called feral children were actually children suffering from the severest form of infantile autism, while some of them were feeble-minded, as was possibly the Wild Boy of Aveyron.*

In the 1940s, two publications aroused worldwide interest, particularly among child psychologists, when they claimed that two children nurtured by wolves, Amala and Kamala, had been discovered in India. This revived an ancient belief in the existence of "wolf children." In the West it was Gesell's lending his authority to this tale which made it important, as it seemed to bear out certain tenets of behaviorism. When a decade later it was once more reported that a wolf child, Parasram, had been found in India, William Fielding Ogburn of the University of Chicago investigated the facts and found the claims to be false. His report, titled "The Wolf Boy of Agra," appeared simultaneously with my essay "Feral and Autistic Children" in the March 1959 *American Journal of Sociology*. Since that time no further claims have been made about children being raised by animals, so one may hope that these two publications succeeded in putting to rest an ancient myth. However, the idea of wolf children is of long standing, and the reasons people believe in them are interesting, so reprinting this article seemed justified.

* J. M. C. Itard, *The Wild Boy of Aveyron* (New York: Century, 1932).

Children suffering from early infantile autism typically are unable to relate themselves in the ordinary way to people and situations from the beginning of life. Their extreme isolation shuts them off from the outside. Some acquire the ability to speak, while others remain mute, but language is not used in either case to convey meaning to others. The autistic child's overall behavior is governed by an anxiously obsessive desire to maintain sameness.

The term "feral child," by contrast, is not a definite diagnostic category but vaguely denotes a very wild child and/or those supposedly raised by animals. From historical accounts of most children called feral, diagnosis cannot be established. But the more detailed the accounts, the more definitely do they seem to designate autistic children. Fortunately, in the case of the two famous "wolf girls" of Midnapore,* Amala and Kamala, a fairly accurate description of the behavior of the older girl and the steps in her partial recovery has been published.

The story of these girls' behavior closely parallels our experiences with autistic children at the Sonia Shankman Orthogenic School, a laboratory school of the University of Chicago devoted to the education and treatment of severely disturbed children. These children have never lived in the company of wild animals and were reared by none but human beings. The similarities are so great and so unmistakable that no other conclusion seems possible but that the two "wolf girls" also had suffered from severe infantile autism, which is entirely explainable without any history of being reared by animals. I could not doubt the veracity of the Reverend Mr. Singh's description of the "wolf girls'" behavior and development, so familiar to all of us who have lived with autistic children. In fact, I was probably more ready than most to believe in the accuracy of his account, and therefore I fell into the error of also giving credence to his report of how he found them.

But as I read Ogburn's story some time after reading Singh's accounts, suddenly the blinders fell from my eyes. Now it became all too clear: Singh's account of his close association with the girls could be, and, I believe, was, entirely correct, but his interpretation of the origins of their behaviors—their having been reared by wolves—was false. He was carried away by his imagination about the single event which

---

*J. A. L. Singh and R. M. Zingg, *Wolf Children and Feral Man* (New York: Harper & Bros., 1940); and A. Gesell, *Wolf Child and Human Child* (New York: Harper & Bros., 1940).

makes or breaks his interpretation: namely, the way in which the children were found. He described flushing three grown wolves out of the hollow of a "white-ant mound as high as a two-storied building" and found "two cubs and the other two hideous beings there in one corner, all four clutching together." Yet when asked, "How often do wolves den in deserted ant mounds?" Singh replied that "this was the only white-ant mound known to be lived in by wolves."

Hindsight is always easy. I can now also see the parallel between Singh's story of finding the girls and the wild fantasies we at the Orthogenic School spun about the pasts of our autistic children when we first met them. Our speculations originated partly in our efforts to find emotionally acceptable explanations for their nearly inexplicable and wholly unacceptable behavior. Later, we came to recognize that this speculation originated mainly in two different psychological needs for us as workers with the very difficult children. First, there was our narcissistic unwillingness to admit that these animal-like creatures could have pasts at all similar to ours (the same narcissism which revolted against the theory of evolution). Secondly, it met our need to understand and to explain these children's behavior, for the more unusual and less acceptable a phenomenon, the greater our narcissistic need of an explanation. Perhaps, too, the more revolting the behavior, the less we wished to devote thought to it, attributing it to an emotional reaction or some similar simple form needing no further thought.*

In the story of Amala and Kamala, the strangeness of the children's behavior and the veracity of Singh's accounts of it were taken as evidence that he must have told the truth about all else: in his story of the way he found them, and in his interpretation that their behavior was due to, and could only be explained by, their having lived with wolves. The mechanism at work here seems to be that the rational mind, which at first would reject the nearly unbelievable story of Kamala's behavior, thus proved to be an unreliable instrument, for this account was correct. Therefore, the rational mind's critical voice was silenced, so far as these stories were concerned, and henceforth everything was believed as told.

This, again, was not surprising to us at the Orthogenic School. Many

---

* For a few years during World War II, the National Socialists of Germany, since they behaved so inhumanly, were viewed as subhuman, and theories that all Nazis were insane found ready acceptance and were defended by psychiatrists.

times when we described the behavior of some of our extremely autistic children—how they urinated and defecated without so much as knowing it as they walked or ran about; how they could not bear clothes but would run about naked; how they did not talk but could only scream and howl; how they ate only raw food; how they would bite us so often and so severely that we required frequent medical treatments—even persons quite familiar with disturbed children would react with polite or not-so-polite disbelief. But later, when they met the children, their doubts changed to complete belief, and then they would have been willing to accept almost anything we told them about the children or their pasts.

Thanks to Ogburn's investigation, we now know that Parasram was not found in the company of wolves. We have, therefore, good reason to doubt that Amala and Kamala were found living with wolves. But, just as it was true that Parasram was found wild, there seems no reason to doubt that Amala and Kamala were found living wild in the forest.

But how did these children survive all alone in the wilderness? How did they get lost in the first place? I believe from our experience with autistic children that the wild children could not have survived very long by themselves, even allowing for the clemency of the Indian climate. Neither their haggard look nor the absence of clothing nor the "hideous ball of matted hair"* proves that they had been lost for long: some of our autistic children persist in keeping their wild looks for months. They can and do tear off all their clothes in minutes. Even after years with us the well-groomed hair of one of our autistic girls could, within hours, be turned by her into a "hideous ball of matted hair," glued together with saliva, remnants of food, dirt, and what-not. One of our autistic girls kept her face well hidden for months behind such a curtain of hair.

Ogburn speculated that the Indian children might be lost, feeble-minded, or the abandoned offspring of prostitutes; these are as likely explanations as any other. My guess would be that they were simply emotionally, and perhaps also physically, abandoned. In the report on the two children of Midnapore we are told by Bishop H. Pakenham-Walsh: "The very primitive people who inhabit the parts where these

* Singh and Zingg, op. cit., p. 18.

children were found, who are not Bengalis, do fairly frequently expose baby children."* If these people are ready to expose or abandon normal babies, is it so farfetched that they may also expose older children who act like babies (as autistic children do) or children who seem extremely abnormal to them? Also, how old are "baby children"? How old are the children before people normally stop exposing them? All these questions remain unanswered in the account of Amala and Kamala. †

Our own experience suggests the explanation that the girls in question were probably utterly unacceptable to their parents for one reason or another. This is characteristic of all autistic children, no matter of what age; the parents manage to disengage themselves from them by placing them in an institution (as is the usual case in the United States today), or by setting them out to fend for themselves in the wilderness, or, the most likely explanation in this case, by not pursuing them when they run away.

Our experience with the parents of autistic children, many of whom are good, well-educated, middle-class people, leaves little doubt that in their deepest emotions they wish to be rid of these utterly unmanageable offspring. They cannot, of course, afford to become conscious of such wishes or to act upon them because of the demands of conscience, the behavior expected of parents in the United States, and the near-impossibility of a child's getting permanently lost in our cities. But there is hardly one such parent, living in twentieth-century America and conscientiously on the watch, whose autistic child has not managed to get lost several times after the age of about three or four. It is reasonable, therefore, to assume that it must be quite easy for such children to get separated from their parents under more primitive conditions of life.

But what promotes the belief that there are feral children in general, or wolf children in particular? First, children labeled thus are not dumb but do not talk; and speech, almost more than anything else, separates humans from animals. Animals cannot talk; it is assumed then that these children have something in common with animals. Second, all normal children, even if feebleminded, need humans to take care of

---

* Ibid., p. xxvi.

† While Pakenham-Walsh, who knew the area, spoke only of "baby children," R. R. Gates, in his introductory remarks to the report on the wolf girls, mentions that in the jungle areas of India "female children are still occasionally exposed" (ibid., p. xiii).

them and will reach out to them; but these children shun human company. Third, some of these children are ferocious in their attacks on others, using claws and teeth, like animals. Beyond that, I can offer only speculation concerning feral children. For example, if the people of the region where the two girls of Midnapore were found believed in the transmigration of souls and were confronted with the behavior of the two girls, it is possible that they thought these girls had been wolves in a previous incarnation, or now represented an incarnation that was part wolf, part human. Such beliefs were unacceptable to the Reverend Mr. Singh, but perhaps they were part of his ingrained thinking before he became a student of Bishop's College in Calcutta.

I have already suggested the role that human narcissism may play in making credible the stories of feral children. As long as we could believe that insane persons were possessed by ghosts or devils, their "wildness" was less of a shock to our self-image as human beings. But the origins of the subhuman, animal-like behavior of these children are, in our enlightened age, no longer sought in the world of spirits. In this day of reason, we think, of course, of childhood environment as the source of their behavior. But their wildness, their total withdrawal, their "contrariness," their violence, their various types of inhuman, animal-like behavior overpower us and our attempts at a rational approach, and despite all our knowledge, we too are thrown back for moments to feel that they are possessed—that they are "animals." To quote a typical response after a rather mild example of such behavior shown by Anna, one of our wild children: "As I watched her continual application of saliva to all parts of her body, her biting and chewing of her toes, I thought to myself, 'She is an animal, destructively washing herself.'" So the easiest solution to the problem of their behavior is to believe it the result of an animal upbringing.

There are other and more specific reasons to suggest comparing these severely disturbed autistic children with animals. During one year at the Orthogenic School, a single staff member had to have medical help more than a dozen times for bites she suffered from Anna. All the children there regularly bare their teeth when annoyed or angry. Different, and again reminiscent of animals, is their prowling around at night, in marked contrast to their quiet withdrawal into a corner during the day. One of these girls could finally be reached and brought to accept human closeness only when her favorite counselor roamed through the building with her for many hours during the night. And only then would she accept food from us.

Then there is these children's great preference for raw food, particularly raw vegetables. Some will go to almost any lengths to get raw onions and lettuce and similar food, and go into violent temper tantrums if they do not get them immediately. Others lick salt for hours, but only from their own hands. Others, again, build themselves dens in dark corners or closets, sleep nowhere else, and prefer spending all day and all night there. Some build caves out of blankets, mattresses, or other suitable objects. They do not permit us to touch either them or their abodes, and at least two of them would eat only if they could first carry their food into their self-created caves or dens, where they would then eat without using utensils.

Some of these children, on seeing animals, respond as though they had found a dear, long-lost friend. One girl, for example, became extremely excited on seeing a dog; she showed a strong desire to run toward it and cried or howled like an animal, particularly like a wolf. She fell on all fours, jumped like a dog with her head down, and made biting gestures. Now, had we believed in the feral origin of this girl—whose total life history, incidentally, was well known to us—we would probably have been convinced that, on seeing that wolflike creature, she was filled with memories of her happy times among wolves and was reverting to what she had learned from them.

It could be said that despite such similarities between the behavior of some of our autistic children and that of the wild children described in the literature, these similarities are only superficial and due to chance, and that closer inspection would reveal important differences. So to decide whether Amala and Kamala were autistic children, we have to determine whether they showed all characteristics typical of the behavior of our autistic children and of infantile autism as reported in the literature.

Singh, in describing the children's behavior, states as most typical of the two wolf girls first what he calls their aloofness, and second their shyness or fright:

> The presence of others in the room prevented them from doing anything, even moving the head from one direction to the other, or moving

about a little, changing sides, or turning about. Even a look towards them was objectionable. They wanted to be all by themselves, and they shunned human society altogether. If we approached them, they made faces and sometimes showed their teeth, as if unwilling to permit our touch or company. This was noticed at all times, even at night. . . . For nearly three months . . . there was a complete disassociation and dislike, not only for us, but for their abode among us, for movement and play—in short for everything human.*

A child psychoanalyst described what he considered most character-istic of one of our ten-year-old autistic girls: "Her most pervasive behav-ior trait is her overwhelming panic reaction to the slightest interference from the outside, often occurring without visible external motivation."

This is behavior typical of all autistic children. But how do Singh and Zingg explain it? According to them, withdrawal from the surrounding world was related to the following:

After their rescue and subsequent capture they were looking for the cubs and the wolves. It was noticeable that they wanted their company and association, but finding that they could not get them here, they re-fused to mix with the children or with anybody. . . .

They could not find their mates in the jungle; they could not prowl about with the wolves; they missed their cozy den, and could not get to feed on meat or milk. Consequently, the thought of their old environ-ment preyed heavily on their mind, and their thought was to regain their former habitation and company. This fact made them meditative and morose.†

But how could it have been "noticeable that they wanted" the com-pany of wolves, or how could it have been deduced that "the thought of their old environment preyed heavily on their mind" and that "they missed their cozy den"? Formerly autistic children whom we have suc-ceeded in rehabilitating to the point where they could tell us about their autistic past have had only the dimmest notion of the vague fantasies which occupied their minds during their state of total withdrawal. We can say with certainty that those who were mute for long periods and were later able to reflect upon it recalled only having been in vague

* Ibid., pp. 15–16.
† Ibid., pp. 15, 17.

states of terror, interrupted by equally vague fantasies of a bliss without content which, in the literature, has been discussed as oral reunion fantasies. But even the latter explanation gives much too specific content to what are either vague and basically empty states of withdrawal from content and relations to environment, or intervals of relative comfort and discomfort.

Singh's descriptions—trustworthy as they are—are so flavored by his convictions about the girls' feral past that I would like, before comparing them with our own experiences and with the literature, to quote the only other eyewitness account of Kamala's behavior, because it is more concise and less adumbrated by speculations. We owe an excellent description of Kamala's behavior when she was estimated to be fourteen years old (some six years after she had been found) to Bishop Pakenham-Walsh. He was, apparently, if not also the most intelligent, certainly the most highly educated person who saw her. He reports:

> When I saw Kamala, she could speak, quite clearly and distinctly, about thirty words; when told to say what a certain object was, she would name it, but she never used her words in a spontaneous way. She would never, for instance, ask for anything she wanted by naming it, but would quietly wait till Mrs. Singh asked her, one by one, whether it was so and so she wanted, and when the right thing was named she would nod. She had a very sweet smile when spoken to, but immediately afterwards her face resumed an appearance of unintelligence; and if she were left alone, she would retire to the darkest corner, crouch down, and remain with her face to the wall absolutely listless and with a perfectly blank expression on her face. She had an affection for Mrs. Singh, and was most amenable to her directions during the time I saw her. She was not interested in anything nor afraid of anything, and cared nothing for the other children, nor for their games. She walked upright, but could not run.
>
> I saw her again two years later [when her age would have been about sixteen], and except that she had learned a good many more words, I did not notice any mental change.*

During the past years we have cared for at least nineteen children at the Orthogenic School whose diagnosis was definitely infantile autism. We have lived with each for at least one year, and with most of them for

---

* Ibid., p. xxvi.

several. If an intelligent and interested layman such as Pakenham-Walsh had observed most of them during their first year with us (and a few even during their second or third year) for a period of time comparable to that he spent with Kamala, his description might have been exactly like that he gave of this "wolf girl." At present, we have twelve such children, ten of whom, for a year or two, showed the same behavior, though most have since advanced much further intellectually. Three who have been with us for less than two years are now at the stage of behavior described by Pakenham-Walsh as seen in Kamala at about fourteen; a fourth has not yet reached it, since he has not yet said a single word. He has been with us for about a year.

Interestingly enough, two of the children began to say their first words after about a year with us, which closely resembles what was reported of Kamala—that she said her first words after thirteen months, when she began to "prattle like a baby."* From our experience, as well as from Pakenham-Walsh's description, I doubt she prattled like a baby, for that is the result of a voluntary reaching-out and an enjoyment first of vocalization and later on of verbalization. These autistic children, even after they have acquired the ability to say a few words—or perhaps, I should say, have overcome their reluctance enough to venture a few words—prefer not to use words but to let us do the talking for them, as was noted in Kamala after six years. The soft, hesitating, often echolalia-like saying of preferably only short, single words which characterizes autistic children's speech is very different from what develops out of the usual happy prattling of babies. Also in contrast to normal children are the autistic children's wild, ear-piercing screams which make their barely audible, strained enunciation of single words appear to be even more minimally invested with the positive wish to talk.

Kamala's behavior, as described, is also typical of the behavior of children suffering from infantile autism as reported in the literature. In their classical descriptions of this disease, Kanner and Mahler† state the most characteristic feature of infantile autism to be a profound with-

---

*Ibid., p. 121.

†L. Kanner, "Autistic Disturbances of Affective Contact," *Nervous Child*, II (1942–43), 217–50; "Early Infantile Autism," *Journal of Pediatrics*, XXV (1944), 211–17; *Child Psychiatry* (Springfield, Ill.: Charles C. Thomas, 1948), pp 716–29; and "Early Infantile Autism," *American Journal of Orthopsychiatry*, XIX (1949), 416–26; M. Mahler, "On Child Psychosis and Schizophrenia," *Psychoanalytic Study of the Child*, VII (1952), 286–303; and M. Mahler and G. Gosliner, "On Symbiotic Child Psychosis," *Psychoanalytic Study of the Child*, X (1955), 195–211.

drawal from contact with people, an obsessive desire for the preservation of sameness that none but the child himself may on rare occasions disrupt, and this while retaining an intelligent and pensive expression. Equally characteristic is either mutism or the kind of language apparently not intended as communication. The children are unable to relate themselves to people and situations from the beginning of life, are referred to as self-sufficient, act as though people were not there, and give the impression of silent wisdom.

Kanner's first case, Donald, at the age of five displayed "an abstraction of mind which made him perfectly oblivious to everything about him. He appears to be always thinking and thinking, and to get his attention almost requires one to break down a mental barrier between his inner consciousness and the outside world."* This sounds like Kamala's crouching in a corner for hours, as if meditating on some great problem, so indifferent to all that was going on that her attention could not be drawn to anything.†

Of Kanner's "Case 9" we are told that "the most impressive thing is his detachment and his inaccessibility. He walks as if he is in a shadow, lives in a world of his own where he cannot be reached. No sense of relationship to persons. He went through a period of quoting another person; never offers anything himself. His entire conversation is a replica of whatever has been said to him."§ The similarity to the wolf girls' aloofness and shyness is striking, and this boy's never speaking spontaneously approximates Pakenham-Walsh's description of Kamala.

It might still seem that some of the specifics of Kamala's behavior (Amala was so much younger, and died so early, that very little of Singh's account deals specifically with her) are so different from the behavior of autistic children as to justify Singh's belief in its feral etiology. To find out whether this is so, I have made a content analysis of the wolf children's behavior. Now among Singh's descriptions, only one item stands out as very strange, and it is the one repeatedly referred to as explicable only by feral experience. It is also the only one for which we have no parallel among our autistic children at the Orthogenic School. This is Amala's and Kamala's inability to walk erect when they were first found.

---

* Kanner, "Autistic Disturbances," p. 218.
† Singh and Zingg, op. cit., p. 15.
§ Kanner, "Autistic Disturbances," p. 236.

While several of our autistic children have preferred to crawl on all fours for some time, and others for a long time would walk only bent over, none was actually *unable* to walk erect when we first met him or her.

Nevertheless, some facts in Singh's account of the children's lives might suffice to explain this phenomenon. On their capture, the girls were immediately placed in "a barricade made of long poles, not permitting the inmates to come out. The area of the barricade was eight feet by eight feet." Singh left them there within those narrow confines and returned five days later to find them deserted by their keepers and left without food or drink. "The situation [was] very grave . . . the children lying in their own mess, panting for breath through hunger, thirst and fright. The feeding was a problem. They would not receive anything into their mouths." Finally he got them to suck some tea from a wick, like babies. Before the girls had time to recover, a journey of seventy-five miles was undertaken, lasting for seven days, during which they were transported in a jolting bullock cart. Thus they spent another seven or eight days in narrow confinement. When they arrived at Midnapore, "they were so weak and emaciated that they could not move about."

If this had happened to some of our autistic children, we would assume that complete and prolonged deprivation of food, drink, and a chance to move about are sufficient to explain total regression to infantilism, such as not walking and being able only to suck. Most of the descriptions we have of the Indian girls' way of walking refer to the time after their arrival at Midnapore. In an entry dated twenty days after (i.e. November 24, 1920), Singh mentions "extensive corns on the knee and on the palm of the hand near the wrist which had developed from walking on all fours." The sores healed, but, he adds, only "on the nineteenth of December we found them able to move about a little, crawling on feet and hands."*

Thus no moving about was actually observed in Amala and Kamala after their capture, and probably none took place from the day of their capture until some sixty-two days later, when they began to crawl like normal infants: a type of behavior which can be fully explained by the deep regression they had experienced in all other ways.

* Singh and Zingg, op. cit., pp. 8–12.

The belief that the girls' walking on all fours was due to their living with the wolves is pure conjecture.* It seems to me much more reasonable to assume that their walking on all fours was part of a regression to the crawling stage, such as we see frequently in some of our autistic children.

A characteristic of the "wolf children" attributed to the feral past is that their eyes were wide open at night, like those of a cat or a dog. We are also told that they could see better by night than by day, though no objective tests support the assertion. This unusual activity of vision is reported as of December 20, the day after they first began to crawl, when they were barely emerging from their deepest immobility and debility.† How Singh could be sure that they could see better at night than during the day, at a time when they could hardly move or do anything else, is beyond me.

Another capacity linked with their feral past is their ability to smell meat or anything else from a great distance, like animals. Hardly anyone who has worked with psychotic children and has reported on them in any detail has failed to remark on their strange hypersensitivity to sensations of smell and touch, in stark contrast to prolonged periods of unresponsiveness to sights. Hearing often takes a middle position, being sometimes blocked out and at other times or in other cases increased. In general, the senses of closeness (touch and smell) and distance (hearing and seeing) are invested in psychotic children inversely to what is usual in normal persons. Elsewhere I have reported on the extremely acute sensitivity to smell of schizophrenic children, who could smell what we could not.§

Kamala's ability to find her way about in the darkness is reported as unusual and likewise due to her feral experiences. But this is not unusual for many of our autistic children, who, in general, rely very little on sight for getting about. For example, one of our autistic, nonspeaking girls at one period kept her eyes shut tight for days. This in no way impaired her ability to find her way about, even when we tentatively put some obstacles in her normal course in the hope of inducing her to open

---

* R. R. Gates, in a footnote to the description of the children's crawling, mentions that A. Hrdlicka in his book *Children Who Run on All Fours,* published in 1931, collected 387 such cases, mostly of white children of civilized parents. This suggests that crawling is neither unique nor necessarily due to feral rearing (cf. Singh and Zingg, op. cit., p. 13).

† Singh and Zingg, op. cit., p. 22.

§ *Truants from Life* (Glencoe, Ill.: Free Press, 1955), p. 222.

her eyes. This she did not do but sensed exactly the place where the obstruction was put and circumnavigated it.

Amala and Kamala are reported to have eaten and drunk "like dogs from the plate, lowering their mouths down to the plate," to which statement a footnote is attached, saying: "Their methods of eating were conditioned reflexes learned from the wolves."* Joe (whose history is given below) has never to our knowledge eaten any other way and still eats only thus, after more than a year with us. Other autistic children eat only by shoveling food into their mouths with a pawlike motion, while again others feed only from their own skins. †

We are told that "the perception of cold or heat was unknown to them," to which, in a footnote, is added that this was "another conditioned reflex from their experience with wolves." § But some of our autistic children have sometimes tried to run out into the street naked even in Chicago's winter weather, when the temperature is quite different from that of Midnapore. We have always caught them quickly, yet they seemed totally insensitive to such experiences and never had so much as a cold in consequence.

Schizophrenic children often behave as though they were totally insensitive to heat and cold, as did Amala and Kamala, whose attitude to temperature is therefore hardly unique and proves nothing about a feral past. ‡

Sensitivity to pain in psychotic children is, in the same way, unlike that in normal children and has to do with the nature of the disturbance and not with a feral past.**

This leaves only one inhuman characteristic in my catalogue—the "wolf girls'" inability to laugh. This, too, is quite characteristic for most, if not all, autistic children. As far as my recollection goes, our autistic children have never laughed until such time as we believed they had definitely moved from infantile autism toward severe neurosis, a much more benign degree of emotional disturbance.

---

* Singh and Zingg, op. cit. p. 27.
† For this and similar strange eating behaviors, see my "Childhood Schizophrenia as a Reaction to Extreme Situations," *American Journal of Orthopsychiatry*, XXVI (1956) 515.
§ Singh and Zingg, op. cit., p. 31.
‡ Cf. my *Love Is Not Enough* (Glencoe, Ill.: Free Press, 1950), p. 300.
** Mahler describes how one of her psychotic patients deliberately scorched her own lips with a cigarette lighter and showed no reaction, and she goes on to say that this child's sensitivity seemed grossly below normal and to explain this as an "indication of the lack or deficiency of peripheral cathexis in autistic child patients" (Mahler, "On Child Psychosis and Schizophrenia," p. 291).

Actually, the catalogue of animal-like behavior for the "wolf girls" is slight. Comparing it with what animal psychologists, such as Lorenz, can tell us about the wide variety of an animal's behavior, not to mention the incredible variety of human behavior, it appears that even our most autistic children show only a few characteristics that lend themselves to comparisons with animals. But these few characteristics or types of behavior are so shocking to us that they assume importance and proportion entirely out of line with their actual frequency or significance in the child's total life. If we were to catalogue the behavior of even wildly acting-out autistic children, two things would stand out: first, that most of the time they do nothing and avoid any contact with the world (cf. the aloofness of the "wolf children"), and second, that if they cease to be withdrawn for short periods, even then they do very few things in comparison with normal children of their age. When they occasionally engage in animal-like behavior, we tend to be so overimpressed by it that we lose sight of the rest.

What was the actual nature of the "wolf children's" past? If feral experiences do not explain their behavior, what experiences do? The early history of the two wolf girls is unknown, but perhaps that of our autistic children may suggest what their actual, as opposed to their imagined, past may have been. I would like to stress here that while we continue to study these children intensively, at the time of this writing we reserved judgment about what causes infantile autism. We were pretty sure of the very important role of certain contributing factors, but whether they were causative or only importantly contributive had not been determined. In 1967 I published a much more comprehensive study of infantile autism under the title *The Empty Fortress* (New York: Free Press; London: Collier-Macmillan).

It should be stressed again that only a small minority of known autistic children are "wild." For example, only a few of Kanner's cases showed some of the traits which characterized Kamala and possibly also Amala; most of his cases were much more like Parasram. At the Orthogenic School, we have worked with both those similar to Parasram and those more like Kamala; both groups have all the essential features in common, with the exception of the animal-like wildness of the latter.

What causes this difference in behavior? For a time, we thought it might originate in the difference in home backgrounds. All Kanner's cases are children of highly intelligent parents, and that is also true of many of our nineteen autistic children. Some of our wildest children had unusual experiences in infancy, as will be seen from the life history of Anna, and her parents would not be described as intellectual. However, two other very wild autistic children did come from highly intellectual homes. At least five of our quieter autistic children, who are very like those described by Kanner, come from nonintellectual homes; and four more came from lower-middle-class backgrounds, where the parents had at best a modest education.

On the quiet type of autistic children, more similar to Parasram, ample material is available, particularly in the case studies published by Kanner. So instead, I shall give the life history of Anna, a wild child with animal-like traits, who has already been mentioned.

Anna came to us at the age of about ten. For years, before she entered the Orthogenic School, her uncontrollable wild behavior had made life unbearable for her family. Her brother, six years younger than she, had been in constant danger of losing his life to Anna's violence, and he had had to be protected at all times from her. Neighbors had often called the police because Anna was so threatening to their children. Several efforts at placing Anna in treatment institutions had failed. In a very well-known institution for disturbed children she lasted barely half a day; in those few hours she managed to throw the institution into such a turmoil, and did so much damage, that she could not be kept. Even in a psychiatric hospital she could remain only a month because it, too, was not equipped to handle such a wild child. There she had to be kept in a maximum-security room, without any furniture, where she spent her days naked because she tore off all clothes that were put on her. Most of the time Anna crouched in a corner in total withdrawal; from this she emerged for short periods of wild screaming, running, jumping, and pounding on walls and door. Since this behavior made it impossible to keep Anna in the children's ward, the hospital had been forced to place her in the adult maximum-security quarters, an arrangement too unsuitable to be continued.

Anna's life had begun in a dugout under a farmer's house in Poland, where her Jewish parents were hiding from the Germans and their concentration camps. Anna's parents were extremely ill-mated. The mother, who found the father utterly unattractive, had rejected him for years while he courted her hopelessly. Both felt that they were of unlike temperaments and background. By the time World War II broke out, the father had given up hope of winning the mother, but the German invasion of Poland soon changed the situation. This man foresaw what would happen after Germany occupied Poland, and so he collected a large amount of wool and made arrangements with a gentile peasant friend to store it in a dugout under his farmhouse, where he had set up a loom. When the Germans began to exterminate the Jews, Anna's father took permanent refuge in his small earthen cellar. But first, he tried once more to persuade the woman he loved to join him. This proposal she again rejected without hesitation. She had no use for him, she said, and would rather be killed by the Germans than live with him. Soon things grew much worse: most of her family was killed. At that time the father, who could no longer leave his hiding place, again sent word to her through his gentile friend, asking her to join him. By then she had been left all alone and had no place in which to hide from the Germans. Very much against her will she took refuge with the father in his hole under the ground; his peasant friend was willing to let them both hide there. But her condition for accepting the refuge was that they have no sexual relations.

The father managed to support them, and in part also the peasant who hid them all during the German occupation, by weaving in his underground hole. The peasant sold the sweaters he wove, and on what he got for them (clothing being at a premium), he and the two in hiding were able to live. But the dugout was so small that there was not enough space for the parents to so much as stretch out at night unless the loom was taken down. Then they could bed themselves down for the night, the wool serving as bed and cover. So every night the loom was taken apart, and every morning it was reassembled. Several times the Germans searched the farmhouse, but they did not find the two in their cellar; its trapdoor was covered with stamped earth, like the rest of the farmhouse floor.

At least once (according to other stories this couple told us, it was several times), the Germans shot into the farmhouse. With the passing of time, life under such conditions became ever more difficult, the two being forced on each other without respite. Nevertheless, for over a year Anna's mother refused to live with her husband as man and wife. She

rejected him because she felt him to be beneath her culturally and so-
cially, and repulsive physically. According to Anna's father, although he
was incensed at the continued rejection, he respected her wishes and
did not force himself upon her.

About what happened then, the parents' two stories disagree. According to the father, they trembled for their lives every day, but he at
least had his work to keep him going, while Anna's mother was beginning to lose all will to live. In desperation he decided that if she had a
child, it would restore her wish to live and maybe even make her accept
him. So he persuaded her to have a child, and she agreed to have sexual
relations just for that purpose. Only because of these circumstances did
she become pregnant.

According to the mother, the father pursued her sexually all along.
After a year, no longer willing or able to stand the presence of a woman
whom he loved so much and who rejected him, he threatened to kick
her out of their refuge; she must either surrender or leave—which was
tantamount to being killed by the Germans. Only under such duress did
she finally give in.

When in the spring of 1943, Anna, the child of this relation, was
born, she did occupy the mother and give her some interest in life, but
it made existence even more difficult in their narrow confinement.
When Anna tried to cry, as infants do, one of the parents had to hold a
hand over her mouth, since any noise, particularly a baby's crying,
would have given them all away. Also the peasant, who with reason
feared for his life if it should be learned that he was hiding Jews, became
more and more fearful and angry when the infant made any noise or
otherwise complicated matters. So the parents and the farmer, each
afraid of the Germans, did their best to see to it that the infant was totally quiet at all times and as little of a bother as possible in all other
respects.

As long as the mother could nurse her, Anna had at least enough
food. But her milk gave out before Anna was a year and a half old. Then
all she could feed Anna was raw vegetables or suchlike, since they could
not cook. Not until 1945, when the Russian occupation replaced that of
the Germans, did things improve, but by then Anna had become unmanageable. Nightly she would run, jump up and down, and scream,
sometimes for hours, sometimes all night. She never fell asleep before

two or three in the morning. When she was not screaming or being violent, she was doing nothing, "thinking, thinking, sitting by herself and thinking her own life."

Eventually, the parents managed to reach Germany and entered first one, then another, and finally a third DP camp. But once in Germany and relative freedom, the mother began having adulterous relations. When her husband learned of it, new and violent fights broke out between the two. The mother wanted to leave him once and for all, but Anna stood in the way. The mother wanted to keep the child, but her lover did not want Anna. The mother was ready to give Anna up because she wanted to live with her lover, but was unwilling to surrender Anna to the father. So she suggested that Anna should stay with her own mother. To this the father would not agree; he wished to emigrate to the United States, where he had relatives, and to take Anna there.

During the years in Germany, the parents frequently contemplated divorce, but at the last moment the father would never consent to it, fearing that Anna would probably be given into the custody of the mother, who had no use either for Anna or for him. There were violent outbursts in front of Anna. As one of them put it: "We screamed and fought all the time over the child." The father's feelings about his wife can best be expressed by his lament: "I so often gave my life for her, and she only betrayed me."

Long before Anna came to this country, even before her brother was born, she was examined by an American physician in one of the German DP camps and immediately recognized as an autistic child who needed treatment in an institution. Since we are here concerned with the background of so-called feral children, and since Anna was recognizably both wild and autistic when about five or six years old, nothing more needs to be said of her early history. But since it was mentioned earlier that the staff members—a nurse trained in child psychiatry—who worked most intensively with Anna needed to be treated over a dozen times for human bite during Anna's first year with us, it might be appropriate to tell how Anna's biting of staff members abruptly stopped in her second year with us. She was once again biting this staff member, who by then had become deeply devoted to her. While before she had tried to prevent Anna from biting her as best she could, this time, out of her devotion to Anna, despite the pain she experienced from the biting, the staff member told her, "Watch out, Anna, you are going to hurt your teeth." This, because of the relationship that had become established between the two, must have made a deep impression on Anna. Being told that the staff member's concern was not so much with the pain the bite inflicted on her but rather with the pain Anna experienced which made her bite seemed to shock Anna, and she immediately let go. From this moment on, Anna never again bit this staff member, and soon thereafter her biting people stopped entirely. She became much less wild and more human.

While thus there was good progress from wild autistic behavior to much more human reactions, after another year and a half we had to stop working with her, since it seemed clear that while she had made considerable progress toward human behavior, the early damage done to her was too severe to achieve full rehabilitation, which is our goal.

We can say with conviction that it is simply due to chance that our two wildest girls were foreign-born and first saw the world in time of war. Thousands of children were born in DP camps and developed normally, and most of our autistic children were reared in what seemed like good middle-class homes. Even more than deep inner parental rejection, total emotional isolation makes for autistic withdrawal, though, as said before, we reserve final judgment until we know more. In general, our autistic children seem potentially very bright and very sensitive; this is why they react so strongly to emotions in their parents which they somehow comprehend as a threat to their existence. To protect their lives, they stop existing as human beings, or so it would seem. Another example is Joe, one of our wild, autistic children who came from a middle-class family.

Joe was the son of highly intelligent and ambitious native-born Americans, exactly what Kanner describes as typical of all autistic children. Joe was nine when we first met his parents. By then, what they recalled of their attitudes toward him as an infant was highly colored by feelings of guilt, but clearly this was a case of extreme neglect and isolation.

The earliest investigation of Joe's history took place when he was not yet three years old. Several more psychiatric studies preceded his coming to the Orthogenic School and our interview with his parents. From each study the same picture of Joe's early life emerged. Both parents began psychotherapy a few years after Joe's birth, and they gave us permission to confer with their therapists, who stated that they each gave us a truthful account of their early handling of Joe—accounts which also tallied with their personalities and with their past and present attitudes, as these were made plain during treatment.

Joe was born within ten months of the parents' marriage, a time when both parents were overburdened and physically and emotionally exhausted. The father, in his third year in medical school, held two jobs, one being night work, to support himself and his family. Understandably, he was always on edge. The task of taking care of a baby frightened both parents. As was typical of the father all his life, when in fright, he attacked. The mother's reaction to having a baby was one of fear and panic, which only increased the father's anger. What the father called his anger and fighting back at the baby is described by the mother as violent rages, which kept her in constant fear. Finally, she said, after living "in fright and trembling," she suddenly turned and started a "counteroffensive," her husband appearing to her simply as an enemy to be vanquished.

While the mother stated that she was "thrilled at the idea of having a child," the father reports that her attitude changed immediately after Joe's birth. She became depressed and showed great fear, if not panic, at nursing him. Indeed, she became fearful of everything about Joe, particularly about whether he would get enough to eat. At the same time she was distressed by sore nipples and confused about how often she should feed him.

Joe was obviously not a happy baby. He rocked a great deal, scratched his face severely, and cried a lot. He was colicky, and by the end of his first month of life both parents were "fed up with him." They accepted a pediatrician's advice to leave him strictly alone, particularly when he cried. The mother, who had previously felt that Joe's demands on her were monstrously excessive, was glad to follow this advice rigidly. After a few weeks his prolonged daily crying spells stopped, but he was still left alone most of the time. His mother related, for example, that when Joe was about six months old, "we again had a violent quarrel one day. We screamed and physically fought each other for half an hour, or longer. Before the fight started, I had just put Joe down, and it all took place within his hearing. He just sat there without moving or any reaction."

When Joe was not yet a year and a half old, the mother went into the hospital to avoid a miscarriage, and since the father was a physician, it seemed simplest to place Joe in the pediatric ward. This precipitated a regressive episode in which he resumed persistent thumb-sucking and rocking and ceased to speak the few words he had already learned. Some weeks later the mother aborted and had to be hospitalized for a time; again, despite the bad effect they knew it had on Joe, they put him in the pediatric ward for the sake of convenience. By then, both parents had lost interest in Joe. The father withdrew entirely into his work, the mother became engrossed in a new pregnancy, and Joe spent most of his time alone, either in the yard or at a nearby beach. He had nobody to play with; he did not move about; he spent all his waking day simply clinging to one toy or another, such as a ball.

The parents first became aware of the seriousness of Joe's difficulties when he was two and a half, at which time the birth of a brother intensified his symptoms: twirling, rocking, thumb-sucking, and lack of speech. When they tried sending him to a nursery school, his total withdrawal became even more apparent. Treatment was attempted but failed.

The parents wished to believe his difficulties were organic, but complete physical examinations at three outstanding medical centers revealed no supporting evidence: each time the conclusion was that his difficulties were emotional in origin. The findings agreed on Joe's extreme intellectual retardation and the severity of his emotional disturbance, as evidenced by his total withdrawal and self-preoccupation and his inability to relate himself emotionally to others or to make any meaningful contacts at all, despite attempts at physical contact made by others. Joe remained withdrawn in his own autistic world, and there was no tangible evidence of fantasy content in his solitary infantile play, or in his primitive hand-and-mouth activity.

One diagnosis was of psychosis of childhood; the two others indicated infantile autism. Treatment away from home was recommended, and Joe, not yet four, was placed in an institution, where he remained without much change until he was about nine and entered the Orthogenic School. By then he did not make any articulate sounds, although he understood simple commands. He tore his food with his hands, licked the plate like a dog, attacked others in all ways, including clawing and biting—in short, behaved like a "feral" child.

To sum up, study of the so-called feral children and comparison of them with known and well-observed wild autistic children suggest strongly that their behavior is due in large part, if not entirely, to extreme emotional isolation combined with experiences which they interpreted as threatening them with utter destruction. Such a psychosis seems to be the result of the inhumanity of some persons, usually their parents, and not the result, as has been imagined, of the humanity of animals, such as wolves. To put it differently, feral children seem to be produced not when wolves behave like parents, but when parents, for some reason or other, reject one of their children to the degree that the child comes to think from an early age that she or he is not accepted as a human being. The child's withdrawal from humanity is his response to what his inner experience tells him: not just that he is unwanted, but that it would be best if he did not live.*

---

* For our successes and failures in treating autistic children, see my *The Empty Fortress*, pp. 413–16.

PART III

On Jews and
the Camps

Janusz Korczak: A Tale
for Our Time

P recious in the sight of the Lord is the death of his righteous
ones," says the Psalmist. If one might ask why the deaths of the
righteous ones rather than their lives are precious to the Lord,
the answer is this: while the Lord is pleased with the righteous ones as
long as they are living righteous lives, only at their deaths can there be
certainty that they never deviated from the path of righteousness.

An ancient Jewish myth at least fifteen hundred years old has it that
there must live on earth at any one time thirty-six righteous people.
Only the existence of these righteous ones justifies humanity's continuation in the eyes of the Lord; otherwise, God would turn his face from
the earth and we all would perish.

As long as these righteous ones walk on earth, nobody must know
who they are; they remain unknown to all other men. To us they may
seem quite ordinary persons; only after their death may we discover
their identity. Then some do become known, and posterity can recog-

This is an enlarged and revised edition of a lecture on Janusz Korczak which was delivered as the
Flora Levi Lecture in the Humanities at the University of Southwestern Louisiana. A small seg-
ment of it was published as an introduction to his *King Matt the First* (New York: Farrar, Straus &
Giroux, 1986).

nize their extraordinary virtue and come to admire them, their lives, and their deeds.

Whoever the other righteous ones may have been in our lifetimes, by now we can be certain about two of them, although the world became aware of them only after they had been martyred. And, as if to prove the saying of the Psalmist, it was their freely chosen death which finally made the utter righteousness of their lives apparent.

One of these two was a Franciscan priest, Father Maximilian Kolbe. The other was a Jewish physician and educator, Dr. Janusz Korczak. Both died voluntarily in German concentration camps during World War II.

Father Kolbe volunteered to be starved to death in the place of another prisoner, enabling him to live and return to his wife and children, while the priest had no such family. So Father Maximilian Kolbe was murdered by being starved to death, while the prisoner whose life he saved lived to tell the story, as did also some other prisoners who had witnessed Kolbe's death, as well as some of the SS guards who could not help being deeply impressed by the courage with which he suffered his terrible fate.

The second of these two righteous men, Dr. Janusz Korczak, steadfastly rejected many offers to be saved from extermination in the death camps. He refused to desert in extremis the orphaned children to whose well-being he had devoted his life, so that even as they died they would be able to maintain their faith in human goodness: that of the man who had saved their bodies and freed their minds; who had salvaged them from utter misery and restored their belief in themselves and the world; who had been their mentor in matters practical and spiritual.

Korczak sacrificed himself to keep his trust with the children, when he could easily have saved himself. He was repeatedly urged to do so by his many Polish admirers and friends, for he was a prominent figure in Polish cultural life by the time he died. Well-wishers offered to provide him with false identity papers which would have allowed him to live freely; they arranged ways for him to escape the Warsaw ghetto and live safely outside of it. Children whom he had salvaged in the past, now grown up, implored him to allow them to save him, for he had been their savior. But as the head and leading light for thirty years of the Jewish orphanage in Warsaw, Korczak was determined not to desert any of the children who had put their trust in him. As he said to those who beseeched him to save himself: "One does not leave a sick child in the night," and "One does not leave children in a time like this."

At the German occupation of Warsaw, all Jews were forced into a ghetto, where they were destined to perish. The orphanage which Janusz Korczak directed was also to be relocated there. Knowing full well the great personal risks involved, Korczak went to the headquarters of the German command to plead the case of his children. As was his custom on similar occasions, he went there wearing his old uniform as a Polish army doctor, refusing to wear the obligatory yellow star. When told he should not bother with Jewish children but devote his physician's skill only to Polish children instead, Korczak declared that he was Jewish. So he was put into prison and tried for such "brazen behavior."

As often before and afterward, some of his previous charges came to his rescue and bought his freedom. From then on, they tried ever more fervently and repeatedly to persuade Korczak to leave the ghetto and save himself, arranging safe escape routes, false papers, places to live. But Korczak steadfastly refused to desert his children, although he knew what the end would be. He worked even more ceaselessly for the welfare of his charges, using his influence and old connections to beg for food, medicine, and other needs, and in this he was astonishingly successful. Even the smugglers knew and admired Korczak and his work, and so they helped him and his children as best they could.

The Nazis ordered that on August 6, 1942, the two hundred children who were then left in the Jewish orphanage of the Warsaw ghetto were to be taken to a train station, there to be packed into railroad carriages. Korczak, like most other adults in the ghetto, knew by then that the carriages were to take the children to their death in the gas chambers of Treblinka.

In a successful effort to assuage the children's anxiety, Korczak told them that they would all go on an outing in the country. On the appointed day he had the oldest child lead them, carrying high the flag of hope, a gold four-leaf clover on a field of green—the emblem of the orphanage. As always, even in this terrible situation, Korczak had arranged things so that a child rather than an adult would be the leader of other children. He walked immediately behind this leader, holding the hands of the two smallest children. Behind them marched all the other children, four by four, in excellent order, sure of themselves, as they had been helped to be during their stay at the orphanage.

The impression received by those who saw the children walk by was that they were holding their heads high, as if in silent protest, or contempt of their murderers; but what these observers interpreted was probably only the children's self-confidence, which they had gained from their mentor. When their procession arrived at the place to which they had been ordered, the policemen, who until then had been busy whipping Jews into the carriages and cursing them while doing so, suddenly snapped to attention on beholding Korczak and the children and saluted them. The German SS officer who was commanding the guards was so startled by the dignity of Korczak and the children that he asked in wonder: "Who is this remarkable man?" It is reported that even there, at the train station, final attempts were made to save Dr. Korczak. One of the guards told him to leave—that only the children had been ordered to the train station and not he—and tried to move Korczak away. But Korczak refused, as before, to separate himself from the children, and went with them to Treblinka.

For many years preceding this, Dr. Janusz Korczak had been well known all over Poland as "the Old Doctor," which was the name he used when delivering his many state radio talks on children and their education. Through these he became a familiar name even to those who had not read any of his many novels—for one of which he had received Poland's highest literary prize—nor seen his plays, nor read any of his numerous articles on children, nor learned about his widely known work with orphans. For example, in 1981, speaking at a symposium on Janusz Korczak, the Polish theology professor Tarnowski reminisced about how, as a youngster, he had admired the radio chats of "the Old Doctor" without knowing that the person he was listening to was the well-known author who had written one of his favorite books, *King Matt the First*.

Korczak's radio talks were sensational for the young Tarnowski, as they were for nearly all other listeners, because they proved to him for the first time in his life that an adult could enter easily and naturally into the world of the child. Korczak not only understood the child's view, but deeply respected and appreciated it, while all other adults seemed unable to do true justice to the world of children.

What Korczak taught best was, to quote the title of one of his most significant books, "how one ought to love a child."

Korczak loved children deeply; he devoted all the moments of his life to them. He studied them and understood them more thoroughly than most. Since he truly knew children, he did not idealize them. As there are good and bad adults, all kinds and sorts, so too Korczak knew there are all kinds of children. Working for them in many ways throughout his life and living with them in the orphanage, Korczak saw children for what they were, and was at all times deeply convinced of their integrity. He suffered from the fact that often children are treated badly, not given the credit they deserve for their intelligence and basic honesty.

Korczak was very critical of our educational system, which, then as now, weighed children down with irrelevant and unimportant information, when education's main task ought to be helping and preparing children to change their present reality into a better future. Most of all, Korczak was convinced that the power relations between adults and children are all wrong; that they must be changed so adults would no longer be convinced of their right—even viewed as an obligation—to arrange the life and world of the child as they think best, without considering the child's feelings about it. In Korczak's opinion, only an education which takes very seriously the child's view of things can change the world for the better. His deepest belief was that the child, out of a natural tendency to establish a viable inner balance within himself, tends to improve himself as best he can, when given the chance, freedom, and opportunity to do so. To give these chances to children was the center of all his efforts.

Those who, like Korczak, single-mindedly devote themselves to making this a better world for children are usually motivated by their own unhappy childhoods. What they suffer then makes such a lasting impression that all their lives they try to come to terms with it by working to change things so that other children will not have to suffer a similar fate.

Janusz Korczak was born Henryk Goldszmit, the scion of two generations of educated Jews who had broken away from the Jewish tradition to assimilate themselves into Polish culture. Korczak's grandfather was a highly regarded and very successful physician, his father an equally successful and well known lawyer. In all external respects, little

Henryk's early life was spent in very comfortable circumstances, in the well-to-do upper-middle-class home of his parents. Yet he was familiar with emotional difficulties from an early age on—his father held often grandiose and unrealistic notions of the world, and had a poorly developed ability to relate to reality. For example, he postponed registering the birth of his only son, Henryk, in consequence of which it is still unknown whether Henryk was born on July 22 of 1878 or 1879.

Even when Henryk was an infant, although all seemed well, his family lived in an atmosphere of psychological, cultural, and social alienation, which must have contributed to the father's basic mental instability. Being by birth Jewish, Henryk's parents were alienated from the Polish culture they embraced. Yet by having made themelves part of this culture, they had alienated themselves from the culture of Poland's Jews, which at that time was unique and vital. Nearly all Jews of this period living in Poland spoke and read Yiddish; their lives were dominated by Jewish religious traditions and observances. All they did and thought was informed by their religion. By contrast, Henryk's parents were nonpracticing Jews who spoke only Polish. So although he was well cared for as a child, Henryk knew practically from birth what it meant to be an outsider. He remained an outsider all his life.

When Henryk was only eleven years old, his father began to suffer from serious mental disturbances, which eventually required his placement in a mental institution. He died there when Henryk was eighteen years old. With the decline of Henryk's father, the family's breadwinner, the family encountered economic hardships. From then on, Henryk had first to contribute to the family's livelihood and later to provide for it. As a schoolboy, he earned some money by tutoring other youngsters. When he became a university student, he began to support himself, his mother, and his sister by writing.

It was at this time that he adopted the pseudonym by which he would subsequently be known. Wishing to enter a literary competition, and fearing that he had no chance to win if he used his own, clearly Jewish name, Henryk submitted his work under the Polish-sounding name of Janusz Korczak, which he took from a Polish novel he happened to be reading at the time. Although he did not win this literary contest, he continued to use this pseudonym thereafter.

By that time, although choosing to be a medical student, Korczak was determined to devote his life to the betterment of the lot of children.

Typically, he introduced himself to a female fellow university student by saying that he was "the son of a madman who is determined to become the Karl Marx of children." As Marx's life was devoted to the revolution which would liberate the proletariat, so Korczak's would be consecrated to the liberation of children, which would require revolutionary changes in the way they were viewed and treated by adults, who suppressed children even more painfully than the proletariat were suppressed in Marx's view. When asked what such liberation of children would imply, Korczak answered that one of its most important features would be granting them their right to govern themselves. Even at this early period he was convinced that children are able to govern themselves at least as well as their parents and educators govern them, if not much better. During his university years Korczak thought that the best way in which he could help children was to become a pediatrician, so this is what he became.

Early on, Korczak was already sure that he would not marry, because he did not wish to beget children. When the university student to whom he revealed these life plans asked him, astonished, why if he was determined to devote his life to children he did not want any of his own, Korczak answered that he would have not just a few, but hundreds of children for whom he would care. As far as we know, he never specifically said why he did not want to marry or have children, but it seems probable that he was afraid he might have inherited his father's tendency to insanity and feared to pass it on, or have a child suffer from such predicaments as he had experienced because of his father's mental instability.

As a medical student specializing in pediatrics, Korczak worked in the slums of Warsaw. He hoped that by combining medical treatment for children's physical ills with spiritual assistance, he would be able to effect fundamental changes in their living conditions. His first novel, *Children of the Street*, published in 1901, was written in anger at the degradation in which these children were forced to spend their lives.

After receiving his medical degree in 1905, Korczak began working and living in a children's hospital, to be close to the children at all times. In the meantime, he continued to publish writings on various subjects, some of them literary, others educational, medical, and sociopolitical. Another novel, largely drawn from his own life experiences, was titled *The Child of the Salon*. Here he took up themes which had occupied his mind as early as his fifth year, when he decided it was necessary that money and currency be abolished, so that there would no longer be any dirty, neglected, and hungry children (with whom, at five, he was not permitted to have any contact). As there should be no children living in elegant drawing rooms, isolated from less fortunate children, there also should be no children of the slums.

When the Russo-Japanese war broke out in 1905, Korczak was required to serve as an army doctor, an experience he found most upsetting, but which brought him into even closer contact with the suffering poor. Over the following eight years, in a slow development, he decided to give up the practice of medicine and devote his life entirely to helping suffering children. He once explained this shift in his life's work thus: "A spoon of castor oil is no cure for poverty and parentlessness." He meant by this that not even the best medical treatment can undo the damage which utter deprivation causes in children.

So in 1912, then in his early thirties, Korczak became director of the Jewish orphanage in Warsaw, leaving the children's hospital where he had worked and lived up to then. From then on until his end, he lived and worked at the orphanage, the only interruption being his service as a physician in the Russian army during the First World War. But even while serving in the battle zone and having hardly any time for himself, Korczak's main concern was with the children. Instead of resting from his arduous labors as a front-line physician when he had a chance, instead of sleeping at night, he wrote what became probably his most important and influential book, *How One Ought to Love a Child*. After the end of the First World War, he also became codirector of a Catholic orphans' home which he named Our Home, and which served both Jewish and Catholic children.

Most of Korczak's writings on children dealt with how one ought to relate to and come to understand them; how one ought to treat and educate them; and most important of all, how one ought to respect and love them. His writings are aphoristic in nature, since he believed that any systematic treatment of these subjects tends to become abstract, and thus to do injustice to the ever-changing expressions of a child's vitality. Repeatedly, and with ever different examples, Korczak asserted that the reason most experts do not really know children is that they study them in the laboratory or in the abstract, instead of proceeding clinically and observing them while living with them day in and day out. One of his ideals in respect to the study of living things was the French entomologist Jean Henri Fabre, who all his life observed and studied insects without ever harming any of them, let alone killing them, while his colleagues ended up by killing what they had tried to study.

Korczak's method of teaching his students at the Institute for Pedagogy in Warsaw, where he taught for many years, may be illustrated by his taking them to observe the workings of a child's heart as it could be seen on the screen of an X-ray machine. The child had to stand in front of a screen in a darkened room and was naturally apprehensive about the darkness, the unaccustomed surroundings, and the strange machinery. Speaking very softly, so as not to add to the child's fears, and deeply moved by what could be seen on the screen, Korczak enjoined his students to take a good look and never forget what they saw: "How stormily a child's heart beats when he is frightened, and this it does even more when his heart reacts to an adult's annoyance with him, not to mention when he fears to be punished."

Many of Dr. Korczak's ideas are now commonplace, but they were radically new at the beginning of this century when he first conceived them. He again and again stressed the importance of respecting the child and all his ideas, even when we cannot always agree with them. He insisted that it is wrong to base educational measures on our notions of what the child will need to know in the future, because real education ought to be concerned with what the child is now—not what we wish him to be in the future. What we do not realize today is the degree to which we owe these and many other "modern" ideas about children to Dr. Korczak's influence. Some of these ideas were also shared by a very few other contemporary educators, such as Dewey. But while educators like Dewey only conceptualized, Korczak set his ideas into daily practice by living with the children on their terms, which he helped them to discover and set into practice.

Others, like Neill of Summerhill fame, began to set into practice more than a decade later what Dr. Korczak pioneered on a daily basis, and Neill's beliefs were based partly on the practice and experiences of Korczak. Even Neill, who was probably the most radical reformer of children's lives after Korczak, did not go as far as Korczak did in insisting that children must govern themselves. Korczak helped his children create a children's court, and he submitted himself to its judgments.

Korczak knew well that despite his utter devotion to children, he himself was the product of a faulty upbringing and therefore not free of shortcomings; his character to some degree had been botched up by the way he was brought up, as is true for all of us. So for him personally, the children's court was an even more important institution of the children's society he had created in the orphanage than even the children's parliament, their newspaper, or their other independent enterprises. He reported that during a six-month period he found himself accused at least five times before this children's court. Once it was because, carried away by his emotions, he had slapped a child who had severely provoked him. He readily admitted his guilt, and that the seriousness of the provocation could not serve as an excuse for slapping the child. Another of his misdeeds had been to send a rambunctious child out of the dormitory so the other children would be able to sleep. His guilt had been that he had acted on his own decision, whereas he ought to have let the rest of the children decide whether they wanted to sleep at the price of having the offending child put out of the room. Another time he was tried and found wrong by the court of children because during a trial he had offended one of the child judges. And still another time he had accused a girl of theft, instead of letting the court of children decide whether she was guilty.

We owe to one of the child judges who found Korczak guilty of his fifth offense a vivid image of the court proceedings. Korczak had playfully put a little girl up in a tree, and when she had become fearful he had joked about it. He was found guilty, according to Rule 100 of the children's court. The judge's decision was: "Without the accused himself excusing, defending, or condoning his action, the court nevertheless finds him guilty." As soon as the verdict was rendered, the girl who had accused Korczak threw herself crying into his arms and lovingly embraced him.

With such arrangements one might think that life in the orphanage was chaotic, or anarchic. It was far from that, however: the children's self-regulation and the children's court saw to it. Korczak himself knew very well that self-control was a most necessary ingredient for being able to live a good life. He asserted that when everything is permissible, then no willpower can develop; but willpower is most necessary if the child is to meet the rigors of life successfully.

Not only when he was accused did the Old Doctor gladly submit himself to the judgment of the children—he sought it always, about everything he did. For example, Korczak read to the children out of his books, asking them for their criticisms, which he took very seriously. Again and again, he said and wrote that the children were his best and most important teachers, that he had learned all he knew from them.

It was the personal courage and depth of feeling with which Korczak lived out his ideas that made him unique. The flavor of these feelings may be conveyed by a reply he gave to a question about the principles underlying his actions. He replied: "I kiss the children with my eyes, with my thoughts, as I ask myself the question: Who are you, you who are such a wonderful secret to me? What are the questions you dare not ask? I kiss them through my arduous desire to discover in which way, in which manner, in regard to what problems I can help you. I embrace children in my mind as the astronomer tries to embrace in his mind the star which is, which has been, and which will be." And children were indeed the stars he tried to reach, by which he guided his life.

Maybe Korczak's philosophy is best expressed by the words with which he said goodbye to a group of orphans as they were ready to "graduate" from the orphanage, whose services they had outgrown. He told them:

> We say goodbye to you and wish you well on your long travel into a faraway country. This your trip has but one name, and one destination: your life. We have thought long and hard how we should say goodbye to you, what advice to give you on your way. Unfortunately words are poor and weak vehicles to express ourselves. So we can give you nothing on your way.
>
> We give you no God, because Him you have to seek in your soul, in a solitary struggle. We give you no fatherland, because that you have to find through the efforts of your own heart, through your own thoughts. We don't give you love for your fellow men, because there is no love without forgiveness, and to forgive is a laborious task, a hardship which only the person himself can decide to take upon himself.
>
> We give you only one thing: the desire for a better life which does not yet exist, but which will someday come into being, a life of truth and justice. Maybe the desire for it will guide you to God, to a real fatherland, and to love. Farewell, don't forget it.

In order to help other adults and children overcome their alienation, which is deadly for both, Korczak wrote a novel, *When I Am Little*

Again, in which he posed both as an adult and as a child, as a teacher and as a pupil, trying to make each of them understand the other's problems, joys, and frustrations, comprehend the other's life. But this book's approach did not turn out to serve his purpose as well as he had hoped.

So Korczak tried once more and produced his most successful, most widely read book: *King Matt the First,* published in 1928. This was the book which, Professor Tarnowski stated in his recollection of his childhood, changed his view of adults, because he realized that the author of this novel, at least, fully understood children, the way they feel and act. *King Matt the First* is the story of a boy who on the death of his father becomes king, and he immediately sets out to reform his kingdom for the benefit of children and adults alike. Both in the original Polish and in its German translation this story has become a children's favorite; it was finally published in this country in 1986.

King Matt is none other than Korczak himself re-created as a child, courageously doing battle against all the injustices of the world, most of all those inflicted on children. All is told from the perspective of this utterly sincere boy who, while always remaining a child, pursues with great courage and determination his goal: to remake a world very much like ours into a good world for children and, in so doing, create a better world for adults. Korczak appears in the story also in his adult form, as the old doctor who foresees the troubles into which King Matt will run, whose heart bleeds for King Matt. The old doctor tries to help but fails in his efforts: the world is simply too insensitive to the needs of children; it does not understand what is right for them, does not appreciate their sincerity, their ability to take care of their own affairs, nor how they could help this become a much better world for all of us.

What makes this fable unique is the exquisite insight into the psychology of children it reveals, including the immaturity of some of their plans, which eventually becomes their undoing. It is marvelous how in this story a modern world and its people exist side by side with the completely imaginary world, one brought into being through the hopes, aspirations, and fantasies of a spunky, exceedingly bright, imaginative, sensitive, and completely honest little boy.

King Matt the First is a rare masterpiece in revealing to us how a child sees the world of adults and its operations, and how, given the freedom to do so, he spontaneously reacts to it. By describing Matt's experiences, the story tells how a child again and again will trust adults, only to be deeply and painfully disappointed by them. It shows how devious adults are in their dealings with children as well as with other adults, and how much more direct and honest children are in their dealings with adults and with each other. Further, it demonstrates how even some adults who mean well are unable to truly comprehend the essence of children's deepest concerns, desires, and hopes. Most impressive of all, this story renders a true picture of how in the child deep seriousness and naive but real wisdom in understanding the world are at all times inextricably interwoven with the need for childish play, for deep friendship with adults and peers, for a life of the imagination—but paramount, a life of freedom, dignity, and responsibility.

King Matt is a late flower in the venerable tradition of the *Bildungsroman* so characteristic of the best literature of the Enlightenment. Goethe's *Wilhelm Meister*, Gottfried Keller's *Der Grüne Heinrich*, and Romain Rolland's *Jean Christophe* are but three examples of the genre, which relates the emotional, moral, and personal development of a hero under the impact of the vagaries, trials, and tribulations of his existence. While all other novels of this type follow the inner growth of the hero into maturity, *King Matt the First* tells only about personal development during childhood. In this, as in so many other ways, Korczak's novel is truly unique.

That Korczak would have written such a novel of enlightenment is hardly surprising, since his entire life was devoted to spreading enlightenment concerning children. *King Matt the First,* in addition to being quite entertaining, is full of insights into how children see adults, what they want from them and out of life. Particularly revealing is the list of reforms which King Matt's children's parliament wishes to see enacted.

Of these reforms, for personal reasons one of them in particular pleased me: the children's wish to abolish being kissed by adults. Many years ago I suggested this idea, without any awareness that Korczak had done the same much earlier, because all children I knew who dared to express their opinion on such matters were uniform in their abhorrence of being kissed indiscriminately. My suggestion was met with the strongest objections. This, among other experiences, taught me how difficult it is for adults to accept that children do experience things differently than they, and how ready adults are to forget how they felt as children. Most adults are convinced that what to them is an obvious expression of love and affection must be the same for children; they do not realize that children and adults can experience the same event very differently. Children enjoy and need bodily contact, not in a form which is part of adult sexuality, such as being kissed, but rather through being held, carried, and cuddled—that is, through involvement of the whole body in pleasurable kinesthetic experiences, rather than a contact concentrated on a particular bodily organ, such as the mouth. All through his lectures and his writings Korczak told how children are delighted when adults show them affection in the way they desire to receive it: foremost, by taking them seriously, and secondly, by treating and playing with them on the level they enjoy.

Part of the Enlightenment tradition within which *King Matt* is written is the Rousseauist notion of the noble savage who, although primitive in outlook, customs, and behavior, is actually more decent and moral than his European counterparts. This notion is found in *King Matt,* along with the other that children are more decent and moral than are adults. It is a black king in *King Matt* who is eager to set the reforms suggested by Matt into practice, trying to become a better person and make things better for his people. Only the black kings are Matt's true friends, ready to give their lives for him, while the white kings, despite nice promises, in the end betray him scandalously.

The story ends when King Matt's carefully but all too childishly planned reform collapses as the result of his being nefariously betrayed by the world of adults, and because the children, being children, all too carelessly and childishly and, on occasion, selfishly execute his plans.

As Korczak succeeded ever more with children, he became ever more isolated from the outside world. The more it became known with what fervor he fought for the freedom of the children to arrange their own lives, to develop themselves in their own chosen ways, the more he himself became an outsider. It was mentioned that his parents had been outsiders in respect to the dominant Polish culture they had made their own because they were Jewish, and had been outsiders to the Jews because they were fully assimilated to the Polish world. In addition to this alienation Korczak had inherited from his parents, he now became alienated from the Polish right as a radical reformer, and from the Polish left because he single-mindedly fought for the liberation of children, not believing that it would automatically come as part of a socialist revolution.

To the various Polish literary groups, Korczak was suspect despite his great literary successes, because he did not adhere to any of the various literary movements and did not get his impetus from them, but from children. Educators feared and rejected him because he severely criticized their methods. Alienated from all these adult circles, he drew all the closer to the world of children, who, like him, were alienated from the world of adults. Yet to undo the alienation of children from adults and vice versa was the goal for which he lived and worked his entire life.

From the time of the German invasion of Poland in 1939, Korczak knew the end was coming. His growing sense of desolation made him anxious to leave a final testament. The diary he wrote during the last months of his life in the ghetto, mainly during the months of May and August 1942, represents, to quote his words, "not so much an attempt at a synthesis as a grave of attempts, experiments, errors. Perhaps it may prove of use to somebody, sometime, in fifty years. . . ." These were truly prophetic words, because it will soon be fifty years since the Old Doctor wrote them, and now his works and deeds are becoming more widely known, understood, and appreciated than ever before.

In July 1942, less than a month before Korczak's end, his devoted followers and friends made another attempt to save him. His Aryan collaborator and friend Igor Newerly brought him false papers, which would have permitted Korczak to leave the ghetto with Newerly. While all Newerly's entreaties failed to shake Korczak's determination not to leave his children, to show his appreciation for Newerly's efforts Korczak promised that he would send him the diary he had kept during his ghetto years. As always, Korczak kept his word, and a few days after he and the children were taken to Treblinka, Newerly received the diary. He bricked it up in a safe house, and after the end of the war rescued it from there. It has been published with the title *Ghetto Diary*, and aside from *King Matt* it is the only one of Korczak's many books which so far has appeared in English.

In this diary Korczak mentions the last play which he chose to be performed by the children for a ghetto audience, shortly before he and the children were murdered. Although it was forbidden for Jews to perform plays by Aryan authors, the play chosen was Tagore's *The Post Of-*

fice. (Korczak, as usual, disregarded the risk of punishment for flouting the orders of the SS.) The play's central figure is a dying boy whose end is made bearable to him because he is made to believe that the king will visit him, and that his dearest wish will be fulfilled by the king. Korczak must have chosen this play because he already knew how he would try to make their dying bearable to his children. When after the performance he was asked why he chose this play, he answered that eventually one had to learn to accept serenely the angel of death.

Korczak had learned to do this, and he made it possible for his children to do the same. On the last pages of his ghetto diary, he wrote this confession: "I am angry with nobody. I do not wish anybody evil. I am unable to do so. I do not know how one can do it." Up to the last, he lived according to what the rabbinical fathers once wrote. When asked, "When everyone acts inhuman, what should a man do?" their answer was, "He should act more human." This is what Korczak did to the very end.

After World War II, Janusz Korczak—his work and his life—became a legend, and not only in Poland. He and his work are now well known among European educators, and in many countries outside of Europe. His work is studied at European universities, and symposia are devoted to it. Many monuments have been erected to honor him; a play, *Korczak and the Children,* has been widely performed. Books have been written on his work; his own writings have been republished and translated into many languages. He was posthumously given the German Peace Prize. The hundredth anniversary of his birth, 1978–79, was declared Korczak Year by UNESCO, and in Poland and many other countries. Pope John Paul II said once that for the world of today, Janusz Korczak is a symbol of true religion and true morality.

The memorial at Treblinka to the 840,000 Jews who were murdered there consists of large rocks marking the area in which they died. These rocks bear no inscriptions other than the name of the city or the country from which the victims came. One rock alone is inscribed with a man's name: It reads: "Janusz Korczak (Henryk Goldszmit) and the Children." This, I feel, is the way he would have wished to be remembered now— as the most devoted friend of children.

Hope for Humanity

I was deeply moved by the book *Anne Frank Remembered*, by Miep Giese with Allison Leslie Gold. Miep Giese, about whom Anne Frank wrote in her diary, "it seems we are never far from Miep's thoughts," knew Anne well, watched her grow up, and came to love her. Thus she can and does tell us much about Anne. But I was moved by Miep's story because it tells about an average, ordinary person's great humanity.

It is due to Miep Giese, more than to anyone else, that Anne Frank could write her diary, since it was Miep who, at great risk to herself, provided the Frank family—and the others who hid out with them—with the food that kept them alive, and with the human companionship they needed to be able to endure their desperate isolation.

Miep was born in Vienna in 1909. Because of the severe deprivation she experienced during World War I and the hungry years that followed it, she was a very sickly, nearly starved child. There were many like her, and some neutral countries tried to save these children. One of these efforts was made by Dutch socialist workers, who took the children of

After having devoted an essay to bringing Janusz Korczak to my readers' attention, I thought it appropriate to do the same for Miep Giese, at least in the form of a review of her moving book. It appeared in the *Washington Post Book World* in the form in which it is here reprinted.

Viennese socialist workers into their homes. Thus Miep, in December 1920, was taken in by the Nieuwenhuises, a Dutch working-class family of very modest means. They already had five children of their own, but, as they put it, where seven could eat, there eight could eat. The plan was that these Viennese children should be fed for three months, and then be returned to their parents in Vienna. But by the end of the three months Miep was still so sick and weak that her foster parents kept her on, and, except for one short visit to her parents, she grew up with the Nieuwenhuises as if she were their own child.

It might be thought that it was her early experience of being rescued which made Miep feel obliged to rescue others. But from reading her story, I am convinced that she risked her life in efforts to rescue those in dire need not out of a feeling of obligation, but out of sheer human decency. She did what she felt was right, with disregard for her own safety, because she was the person she was.

At the very beginning of her book, Miep tells how she saw and still sees herself:

> I am not a hero. . . . More than twenty thousand Dutch people helped hide the Jews and others in need of hiding those years. I willingly did what I could to help. My husband did as well. It was not enough.
>
> There is nothing special about me. I have never wanted any special attention. I was only willing to do what was asked of me and what seemed necessary at the time.

In 1933, when Miep was twenty-four years old, she took, more or less by chance, a job with Mr. Frank, who had so recently escaped from Germany that his wife and two small girls had not yet joined him in Amsterdam. When they did, Miep and later her future husband, Henk Giese, became friendly with the Franks over time, and also with their group of German Jewish refugees. Their lives proceeded normally, without mishap, until the German occupation of Austria in 1938. At that time, Miep was ordered to appear at the German consulate, where she had to give up her Austrian passport for a German one. Shortly thereafter, she was visited at the home of her foster parents, where she lived, by a German girl who had been given her name by the German consulate. This girl invited Miep to join a Nazi girl's club. When Miep refused, the visitor insisted and pressed her for the reasons for her refusal. In reply, Miep mentioned, among other reasons, the way Jews were treated in Germany. At the time, she paid no further thought to this incident, which, after the occupation of Holland by the German army, had serious consequences for her. Then she was again ordered to present herself at the German consulate, and because of her refusal to join the Nazi girl's club her passport was invalidated and she was ordered to return to Vienna within three months. In desperation, she sought help from the Dutch authorities, who told her that the only way she could remain in Holland was to marry a Dutchman. She and Henk Giese had planned for some time to get married as soon as they could find an apartment to live in. Now they decided to get married immediately. They were able to do it, but just in the nick of time, because of difficulties Miep had in securing the papers she needed from Vienna.

Soon after the occupation of Holland the persecution of Jews, particularly those who were German refugees, became unbearable, and the deportations to the camps began. So, in 1942, Mr. Frank decided to go into hiding in the rear part of the building in which his office was located. By then he had already handed over his business to some gentile Dutchmen, but he continued to work at it. Before he began his arrangements to go into hiding with his family, he asked Miep, "Are you willing to take on the responsibility of taking care of us while we are in hiding?" She answered, "Of course." Mr. Frank warned her, "Miep, for those who help Jews, the punishment is harsh; imprisonment, perhaps . . ." She cut him off: "I said, 'of course.' I meant it." And that was it; no further questions were asked or answered. The less one knew, the less one could reveal when interrogated.

Well before the preparations for the Franks to go into hiding were completed they were forced to do so, because Anne's sister, Margot, was ordered to present herself to be shipped to Germany to do forced labor. Although all mixing of gentiles and Jews was treated as a crime, to be punished severely, on learning about the situation, Miep and her husband went to the Franks' apartment and took as many pieces of clothing and other necessities as they could stuff in their pockets and hide under their overcoats to carry into the hiding place, now that this could not be done openly without risking detection.

By then all Jews had to wear the Jewish star, which made it risky for a gentile to walk with a Jew. Nevertheless, very early the next morning, Miep escorted Margot into the hiding place. Mr. Frank appeared at the regular working hour, and later in the morning Mrs. Frank and Anne came there, ostensibly to visit Mr. Frank. Such pretenses were necessary, to prevent the people who lived in the same apartment building as the Franks from becoming suspicious or guessing where they had hidden. If such a disappearance was not reported to the German authorities, those who had kept it a secret were considered criminals.

Mr. and Mrs. van Daan joined the Franks in their hiding place after a short while, together with their son, Peter, who later played an important role in Anne's life. How carefully one had to proceed when one went into hiding is illustrated by how it was handled when Dr. Dussel, a German Jewish dentist, asked Miep, whom he knew he could trust, to find him a hiding place. She told the Franks about him, and they decided he could join them in their hiding place. Miep did not dare to tell him where he would hide, for fear that through some mistake or mischance he might tell his gentile wife and the secret would be revealed somehow. So he and his wife were made to believe that Miep had found him a hiding place out in the country. All Miep told him was that on the next Monday morning at eleven o'clock he was to walk up and down in front of the main post office. A man would pass by him as if by chance and tell him, "Follow me." This he must do without a word. He was not to carry anything, because this would arouse suspicion. Having said that, she wished him a good journey. They said no more, since they knew danger lurked everywhere for a Jew on his way into hiding. The man who contacted him in this way was Mr. Koophuis, the man to whom Mr. Frank had turned over his business. He had never met Dr. Dussel, nor had Dr. Dussel ever been to the business place of Mr. Frank. Thus Dr. Dussel had to put his safety, really his life, into the hands of a complete stranger. He was most surprised when he was not guided out into the country, but to where the Franks were in hiding. Thereafter, once a week Miep brought Mrs. Dussel a letter from her husband, and his wife gave to Miep her letters and parcels for him. She knew better than to ask any questions, and believed that Miep exchanged these things through some distant contact. Only in this way could Mrs. Dussel, when interrogated about her husband, not reveal anything about his whereabouts.

How absolutely necessary it was to keep things secret is further illustrated by the fact that Henk Giese told his wife—whom he provided with false ration cards so that she could feed those in hiding—that he had joined the resistance only many months after he had done so, and he told her then only because she would need to know how to keep informed should he be caught or suddenly need to go himself into hiding.

To find a relatively safe place for a Jew, or any other endangered person, was only the first of an endless series of difficult problems for those who hid them. A daily problem was how to feed them, since the small rations were hardly enough to feed those who had ration cards. Either faked ration cards had to be secured through the resistance, with all the dangers attached to them should the fake be discovered, or else food had to be secured on the black market, which was expensive, difficult, and also dangerous. Particularly serious problems arose when a person in hiding fell ill, as did a young Dutch student whom the Gieses hid in their own home. No physician could be called, however serious the illness was, and taking him to a hospital was out of the question, because not only might the patient lose his life on being caught by the police, but also the person who brought him to the hospital might be killed as well. As Miep tells it:

> By winter of 1943 . . . all Jews in Amsterdam were gone. About the only way a Jew was seen now was floating facedown in a canal. Jews were thrown there by the very people who had hidden them, for one of the worst situations that could arise for us helpers was if someone in hiding died. What to do with the body? It was a terrible dilemma, as a Jew could not properly be buried.

But all that Miep, her husband, and their helpers did for their hidden friends was in vain. It is not clear who betrayed the Franks and their friends, or how the police found out about their hiding place, but on August 4, 1944, the Nazi police came to take away not only those in hiding, but also Mr. Koophuis, who was running the business, and Mr. Kraler, the second in command, since it was obvious that they knew about the hiding place. Only through a near-miracle did Miep escape being arrested too. From his accent, Miep recognized that the policeman in charge was Viennese, and so she told him that she was Viennese, too. When he saw from her identification card that she had been born in Vienna, he became confused. Although he threatened and cursed her, calling her a traitor who deserved terrible punishment, he eventually did not arrest her, as a favor to a fellow Viennese.

Mr. Koophuis and Mr. Kraler, as gentile Dutchmen, were soon separated from the Franks and their friends, who were sent into concentration camps. The two businessmen were imprisoned; after a while the first was released, while the second managed to escape. The annex in which the Jews had been hiding was immediately locked and everybody was forbidden to enter it, since all Jewish possessions became Nazi property and were carted away. But before this happened, Miep, who had a second key to the annex, risked herself once more by entering it. Looking around at the devastation, she spied Anne's clothbound diary, and the old accounting books Miep had given her to use after the original had been filled. Miep collected all of Anne's writings she could find, took them with her, and hid them in her desk.

Miep knew how important Anne's diary had been to her, and how secretive she had been about it. As interested as she was in its contents, she felt that she ought not to pry into Anne's private thoughts, which she had tried so hard to keep secret from everybody. So Miep did not read the diaries then, but kept them inviolate, in the hope of someday being able to return them to Anne. Alas, this was not to be. After the war ended, only Mr. Frank returned. Bereft of his family, he lived for the next seven years with Miep and her husband as part of their family. Then he emigrated to Switzerland, where his old mother still lived.

It was Miep's respect for Anne's privacy which preserved Anne's diary for posterity. After it was known that Anne had died, and after Mr. Frank had already permitted publication of some diary excerpts, he was finally able to persuade Miep to read the entire diaries. She had up to then steadfastly refused to do so, because she did not want to pry into what Anne had so obviously wanted to remain her private thoughts. But as Miep read the diaries, she realized that had she done so sooner, during the occupation, she would have had to destroy them.

I was surprised by how much had happened in hiding that I'd known nothing about. Immediately I was thankful that I hadn't read the diary after the arrest, during the final nine months of the occupation, while it stayed in my desk drawer right beside me every day. Had I read it, I would have had to burn the diary, because it would have been too dangerous for people about whom Anne had written.

Thus it was the human decency of a simple, quite ordinary person that made it possible for Anne to survive long enough in her hiding place to write the diary. It was Miep's courage that made her ignore the risk to herself and her husband, and her wish to protect Anne's privacy that alone preserved Anne's diary. Without Miep, the diary would not have existed. Her courage, her humanity, and her decency give us hope for humanity.

Children of the Holocaust

The terrible silence of children who are forced to endure the unendurable! Their agony is mute: with all the strength available to them they need to bury in the depths of their souls a wound, an anguish which never leaves them, a sorrow so cruel that it defies all expression. And this remains true for a lifetime, not only during the destructive events, the time immediately following them, and all through childhood, when we all have a hard time putting into words our resentments, deep concerns, and fears. Such an injury hurts so much, and is so omnipresent, so vast, that it seems impossible to talk about it, even when a whole lifetime has passed since it was inflicted. For those who continue to suffer from it, it is not something that happened in their past; the hurt is as present, as real, many years later as it was on the day it happened. Despite all outer appearances to the contrary, it is not possible for these victims of past events to have normal lives in the present.

Of the 75,721 Jews who were deported from France from 1942 to 1945, barely 3 percent returned. A pitifully small number of Jewish chil-

This essay, in somewhat different form, appeared in French as a postscript to Claudine Vegh's *Je ne lui ai pas dit au revoir* (Paris: Gallimard, 1979). It is here published for the first time in English.

dren survived the German occupation of France by being taken in by French families or by being otherwise hidden. Claudine Vegh was one of these very few; a childless French couple in the unoccupied zone claimed her as their own child. She describes something of this experience in her book, which consists mainly of her conversations with seventeen other men and women who, like her, had survived through being separated abruptly from their parents. She describes first how the book came about: she became deeply upset during a Bar Mitzvah ceremony, so much so that she subsequently discarded the research she had begun and planned to submit to the authorities to gain certification as a psychiatrist. Instead, she decided that she must lift the curtain which for more than thirty-five years had hidden her own past and that of other Jewish children who, like her, had survived the deportations during the Hitler years in France. She tried to discover what their experiences had done to them and to her, and why, and by what miracle, they had survived.

Claudine Vegh begins her deeply moving account—her own history and also the similar story of others—with her experience while participating in a ceremony which, under normal circumstances, would have been one of rejoicing: the Bar Mitzvah of a friend of her daughter. But instead of showing the pride, the happiness which one would expect to fill a mother as she attended this religious ceremony celebrating her son's entrance into adulthood, the mother of this boy withdrew into herself, covered her face, and began to cry at the height of the ceremony. Another mother who was attending was upset by this distress on such a happy occasion, and remarked about it to Claudine Vegh. This led Ms. Vegh to remember the feelings she had experienced when her own son, a year earlier, had had his Bar Mitzvah. She also had experienced great distress at that time.

All this made her keenly aware that the moments which normally provide great happiness in life do not do so for those who have suffered grievous emotional mutilation in their childhood. For them, the important moments in their lives attain quite different meanings and dimensions. Because of what they have suffered in the past, in such moments their grief becomes much more acute. These special events reactivate the terrible traumatizations they suffered in childhood, bring them back to mind in full force. All events which, under normal circumstances, would be experienced as happy make these wounded ones feel more painfully the irreparable losses which they have suffered in childhood, and make them feel more keenly that normal life is lost forever to them.

Charles, one of those Claudine Vegh interviewed, remarked: "I do not know what it means to be happy, I do not know what this means, I have never known it." It is put even more concisely by another named Lazare: "It is in the moment of happiness, when it feels most terrible." Louise, who tried to keep herself composed and tranquil, knew deep down that in reality her life was "an eternal balance between anger and tears."

It requires a distance of twenty or more years to comprehend how the particular tragedy one experienced in childhood has transformed one's life. Saul Friedlander, in his book *When Memory Comes,* writes: "Only at a later period in my life, in my thirties, did I understand to what degree the past modified my view of all things, how much everything essential was experienced by me transformed as if seen through a very special prism which was impossible to get rid of." In the moment when Claudine Vegh realized that she experienced the events of the Bar Mitz-vah as if seen through such a prism, evoking emotions entirely different from those which one would view as normal, she made the decision to abandon the psychiatric dissertation on which she had already done a great deal of work. Instead, she decided to embark on a very different investigation which was much more significant: to highlight the nature of the particular prism through which the world appeared to her.

Her decision made excellent sense for a person preparing to become a psychiatrist. To be able to help others with their difficulties in coping with life, the psychiatrist must understand what has made each patient the person that he or she is. More important, psychiatrists must know how they themselves became what they are, and in what respects they see and experience things differently from those they are planning to treat. This is good reason for exploring not only one's own history, but also that of those others who have suffered as one has oneself. But the results of Claudine Vegh's research are of much greater significance than the normal psychiatric dissertation.

Through the conversations she conducted with those who, as chil-dren, had suffered as she had, Claudine Vegh explored one of the great-est tragedies of our time and the permanent consequences it had for its victims. She felt the need to examine how these victims had managed to survive, at least in some fashion, and was probably also motivated by the hope that her research could help her free herself of the terrible burden of her past. She probably felt also, maybe unconsciously, that if others who had suffered like her could share their burden, maybe she could do the same, once she understood what was involved.

We, as readers, owe her gratitude for the courage with which she undertook a most difficult and most painful task. Her research sheds light on ordeals that demand recognition, that must be understood in their magnitude and with due compassion if we want to live in peace with ourselves. Whether we are close to such things or far away from them, we also live in a world of round-ups, of deportations, of concentration and extermination camps. We are part of this world of suffering children, however far we were removed from it at the time. What happened there, the fate of the victims, has left its imprint on all of us and on the world in which we live.

Why were the young victims unable to speak about what happened to them? Why is it even some twenty or thirty years later so very difficult for them to talk about what happened to them during their childhood? And why is it nevertheless so important to talk about it, for them and for us? I believe these questions are closely related: because what one cannot or wishes not to talk about is just what one also cannot put to rest, cannot come to terms with—precisely this is what we must try to do, however hard and painful it may be. If these ancient wounds are not dealt with, they will continue to fester from generation to generation. As Raphael said: "The world must know that these deportations [of their parents and of themselves] have marked us into the third generation. It is horrible."

If there should be any doubt about whether these old horrors continue to mark the following generation, Helen Epstein's book *Children of the Holocaust** dispels it. Her parents were survivors of the extermination camps. The experience of her parents and their inability to speak about it severely damaged her life, even though she was born and raised in the safety of the United States. Very different from those whom Claudine Vegh interviewed, she was never torn away from her parents, never had to hide herself and deny who she was and what her background was to save her life, as did those whose stories form Vegh's book. On the

*Published in New York by G. P. Putnam, 1979.

contrary, Helen Epstein's parents made the most strenuous efforts to shield their child from knowing and suffering from their past. Despite their efforts, however, their daughter did suffer from her parents' burden, from sensing how much they suffered without ever speaking to her about it. As an adult, Ms. Epstein wished to find out whether her fate was unique, or whether other children who had parents of similar backgrounds had shared it. She sought them out and induced them to talk, not very differently than Claudine Vegh did. Like Helen Epstein herself, those whom she interviewed had been raised in physical security. Nevertheless, she found them all oppressed by the experiences of their parents, as she had been. Different as their histories were, they all had suffered from their parents' inability to talk about their ordeals, and about the consequences these ordeals had for them.

Helen Epstein uses a moving image to describe her suffering: that of forging an iron box which she buried deep within herself, a box which made life most difficult and painful for her. "For years," she writes, "my misery lay in an iron box buried so deep inside me that I was never sure just what it was. I knew it carried things more secret than sex and more dangerous than any shadow or ghost. Ghosts have shape and name. What lay inside my iron box had none. Whatever lived inside me was so potent that words crumbled before they could describe it."

It is the incapacity to name and describe what oppresses one so fiercely that forces one to bury the oppressive things so deeply within oneself that one can no longer reach them. Things thus repressed so deeply nevertheless seem to have an independent existence that corrodes one's life, destroys the right to enjoy things, even the feeling that one has a right to live. As Jean, one whom Claudine Vegh interviewed, asks: "Why can't I take advantage of life?" He expresses the fear that encased in his "iron box" might be feelings of violence, the consequences of what was done to him. He says: "You know, I have fear of the violence I sometimes feel well up in me. It feels as if I would be in revolt against life itself. And what is most bizarre, I feel I have no right to live!"

Saul Friedlander's parents had entrusted him, their only son, to a French Catholic lady. To save him she had him baptized, and for greater safety, educated him in a Jesuit school. He felt so much a Catholic that he intended to become a Jesuit priest. But at the moment he was about to enter the seminary, his background was revealed to him, and the fact that his parents had died in Auschwitz. From this moment on, his life was a most difficult struggle with his fate, as he movingly describes in his book *When Memory Comes*.* Eventually, he found his way back to his Jewishness. Although he is now happily married, has children, and is well established as a professor of history both at Tel Aviv University and at the University of California in Los Angeles, he too continues to suffer from an inner hurt, which he describes somewhat as Helen Epstein did. He writes: "I now preserve, in the depth of myself, certain disparate, incompatible fragments of existence . . . like those shards of steel that survivors of great battles sometimes carry about inside of their bodies."

He also writes: "It took me a great deal of time to find the way back to my past. I could not trace the memory of the events themselves, but when I tried to speak about them, or to take a pen to describe them, I found myself immediately strangely paralyzed."

What is the cause of this paralysis? Why did those whom Claudine Vegh interviewed erect, as she herself had, a wall of silence as soon as they experienced the loss of their parents? It is this unwillingness, or more likely inability, to talk about it that Claudine Vegh dramatically describes. As the lady who rescued her urged her own parents to separate themselves from their child and go into hiding to save themselves, and they hesitated to leave her, their only child, Claudine urged them on herself: "Quick, leave, I'll stay here." It was probably the pain of not having parted from them in a better way, and then never seeing her father again, which made her give her book the title *Je ne lui ai pas dit au revoir*—"I Didn't Say Goodbye to Him."

I believe Claudine's urging her parents to leave her quickly was due only in small part to her fear for their safety. It is more likely that the little girl could not have accepted remaining with her new parents if she let herself think that she might never again see her true parents. If she thought that she might lose them forever, she would have tried at all costs to remain with them. So she hurried their departure to shorten a separation which would otherwise completely destroy her. Had she permitted herself the time to give in to her feelings, the time to say goodbye to them, she could not have let herself be separated from them. By hur-

---

* Published in New York by Farrar, Straus & Giroux, 1979.

rying them on to leave, she prevented herself from having the time to think and to feel. She could separate herself from them only by pretending that the separation was strictly a temporary one.

When, after the liberation, Claudine's mother returned to her, and Claudine was told that her father had died, her reaction was equally prompt and decisive. As soon as she met her mother, without shedding so much as a tear, she told her : "I know. I at least have one of you left. Let's never talk about it." And for twenty years she remained unable to speak about it, not even to utter the word "father," nor did she permit any reference to this aspect of her childhood.

Hers was not a unique response to what had happened to her. On the contrary, it seems to have been a typical reaction of children who lost their parents in the holocaust. It was a strange world, she writes, the world of the children who had lost their parents. Those she met, still as a child, after the liberation in a camp for such children in France, never spoke of their parents, their families, their past, or their homes. "Never to talk about these matters was a rule nobody had ever imposed. Speaking about their unhappiness, their sorrows, shedding tears, was completely unacceptable to them, and also to me." Why did they so totally repress their feelings? Why did they deny facts which were so evident and of such extreme importance to them, facts which were the most significant aspect of their lives?

What had been done in their childhood to those who finally, thanks to Claudine Vegh's efforts, were able to give their experience words had so destroyed them, so ruined their very existence, that they just were not able to talk about it, even to those closest to them. As one of them said: "I have never spoken about it, not even with my wife, least of all with my mother." There are a number of reasons why they cannot talk about it, do not wish to talk about it. It is not that they want to avoid thinking about what had happened, because they have never for a moment been able to forget it; they have been obsessed by it all their lives.

One reason that those whom Claudine Vegh interviewed were so reluctant to speak is that they were convinced that no words were adequate to express what happened to them; no words could put it to rest. A deeper reason is that they realize, or at least think, that others wish that they could make their peace with what had happened to them; and this, they know, is impossible. Those who listen may think they understand the tortures the victim has suffered; but the victim knows that at best they can comprehend only the facts, having no real comprehension of the nature of his sufferings. What good would it then do to speak about it? This is why they could open themselves only to a person like Claudine Vegh, who has suffered as they have. They begin to believe that they may be understood by her, when they realize that she has suffered, much as they have. But even to her, they talked at first only with the greatest reluctance.

The feeling with which their enormous loss has left them is so overwhelming to these victims that it threatens to engulf them, to destroy the walls which they have erected against it so that they might not be at all times inundated by their grief. They had to construct such walls to be able to undertake the difficult task of creating a life after the devastation had ended. It required a strenuous effort to do so, with at best very precarious results; therefore, they do not wish to see their balance threatened.

In order to be able to construct for themselves a *modus vivendi,* the victims hid their true feeling so deeply, in the innermost layers of their very being, that they can hardly reach it themselves. They did this in order to be able to continue to live, to do well in school, to pass exams, to prepare for a profession, and later to be able to marry, to have children, to try to meet the obligations of family life. So the feeling is repressed so deeply, so completely, that all they know is that life is extremely difficult for them, and that in the deepest sense it is empty. Colette, one of those Vegh interviewed, felt this inner emptiness so keenly that she tried to escape it by all means, such as asking herself what sense it made for her to be Jewish when it had led to such sufferings, particularly since her husband was not Jewish and their four children were brought up without any religion. She said: "I have the impression that I have struggled so much all my life and now I have lost the meaning of all this struggle. There is a vast emptiness around me, an emptiness which, despite all my efforts, I am unable to fill." And she sums it all up by saying: "It is really very difficult to live, yes. It is extremely difficult."

All whom Claudine Vegh could induce to talk about their past and their present feelings about it knew that to speak about this past would reawaken feelings too difficult to bear. That is why they dreaded the interviews. Sonia, one of them, told her that she panicked at the thought of what she might say. She, too, feared the emptiness which she would reexperience. She said: "I have the impression of an emptiness of my childhood, an emptiness which troubles me deeply." Paulette, another survivor, began the conversation by saying: "You know, although I agreed to this conversation, I am very anxious, have great anxiety about it."

And this some thirty-five years after the events which they dread to recall. One might expect that after all these years, during which they have lived what look like normal lives, during which they have ripened into maturity, made a place for themselves in society, created a home, had children, the scars would have healed over these ancient wounds. But for them, these are not ancient wounds, long scarred over; on the contrary, these wounds have never healed, and as soon as one touches them they begin to bleed anew, and profusely.

At other times, as the result of other catastrophic events—earthquakes, floods, famines—children have lost their parents. These children also suffer cruelly, but they are by no means incapable of expressing their feelings, of speaking of their parents and their terrible loss. In short, these children can grieve, can cry openly. By doing so, they can slowly come to terms with their fate. In consequence, they do not come to think that the death of their parents has deprived them of their right to live.

The tragedy of those of whom Claudine Vegh speaks is that their fate has prevented them from grieving for their parents, from mourning for them, and this is why their old wounds cannot heal.

At first these children hoped their parents would return, and they hung on to this hope as long as they could. Sonia reports that neither she nor her brother asked a single question about their parents, or why they had been made to change schools. In order to hang on to their hopes they preferred to ask no questions, not even so much as hint at the subject. She and her brother never talked about it with each other or anybody else, she said, "because we always waited and hoped." Similarly, Claudine Vegh, like the others, never made any allusion to her father for over twenty years. I believe the most powerful reason for this silence is that they had unconsciously never given up the hope that the absent parent was not really lost and through some miracle would return. André suggests this unconscious connection between his not speaking about his father and his keeping him alive in his inner self. "I never speak about my father, with no one, because he lives in me, that's all, that is sufficient." For the same reason, Robert continued to believe for years in the return of his parents, continues in his unconscious to believe that he still lives with them, so much so that he says, "I do not know what it means to live," meaning to live in the present; he adds, "I live in the past." His real life is only in the past, at a time when his parents were still alive.

Even under normal circumstances, it is difficult to give up hoping for the return of a parent who has suddenly disappeared without a trace. As long as no irrefutable proof of a death has been found, those who love the missing person will not accept that he has died. Especially for a child, the wish to believe that the missing person is still alive is so strong that some proof is needed before the unhappy fact will be accepted. This holds true even in normal circumstances, and the conditions in which these children existed were far from normal.

Yet if these so terribly victimized children cannot admit that their parents have died or make their peace with this idea, even after many years, it is not only because it is so difficult to give up a hope one has cherished for so long. There are more complex reasons.

After such a loss, in order to be able to face life again, one must first have mourned the loss. Mourning, as Freud has shown, is a very difficult psychological process, but absolutely necessary if one is to overcome the depression into which one has been projected by the loss. Mourning requires that for some time one concentrates single-mindedly on this task, devoting to it all one's psychic energies for days or months. The ceremony of the funeral helps, and the various customs which have developed for coping with the death of a beloved person. Among Jews there is the custom of sitting shivah, among the Irish there is the wake, and there are memorial services and masses for the dead. These customs permit the mourner to accept the loss, at least to some degree, and slowly return to life, despite the depression caused by the loss.

The task of mourning is facilitated when we can prepare ourselves in some measure for the loss. When a beloved parent suffers a period of sickness before dying, our care for the sick parent during this time helps to prepare us emotionally for what is to come, to separate ourselves. Even when this is not possible, usually we can at least say goodbye to the body, participate in the burial and in the funeral rites. All this helps us to understand, little as we are ready to do so, that this person has died; that it is a fact which we must accept.

Even with all these rituals it is nearly impossible to accept the death of a beloved one and to return to life without the help of others. What we need most is the help and support of those closest to us, usually the members of our own family. We need their physical presence and their direct participation in our mourning. It is their presence and the comfort they offer which enables us to believe that not all is lost, that there are people left who wish to help us continue with life. It is not the dead who need people to pay their respects, it is the survivor. This is why since the most ancient times funeral rites have been among the most elaborate of all religious rites.

So there are many reasons why the children whose parents disappeared in the Nazi roundups could not engage in the work of mourning. First of all, they hoped their parents would return. And since, indeed, a few did return, why should their parents not be among them? When there was this possibility, however slight, that one, or both, of their parents might still be alive, it was impossible for the children to think or speak of them as if they were dead. Not to talk about them at all was the only way they had to prevent others from speaking of the missing parents as dead, and preventing others from doing so was the only way the children could continue to hang on to their hopes. But since they could not speak about their parents, not mention what was most important to them, then nothing they could talk about seemed important. Since they had to deny the reality of their parents' disappearance, nothing they could talk about seemed real. For something to be real to us, the reality needs to be validated by others. This is why in mourning, it is so important that we talk about the person who has died. It gives others a chance to convince us that the person has really died. When we don't talk about the death of a beloved person, his death remains to some degree unreal, and then we cannot really mourn it.

Further, these children never received tangible and physical proof of the death of their parents: there was no body to be buried, no grave to be visited. There were no rituals which would have given the signal to begin the work of mourning, to organize it in traditional ways. Even given participation in all normal rituals which help the living separate from the dead, the work of mourning must extend for a long time before it can be completed, certainly for many months, in reduced form for years, often a lifetime. In some cultures one wears mourning garb for a month, in others for a year, which serves as a signal to everyone that one is in mourning. According to Jewish custom, the gravestone is set only on the anniversary of the death or of the funeral, and it marks the end of the official period of mourning. The children of the Holocaust do not know the dates of their parents' death, hence they do not know when their period of mourning ought to have begun, nor when it should have ended.

Without such clear dates for the beginning and ending of mourning, it seems to have no end, and there is a real chance that it may painfully extend over all of the person's life. Saul Friedlander remarks that when people leave one, their presence anchors itself and survives in the memory of those who remain, in their recollections and daily conversations, in the picture albums which one shows to one's children. From time to time one puts flowers on their graves, and their names are there, engraved on the tombstone. But these children were robbed of the chance to enter a specific period of mourning, which would have entailed not only a definite beginning, but also a definite end.

Jean, one of those Claudine Vegh interviewed, confirmed this dilemma. Because of the absence of tangible signs which would testify to the life and death of his parents, it was impossible for him to forget about them, but also impossible to live a normal life. He said: "I often ask myself why I am unable to take advantage of life! If I could completely forget the past, then I could possibly live like other people, happy with what I have, and I would not have to think all the time of what I have lost. I have no photos of my parents, I have no last letter from them, no grave to collect my thoughts around them. All I have is a notice: Disappeared . . . Auschwitz 1943. It is terribly hard." The absence of tangible proofs does not permit normal mourning, which would prevent an eternal grieving.

Some remarks by Sonia make it clear why it is impossible to give up all hope, and to free oneself of its consequence, which is to be always disappointed, until the day when one receives some real proof. She told how she finally realized that her parents had died from a book of Klarsfeld, published in 1978. There she found under the date of April 29, 1944, the names of her parents. It was a terrible shock to find this evidence, even thirty-five years after the event. All these years she had hoped, could not prevent herself from hoping, because without mourning we cannot really believe that the loved person is dead, and without evidence of the death one cannot mourn. Only after she read the proof of her parents' death could she begin to mourn them.

Powerful as the factors were which made it impossible for these children to mourn their parents, they wane into insignificance when compared with the psychological conditions in which the children found themselves as soon as they were separated from their parents.

In order to be able to survive, these children could not permit themselves to mourn, to fall into the depression which is part of it. They needed all their mental energy to find ways to cope, to adapt themselves to a new way of life, to learn to live successfully with people they had not known before, under entirely new and strange conditions. There was nobody familiar around who could give them the loving support they would have needed to absorb emotionally what had happened to them.

Claudine Rozengard, which was Claudine Vegh's name at the time, had the rare luck to be taken in by substitute parents who loved her as completely as if she had been their only child. They thus could offer her quite favorable living conditions; hers were exceptionally rare and lucky circumstances. Even so, she suffered.

The stories of those whom she interviewed show what nearly unimaginable difficulties these children had to overcome, the upheavals they had to cope with, just to survive. The story of a Jewish boy, not yet ten years old at the time, may illustrate this. He was sent by his parents on a small errand. On his return he saw the house in which they lived surrounded by the police. It was enough for him to guess what was going on. He immediately ran away into the open country and hid in a nearby forest. All he had was the address of a person who lived some thirty miles away. He did not dare use a train, out of fear of being discovered. During the day he hid in forests and walked only during the night, avoiding open roads. All he had to live on was the few provisions he had been sent to buy; on them he managed for the two days and nights it took him to reach the address. But this person did not dare to keep him, and sent him on. The same happened to him twice more. Finally, a farmer hid him for a few days and then placed him in a home for feeble-minded children. There he was safe for a while, until even the feeble-minded children became suspicious because nobody visited him, he received no letters, and he was different from them. So they began to ask questions which forced the director to send him to another children's institution, which, fortunately, within weeks of his arrival, was liberated by Allied forces. This boy barely managed to survive, but survive he did. To be able to do so he had to muster all his mental energy and concentrate single-mindedly on survival. If he had given in to the feelings caused by knowing that all his family had been deported, probably to be killed, he would not have had the strength to go on. He had to repress his feelings to be able to do what was necessary for survival; because he did, he is now the only survivor of what was a large family.

I have already mentioned that nearly all rites of mourning have as an essential feature the support provided by family, friends, and the community, and that only this support permits the mourners to reintegrate themselves after their loss. I have also mentioned that children who have lost their parents because of other catastrophes, real as their sufferings are, often manage to survive without irreparable damage. This leads me to my last point: why it was so different for the Jewish children who lost their parents in the Nazi Holocaust.

Children who lose their parents because of other catastrophes feel what the reaction of the world is to their misfortune, and they respond to this positive reaction. They know that the rest of the world pities them, wishes to come to their help, and hopes that their fate will not destroy them. Since everybody seems happy that at least they were saved, and seems to want to help them, this permits them, once the immediate threat to their lives is over, to begin the process of mourning which is appropriate to their age and maturity. In addition, all efforts are made to find the corpses of their parents and to bury them with all the appropriate rites. All this helps these unfortunate children to accept the facts, to accept that they are irreversible, protects them from engaging in false hopes, and encourages normal mourning.

The psychological situation was exactly the opposite in the Nazi-occupied countries. True, Claudine's new parents wanted her to survive and did all they could to make this possible. All the children who survived had people who helped them to do so; otherwise none of them would have survived. And those who helped them took great risks for themselves and their families. But these attitudes, which provided these children with their sole opportunity to survive, did not change the fact that society at large, the government, the powers which controlled all life —the very powers whose obligation it should have been to protect the lives of these children—were determined to destroy them; had first robbed them of their parents and then killed those parents. It was not because of unfortunate chance that these children sustained their loss, as is the case when parents die of illness or in a natural catastrophe. It was because their parents were Jewish that they were slated to die, and so were the children.

There is no way to escape the race into which one was born, and this even a quite young child knows, at least to some degree. One cannot really weep for the loss of a parent when one knows one is also fated to be killed. Despair and the refusal to feel are the only reactions which are psychologically possible.

I found myself during the year I spent at Dachau and Buchenwald in a somewhat similar situation. One was very sad when a comrade was murdered, but one did not shed tears, because one was oneself only a hairbreadth from death. If one had given in to the sadness which is part of mourning, the risk would have been much greater that one would not have been able to muster the strength necessary for struggling for survival, that one would have lost the resolution needed. In such a situation, mourning becomes an obstacle making survival less likely.

Claudine Vegh speaks of an overwhelming feeling: the prevailing danger of death. She mentions it in a somewhat different context. I believe this feeling has its origin in what she felt when she hid herself, trembling with fear of being discovered, what she thought others felt when they hid themselves to escape being sent to the extermination camps. They knew that even though they were in hiding and relatively secure for some time, there was no way to escape one's birth. This is why when she asked one in an interview about his origins, he answered that he was "a Buchenwaldian."

By refusing, by denying, whatever it may be that one denies, one alienates oneself from what is denied. To apply the image Helen Epstein used, one encloses these feelings in a box to which one has lost the key, lost it carefully and definitely. But despite all these efforts, one cannot get rid of this box. It remains something strange within oneself, and it has power over one's life.

Claudine Vegh concludes her book by saying:

We, the Jewish children who lived through the Nazi period, we all have rejected this experience as something that is "outside ourselves." But it does not work. We cannot put outside ourselves what is in reality the most important ordeal of our lives. If we try to do this, then we detach ourselves from our very lives. We must accept these experiences as a most important aspect of our lives. The accounts in this book have shown that this is exactly what has happened. To the degree that we tried to repress these memories, to that degree they ended by dominating our lives.

To those who have participated in the creation of this book, it has become a significant step forward. It ended the attempts at repression and denial, and it is a deferred start to mourn the murdered parents, so that, in a way, the memories are put in the grave and finally the children can live a normal life.

This essay has centered on the lack of mourning rather than on the horrors suffered by those we learn about in this book, their great courage, and the much too heavy burden of their memories. I have concentrated on the mourning because I believe that for them this mourning has given meaning and importance to their conversations with Claudine Vegh. As she relates, they have shown this by withdrawing more and more into themselves as they spoke of their past and of the loss of their parents. They turned away from her as they immersed themselves ever more into their past, left the room, threw themselves on their beds, crying. As they themselves put it, their conversation was "an endless monologue with themselves."

Nevertheless, they ended by saying all this out loud to a person who listened to them with compassion. This is exactly what happens in mourning: one speaks about what one has lost, and in doing so one talks mainly to oneself, but in front of a person who is ready to carry part of this burden, who understands, wishes to help. It is this which gives one the courage, the strength, to grieve, to be in a state of mourning.

That those who were interviewed did indeed take the first steps to engage in a mourning much too long postponed can be seen from their telling Claudine Vegh that on the day following their interviews, they felt better, felt relieved.

Perhaps many others, in the same way, would feel better if they could likewise bring themselves to mourn for the terrible losses they have suffered.

Returning to Dachau

Off and on for many years, beginning long before my own experience made them a very personal and immediate issue, the problems posed by totalitarian societies have occupied my mind. A year (1938–39) of incarceration in the concentration camps at Dachau and Buchenwald made me realize what a central role the concentration camp (or prison) plays as an instrument of control under totalitarianism, and how essential it is in shaping the individual's personality into the type such a society requires. Originally, therefore, it was the psychology and the sociology of the concentration camp that interested me most.

The first article I wrote about the camps was a monograph published

This essay appeared in *Commentary*, XXI, 2 (February 1956). In the many years since it was written, things have changed radically in West Germany. There are no longer any displaced persons living in the barracks of the Dachau camp, nor any American soldiers in what had been the SS quarters. Most important, while at the time this essay was written most adult Germans had lived during the Hitler period, by now the vast majority of adult Germans were either born after Hitler or were small children during the Hitler years.

However, the problem of how to react to what happened in Germany under Hitler is still a real one, not just for the survivors of this period but also for many of their children. So it seemed worthwhile to reprint this article in a revised form. Although more than a generation—some fifty years—has passed since I was a prisoner at Dachau and more than thirty years have passed since I wrote this piece, and despite the several visits I have paid to West Germany in the meantime, on rereading it now I find that it accurately states my present views.

during World War II when information about the camps was still meager. It was met with skepticism from the American audience. In it I described the ways in which the integrity of the human being was undermined by the camp regimen and how one's personality radically changes. That was a beginning, but a more important study remained to be written, one dealing with the problem of reviving, restoring, and reintegrating the personality that had undergone the experience of the concentration camps. That problem, the rehabilitation of traumatized or "destroyed" individuals, has been my vocation for many years, and I have written a number of books on the subject.

Among the reasons I accepted an invitation to spend several months at the University of Frankfurt in 1955 was the knowledge that I would be working with a group of sociologists who might help me to understand the process of rehabilitation. Originally my plan of research was simple: I would interview Germans who had been in concentration camps in order to try to fathom the ways in which they had dealt with their experiences. But a few weeks of careful observation made me realize that I had seen my problem too simplistically.

Although I myself had already said in print that no person who had passed through a Nazi concentration camp could be immune to the effect of its institutions on their personality, I had not realized the overwhelming significance the Nazi experience had for the German population. After a few weeks of talking to natives in all walks of life, and observing the present-day forms of that life—in universities, on the street, or in the workplace—the conclusion became inescapable that every German had in some way or other been an inmate of that wider concentration camp which was the Third Reich. Every German who had lived under the Nazi regime, whether he accepted it or fought it, had been through a concentration camp in a sense. Some, the actual camp inmates, had gone through it as tortured slaves; others, the majority of Germans, had gone through it as trustees, so to speak.

Basically the German citizen had only two stances available to him under Hitler: to preserve his inner integrity by fighting all aspects of the Nazi state—which a small minority did—or to accept it to a large degree and shape his personality in accordance with its demands, which was what the vast majority did. This difference between minority and majority still exists in Adenauer's Germany, and in all probability in the East Zone too. There are those who still cannot extricate themselves from their struggle against the concentration-camp society, and those who still cannot extricate themselves from having assented or been resigned to it.

Psychologically speaking, one might say that both groups were severely traumatized. But since the nature of the traumas was antithetical, they have reacted differently. Those who more or less accepted the concentration-camp society deny the nature of the camps and their horrors; in their case it is obvious that defensive amnesia has set in. When broken through, such amnesia tries to reestablish itself by frantic denials, by alibis and by reaction formations (complaints about what the Americans and Russians did to Germans, what Americans still do to Negroes, and so on). Such a repertory of defensive mechanisms is set in motion when the amnesia needed by an individual in order to continue functioning is attacked from the outside.

But those who fought the Nazi regime are not better equipped to live in tranquility. They do not deny, or block out by amnesia, the fact of the concentration-camp society; on the contrary, they seem to go on reliving that trauma in an "unintegrated" way. I met a man who wanted, most devotedly, to build a better Germany; he was not an isolated individual but an active leader of German intellectual life. After a while our conversation turned to the concentration camps, whereupon he took a two-year-old newspaper clipping out of his wallet and showed it to me. It reported that a visitor to Dachau had been told by his German guide that none but criminals were confined in the camps, that torture was never practiced in them, and that what most people said about them was all lies—no decent citizen had ever been sent to a concentration camp. He was obviously so shocked that such lies found common acceptance, and were published by a respectable newspaper, that he could not discard this evidence of blatant denial of the facts. What struck me was that this man had carried the clipping in his breast pocket for two years—over his heart, as it were—which suggested that he, too, was unable to forget the concentration camps, not for a moment.

On this trip I had been told Dachau was being preserved as a kind of memorial; and I had been considering revisiting it. The newspaper clipping and the dramatic way it had been brought to my attention made me decide to do so.

I had spent the spring and summer of 1938 in Dachau, before being transferred to Buchenwald. In a way, I wanted to have the guide who would take me around deny the horror of the camp; this would confirm my conviction that today's Germans prefer to deny wholly the Nazi experience. But reality, as so often happens, turned out to be entirely different.

On my way to Dachau I stayed at one of the best hotels in Munich, registering as an American citizen and deliberately speaking nothing but English. When I asked how to make arrangements to visit the site of the concentration camp at Dachau, the desk clerk, who until then had been most polite and helpful, suddenly busied himself with another guest. Pressed, he told me that he didn't know if one could visit Dachau or how, and that there was nothing of interest left there anyway. I insisted nevertheless, and again he turned away from me, with the indication this time that I was showing very bad taste. After waiting awhile, I turned to another desk clerk with the same question, and got more or less the same response.

Finally, in the face of my persistence, they said they didn't know how the camp could be reached since it was quite far from the train station, and hiring a car and driving there from Munich would be very expensive. I answered that I would take the train and try to get a ride from the Dachau station. This, they said, might be possible, but they were not at all sure I would be able to get a taxi there. I said I was willing to risk it. Was it not a memorable, though sinister, place that might be interesting to see? Icy silence was the response. Then I asked for the train schedule, and was told that trains ran often to Dachau. When was the next one? I was shown a huge timetable giving all the trains leaving Munich in all directions. It was fastened to the desk facing the clerks, so I had to scan it upside down.

Until then I had not felt very strongly about visiting Dachau, but these hotel clerks gradually awoke a cold anger in me, first at their implicit denial of the importance of the camp, and then at the attitude of disapproval they manifested toward one who seemed interested in it. Once aboard the suburban train from Munich to Dachau, I let myself relive some of the feelings I had known while in the camp itself. I felt the stark contrast between this easy, comfortable half-hour ride and my trip of seventeen years before, with all its brutality involving the murder of good friends and the maiming of others. By the time I walked out of the sleepy Dachau station to one of the several waiting taxis, I was ready for an emotional experience.

I had planned the trip in the spirit of the newspaper clipping that had partly motivated it. I had decided to act like a skeptical Austrian. In my best Viennese dialect I asked the taxi driver how far it was to the camp, whether there was anything to see there, and how much time it would take to visit it. His friendliness and eagerness to do business with a sightseer disarmed me; he encouraged me to visit the place and offered to point out all the interesting sights, claiming to be thoroughly familiar with them.

I then mentioned casually that I had heard a lot of contradictory stories and, having some time on my hands, had felt the impulse to find out the truth about Dachau's camp. I added that people seemed to exaggerate and dramatize things—whereupon he told me it was hardly possible to exaggerate Dachau's horrors. He began to tell me about incidents some of which, curiously enough, I had witnessed myself. He spoke of the petty difficulties he had experienced with the SS men guarding the camp, and of the greater difficulties with them experienced by peasants in the neighborhood. He described to me the killing of prisoners in 1938 and 1939, and the incredibly callous attitude of the SS men involved—exactly what I myself had witnessed so many times. I was just beginning to wonder how it was that this man could accept the truth about the concentration camps with so much equanimity when he gave me the answer, or the clue to it. Suddenly he left his tale of Dachau to reminisce about his four years in a prisoner-of-war camp in Siberia; how he had lived in fear of his life between the Russian guards and the cold, dirt, and hunger. It was as if a story about one prison camp naturally led to one about another.

Here, then, was my answer. This German felt he had suffered under Hitler just as much as those in Hitler's concentration camps had. So he felt free of guilt. As a resident of the village of Dachau, he had not only known of the existence of the camp, but had feared its presence more than most other Germans. True, he had been happy about German military successes as long as they continued, and he commended the greater equality in the distribution of earthly goods (particularly food) under the Nazis as compared with the years immediately after 1945, when some had plenty while he had starved. Nonetheless, he was full of hatred for Hitler; it was, however, mainly for very personal reasons.

Before the war, the SS men from the Dachau camp had filled the taverns in town and monopolized the free girls. Even worse, they had interfered with one of the great pleasures of this man's youth, which was to sit in the tavern with his friends and sound off about everything that displeased him. The constant presence of the SS men had prevented them from talking freely to one another. The cab driver became even more heated when describing to me how that scoundrel Hitler, by locating the camp outside this nice hometown of his, had given it a bad name to the world. Whenever this man traveled elsewhere, he preferred not to say where he lived, since that invariably led to an unpleasant discussion.

If anything could be learned from this little incident, it was that a man like this one, who had had firsthand experience of the proximity of the Dachau concentration camp, could never be made to view it in a favorable light. Nor, unlike most other Germans today, could he put it out of his mind, living as he still did near its site. The camp could not be regarded as a unique experience, a nightmare that could be pushed out of memory; for him, it was a reality he had been forced to learn to live with over the years. Although the Dachau camp had not originally turned him against the Nazi regime, which had, he felt, done a great deal of good for people like himself, he could never accept the camp itself. At the same time, since this same regime had brought him suffering that he could liken to that of the prisoners at Dachau, he did not need to feel guilty or to deny anything. His constant contact with the fact of the camp, so that its horror had impressed itself on him slowly, not suddenly, deprived it of the nightmarish qualities of a trauma that overshadowed all of life or needed to be denied. In his own simple way, he had worked through the reality of Dachau and what it stood for, and his attitude was therefore a matter-of-fact one.

As the taxi driver showed me around Dachau I felt quite comfortable in my role of naive visitor. He pointed out what he could, calmly, neither omitting nor hiding anything he might have been expected to know.

He told me about the tower over the camp's entrance gate. He pointed it out from a distance, regretting the fact that we could not get closer because it was, as I could see, now part of an American army installation, and in a restricted area. Had I addressed myself to the commanding officer, I could probably have obtained permission to go inside, but it seemed pointless. I was not trying to revisit specific sites or buildings; I wanted to receive impressions. And the fact that the dreadful tower was now part of an American army installation removed all its dread. What we prisoners had not dared hope for, and had hardly dared to dream—that the Stars and Stripes would fly over the tower—had become an everyday reality. This being so, what use was there in looking at a collection of stones close up?

We drove along outside the stockade, the electric fence, the watchtowers, the ditch that used to be filled with water. But the logs of the once formidable stockade were weathered, rotting, and askew; the cruel wire was torn and dangling; the bottom of the ditch was dry, its steep sides slowly caving in and overgrown with grass, weeds, and wildflowers. It was the same place, and yet it was not. Only by a deliberate act of memory could I re-create the past, which at every step was belied by the appearance of the towers, the stockade walls, and the grass-covered moat, all looking like ancient ruins—and, most of all, by the presence of American soldiers and armor.

We drove through what had once been the main street of the camp, which was lined with a double row of barracks. Slowly, we approached the one in which I had lived. For a moment I was tempted to ask the driver to stop and let me out, but children were playing in front of it, and I thought better of disturbing their play and privacy for the sake of what by now was empty curiosity.

The camp now houses refugees from the German East Zone, and its administration has tried to improve the looks of the place. The windows—through which rotating floodlights had glared all night into the eyes of the prisoners, men trying to catch a moment of sleep or rest against the next day's torture and threat of death—were now softened by curtains, by the efforts of women to make homes behind them. It was just like any other DP camp, dreary in the main, but at least its inmates had some hope of getting out.

This was not Dachau. It was as if the concentration camp had never existed. It was neither a monument by which to remember a terrible past, nor one that could promise a better future. It simply represented the practical utilization of available facilities, just as the American troops, for utilitarian reasons, are now making use of the excellent facilities the prisoners once built under the whip for the use of SS troops.

I do not believe this erasing of the past was deliberate. The military occupation, and indeed the whole postwar history of Germany, have lent themselves exceedingly well to the obliteration of the Nazi past—or rather, the deepest wishes of the Germans themselves combine with history to do just that. In those surroundings and at that moment, it seemed as if only the cab driver and I remembered Dachau's past, if for very different reasons and perhaps with different feelings.

What about the memorial? We drove into a conspicuously marked-off enclosure, where two American soldiers on guard waved us on in friendly fashion. There was a small space in which three cars were parked, clearly marked by their license plates as belonging to the American occupation forces. The omnipresence of U.S. Army symbols, while most reassuring, in a way took the edge off one's experience of the spirit of the place. The reaction of the clerks at the hotel in Munich to my inquiries had reawakened my old anger; the displaced persons living in the camp and the presence of the American military had once again subdued it. It was no use beating a dead dog, even though when alive it had mauled, maimed, and killed.

The memorial covered only a small area, and included the old place of execution, the gallows, the gas chamber, the crematorium, and two or three (my cab driver was not quite sure) places of mass burial. In the center of all this stood the statue of a concentration-camp prisoner in typical uniform, his face and figure showing the ravages of physical and mental suffering. It was true to life, yet at the same time idealized. Not a great piece of art, but decent and well meant. Perhaps we are still too close to what happened in the camps to express it more symbolically, and hence in a way that would be more aesthetically valid.

In this pleasant grove, interspersed with well-kept flower beds, only the statue of the prisoner and my own conscious effort brought to mind what the memorial was there to commemorate. Of course, I saw signs explaining what each place of horror had been used for. It was hard to imagine, looking at the neatness of everything, that tens of thousands of people had over many years suffered incredible degradation and pain here, had been viciously murdered. True, in a way the orderliness and dispatch with which bureaucratic transactions in human lives were once effected here had been one of the supreme horrors of the place. But this, too, no longer came through from the present neatness and orderliness.

Maybe what oppressed me was the smallness of it all. The little box that had been the death chamber could not have held very many prisoners at once. There were only two openings, each admitting but a single corpse at a time, to the oven of the crematorium. The two burial places, one marked with a wooden cross, the other with a Jewish star—pits into which the ashes of thousands of human beings had been dumped—were each not much larger than an individual grave.

The wilted wreaths, with their faded inscriptions, added to the illusion that everything belonged to a remote past. The walls of the death chamber and the crematorium were covered with graffiti, the names and remarks of visitors—all so typical of the historical monument—but not even these emblems of the tourist aroused more than a mild disgust in me. After all, most of the visitors had been Jewish and American. Why be angry at those who had defaced the walls of the memorial if they were in deep sympathy with those who had suffered here? That they inscribed their names and the dates of their visits meant only that they, too, felt they had been in a historical place, and one with so little connection to their immediate lives that, far from being overawed by the spirit of it, they had tried to establish a connection with it by leaving signs of their presence on its walls. Some inscriptions included angry remarks, but they too seemed out of place if not childish, because of the abyss between what they were meant to express and what they actually said.

If my experience in the camp had been a single event, I could perhaps have recaptured the old feeling of the place. But what made Dachau memorable to me was innumerable experiences: the day I and hundreds of my comrades suddenly went blind, caused by a temporary edema of the eyelids; the shooting of a friend; the suicide of another, who deliberately ran into charged wire; and, most of all, the constant, continuous petty suffering and degradation, and the frantic and desperate way one tried to maintain oneself in the face of all this.

A small group was going around at the same time as we: an American major, a captain, and two or three ladies with them; probably they had come in the cars I saw in the parking lot. The major looked grim and angry as he inspected the gas chamber and the crematorium, but the others seemed indifferent, even slightly bored, if I read their faces right. Also, a teacher was leading a group of German schoolchildren through the place, boys and girls of about ten or eleven, some twenty-five in all. They seemed neither interested nor impressed. The teacher told them something about the number of those who had died here. The children joked, hardly glancing at the small building or the inscriptions. My impression was that they were enjoying their escape from the classroom, but that the place itself meant nothing to them, despite the teacher's objective explanations, which amounted to no more than a flat recital of facts. He, too, seemed uninterested, and after a quick tour left with his charges.

I do not know how others feel when something once a terrible part of their lives becomes a monument to be visited by sightseers. For myself, it was not the right way to reexperience the past. My reaction was similar to the schoolchildren's. I have avoided mass graves all my life because they call up no meaning for me. The tomb of the Unknown Soldier affects me; the mass tomb at Verdun does not. As I stood there in Dachau, the concentration camp was more over and done with for me than when I had thought of it in faraway Chicago. The mass commemoration of the tens of thousands of Dachau's victims gave the remoteness of chronicle to their deaths, as to their lives. I felt stronger emotion when, a few days later, relatives in Vienna pointed out where, to escape the Gestapo, one person had jumped from a window and another had hanged himself. These were single human fates, and there was a great sense of immediacy in their loss.

Driving back to the station, the driver unburdened his heart, and thereby reduced Dachau once more to the human experience it was for him. Why had the camp been located at Dachau, his hometown, not somewhere else? It was all because of an old farmer and his good-for-nothing sons, who did not know how to till the soil. The site of the camp had once been a large farm; then it had been sold to the government, which before the First World War had built a munitions or arms factory on it. When the Nazis came to power, they used it for a concentration camp because it already had barracks on it, and a stockade and barbed-wire fence. It had just been a matter of utilitarian convenience, as it now was for the American authorities to use part of the camp, and for the Bonn government to use the remainder to quarter DPs.

Leaving Dachau, we again passed the barracks, and then came my last view of the camp and of its awful gate, through which some jeeps were now rolling. A large U.S. Army installation, a large DP camp, and a few small buildings as a memorial to the past—I could not quite accept it. For my own reasons, I wished they had preserved the camp just as it had been when it was liberated. Then I probably would have been able to recapture my memories better; then Dachau might have come to life on the tide of old feelings of anger, degradation, and despair. But history (and the crematorium) had been relegated to a small area located, as if symbolically, at the farthest corner of the camp, away from the business of the present.

Waiting at the train station, I listened to German DPs who sipped beer and talked of how they had lost everything. On the ride back to Munich I looked out of the train window over bombed-out areas. I realized, when I left the station at Munich and saw the utter destruction still around me, that unconsciously I had wanted the Germans to dedicate the old Dachau for all time as a monument to my sufferings and those of my fellow Jews and antifascists, but had not wanted them to dedicate any monuments to their own suffering, which were almost equally a result of Nazism.

Of course, the inmates of Dachau had been helpless victims of the Hitler regime, whereas the Germans, or nearly half of them, had embraced it of their own free will. Might it not be, then, that I had hoped unconsciously for the dedication of an unchanged Dachau more as a monument to the vileness of the torturers who established and ran it than as a memorial to its victims?

So this was one lesson I learned: that one cannot dedicate monuments to the depravity of a system by tending carefully the graves of its victims. After all, it is the Christian martyrs themselves who symbolized their faith and religious creed; it was not the cruelty of their torturers, which was only incidental, or seems so to us now, that really counted. I realized that I had gone to Dachau in the wrong spirit. Dachau, to me, was now a symbol more of the cruelty that took human beings and converted them into ciphers to be processed in a gas chamber than of suffering mankind. One simply cannot look at the statue of a concentration-camp prisoner in stone or bronze when one has been a prisoner oneself; the survivor cannot look at the graves of his fellows in suffering and say: Behold the greatness of my suffering, and admire it! One can do something about one's own suffering, and that of others, only by living and acting.

And then I realized that the present state of Dachau was more in keeping with reality, present-day reality, than it would be if it had been preserved as it was at its liberation—as, I am told, Buchenwald is. Preserving a site intact removes it from the stream of history, makes it a monument that is no longer of this time and this place.

Actually, the presence of these refugees commemorates, far better than does the monument, the sufferings of human beings at the hands of their fellows. The extreme misery of Dachau belongs to the past, but misery in general survives; people are still being driven from their homes by fear and terror. The victims of the moment were German, but I did not find any historical justice in that fact. If one believes, as I do, that our first concern must be for the living, it becomes understandable that for the Germans, too, the horrors of the concentration-camp regime fade before the misery of the DPs who have taken it over.

This, then, was what I learned from revisiting Dachau: that I could best preserve it in my mind. Other camp survivors who, like myself, had left Germany could do the same, because our lives did not need to continue in and around Dachau. We had radically separated ourselves from the country of which it had once been a central institution. I could keep the old Dachau intact as an emotional experience. I could digest its impact by working it out emotionally and psychologically, and it would remain the impact of a Dachau that preserved its old physical reality unchanged because I was no longer attached to the physical reality of Germany itself. For me, Dachau had become a problem of human nature and a personal experience, but it was not a particular place in the country that was my home.

The Germans, however, have had to live more closely than I with the memory of their concentration camps. During the war and most of the time since then, they have lived with it every day. They could not detach themselves from the suffering brought about by Nazism by crossing an ocean and entering upon a new way of life. If they wanted to go on living as more than mere survivors of Nazism and defeat, the Germans had to deal with the place Dachau, as well as with Dachau the crime. If they had preserved Dachau in its entirety as a monument to the shame of Nazism, and to the immense suffering it inflicted, it would follow that they should have preserved their ruined cities as a monument to the suffering they themselves had experienced.

So probably the Germans did the right thing when they set aside only a small enclosure at Dachau to the memory of the victims, while using the largest part of the place for DPs, and letting the Americans use the rest of it for an army installation. "Letting," I write, as though it were all their choice. Then I remember seeing vehicles roll by with license plates marked "U.S. Forces in Germany." One sees these license plates everywhere in West Germany, and so I asked myself: Suppose the unthinkable had happened, and the Japanese had overrun the United States? How would Americans have met, dealt with, and worked through ten years of life with the symbols all around them of utter defeat, and with the victors everywhere on their streets? Would they have made a memorial of anything that reminded them of their defeat? I do not know. But I do know now that the only way to live with such a past is not to keep it alive unchanged, encapsulated—but to confine it to an ever smaller place, as had been done with the memorial at Dachau.

Sad as this is in view of my own experience and those of the friends and relatives of the millions murdered by the Nazis, we cannot expect present-day Germans to have a much different attitude toward their victims than they have toward their own devastated cities. Since they are much more matter-of-fact about the ruins of their own homes than I am, I must accept their being more matter-of-fact about Dachau. As if with a vengeance, present-day Germany is turning away from the destruction of the past toward the building of the present and the future. Yes, they do it all with a will and a vengeance, as if they had a need to cover up, forget, and undo the past, including Dachau. So far only the frantic activity is obvious. Will it lead to a better future? This as yet is hard to say, but much will depend on their and our attitudes toward their past.

Freedom from Ghetto Thinking

There is no strong light without its dark shadows, and so along with the great contributions to human culture which the Jews have made during their long history come also some dark areas. I believe it is necessary for Jews to consider all parts of their heritage, and although in this essay I speak as a Jew to fellow Jews, I believe the issues raised are of general interest, because of the horrendous implications of the Holocaust for all mankind.

As a psychoanalyst, I am beholden to the idea that the hidden, denied, and repressed continues to disturb our conscious life unless we drag it out into broad daylight and take a good look at it, so that we may permanently rid ourselves of it. Otherwise, we continue to carry it within us as our secret shame.

It is well known that Jewish history is a strange combination of universalism and provincialism, of the greatest movement for spiritual freedom and of narrow bigotry. Jews first appear in history as the carriers of man's greatest achievement during the early days of humanity, as the

This essay combines the Lessing Rosenwald Lecture of 1962 with an article of this title which appeared in *Midstream* in the spring of the same year. Both were addressed to a Jewish audience. In its present form it has not been published before. (It also contains portions of my *Survival of the Jews* and *Their Specialty Was Murder*.)

discoverers of monotheism, and champions of a life under the Law. But early Jewish history also tells of narrow-mindedness and sometimes vicious nationalism. Later it is among Jews that for the first time man stood up to an arbitrary God, as in the story of Job; in modern times this theme has been beautifully redefined in Archibald MacLeish's play *JB*. But at about the same time that Job asserted man's humanity even against God, we find religious intransigency, such as among the Pharisees. I do not wish to cast aspersions on a very important religious movement that goes under this name, but refer here to the narrow-minded attitude which is customarily meant when we speak of Pharisaism. Many centuries later we find the great culture hero Spinoza a contemporary of the persecution of Uriel Acosta by official Jewry.

Much as Jews would like to overlook it, there are these two strong, contradictory trends in Jewish history. Jews are so wont to take pride in their great contributions to the liberation of the spirit that they tend to disregard the fact that not all is sweetness and light in their history. Since I believe that for their own benefit Jews ought to free themselves of any remnants of the narrow-minded provincialism frequently found in their heritage, I shall dwell on this cultural attribute.

There can be no doubt that because of Hitler and what happened under and after him, the self-image of the Jews has been radically changed. There is anxiety about what the future of Jews is going to be and what their role in the world ought to be. With the creation of the state of Israel, another question was added to these old ones: the problem of what Jewish national and world political positions ought to be. Most American Jews have rejected a narrowly Zionist or nationalistic position. But if they are not Zionists the problem that confronts them, which they inevitably encounter in raising their children, is: What exactly is the meaning of being a Jew?

When I was a child in anti-Semitic Vienna, the Passover prayer for a "next year in Jerusalem" had deep emotional meaning for me. This was not because I was nationalistically inclined—I suffered too much from pan-German nationalism and its concomitant anti-Semitism to find any nationalism appealing—but because the prayer stood as a symbol for the end of the persecution of the Jews. More than anything else, what then bound me to Judaism was the deep ties I felt to all others who were similarly persecuted.

But Jews in America are not persecuted. What then will tie them together in the future? The question is whether a religion, a common tradition, a common history, or such a vague concept as Jewish ethnicity can bind American Jews together for times to come. Most of them feel that they should continue to exist as a distinct group; they wish to do so, because they are convinced that they have a unique contribution to make. But after that, unfortunately, there is not too much agreement as to why this should be so and what this uniqueness consists of.

Jews are not necessarily the only group to experience this problem of maintaining an ethnic identity in America. A short while ago, I was asked by a Japanese-American group to speak to them about the difficult problems they encounter in raising their children, who are confronted by the dichotomy between their Japanese background and their American loyalties. In asking my advice, one leading Japanese-American summed up the problem as follows: As the Issei group (those Japanese who immigrated to the United States) grow older, their difficulties with their own self-image, the contradiction between it and that of their children, has become increasingly more acute, particularly in view of what they feel are the cultural limitations in contemporary society. The first generation of American-born Japanese, the Nisei, appear to be in increasing conflict around the issue of maintaining consistent identification of themselves as Americans of Japanese background, and this confusion is transmitted to their children, the Sansei. Statements such as "We have to keep the best part of our Japanese background" and fears expressed over the younger generation's loss of its Japanese identity ("They have to learn to be proud of their Japanese heritage") reflect the anxieties of many Nisei parents today.

Like the Nisei, children of American-born Jews feel that they have to make an effort to preserve the best part of their Jewish heritage and to teach their children to learn to be proud of their Jewish heritage. Thus, this is a problem for any immigrant group that is justifiably proud of its unique tradition. With the Jewish group this is the tradition of enlightenment, compassion for others, responsibility, civic and social service, and so forth.

How is this tradition realized in the American Jewish community of today? Probably the most interesting and comprehensive study of the attitudes of an American Jewish community in regard to these questions is the American Jewish Committee's Rivertown study.* It was found that, contrary to widespread belief, it was not a common religious philosophy but a common ritual that binds Jewry together. In most other respects, the differences are quite small between most American Jews and the surrounding gentile world of similar socioeconomic status. But these small differences gain in importance, are made secure, are actually enhanced, by very strong efforts at self-identification. It seems that it is congregationalism, the desire to meet and live together with those of one's own kind, rather than religion that binds American Jews together.

While all those responding to the questions asked in this study were convinced that Jews should continue as a distinct group, there was very little agreement as to why they should do so. There was, by and large, because of this self-identification, a feeling of superiority, though it was tempered by humility. There was thus the feeling that the Jews were better people, but mostly because they saw themselves as more philanthropic than others, more concerned with the well-being of their fellow human beings, and more ready to make sacrifices for them.

What did these Jews find "essential" to being good Jews? The item they chose more frequently than any other as crucial in this respect was: "Lead an ethical and moral life." (Some 93 percent of the respondents felt that this was necessary.) The next four most frequently chosen "essential" characteristics were as follows:

Accept being a Jew, and not try to hide it.	85%
Support all humanitarian causes.	67%
Promote civic betterment and improvement in the community.	67%
Gain respect of Christian neighbors.	59%

I do not know how one ought to feel about this list, but as I studied it, I felt that a redefinition of Jewishness is in the process—or perhaps more to the point, a redefinition of the criteria by which the quality of an individual's Jewishness may be measured. Though the ethical life has always been emphasized in the Jewish religion, it had existed side by side with an equally emphasized attention to a highly elaborated code of

---

* Dr. Marshall Sklare, "The Changing Profile of the American Jew: A preliminary report on a Study of a Midwestern Jewish Community."

personal observance. The two were intertwined; in fact, the concept was that by means of ritualistic observances, the individual could be led toward the ethical life.

Such an emphasis on ritualistic observances is entirely lacking in the list mentioned above. True, to accept being a Jew and not try to hide it has an in-group, if not ritualistic, orientation. However, it suggests an equally strong orientation in the direction of popular psychology—the importance of a healthy mental state of adequate self-respect.

From the statements quoted above, it appears that to American Jews, to be a good Jew and to be a good person are equivalent. Jewish ritualism, the study of the Torah and obeying its laws, is thus replaced by a generalized moralism; the leading quality of the good Jew is ethical behavior, general humanitarianism, and a keen civic spirit. This is even more strongly suggested by the fact that only 24 percent of the respondents considered it important for a good Jew to attend services, even on the High Holidays. Thus, adherence to general precepts of morality and ethics is seen as more essential to being a good Jew than adherence to the particular precepts of Judaism. It is as though the respondents said: "Being a good person makes you a good Jew." In previous generations the more typical answer would have been: "Being a good Jew makes you a good person."

While to modern Jews leading a good Jewish life means leading an ethical life of enlightenment and liberalism, if one goes back historically and looks at Jewish traditions, one sees that enlightenment by no means characterized the lives of many of their forefathers in the ghettos of Europe. On the contrary, theirs was a narrow-minded religiosity in many ways, as I fear the Zionist movement represents an honorable but nevertheless somewhat narrow-minded nationalism. Therefore, historically speaking, those qualities and values which American Jews most wish to see maintained and further developed in Judaism are not altogether part of the ancient Jewish heritage. They are rather, to a very large part, the consequences of the period of the Enlightenment, or assimilation.

One contradiction is evident, for example, between the Jewish demand for social equality and egalitarianism and the widespread practice of social withdrawal into Jewish communal life. Despite Jewish insistence that no barriers should restrict housing and that all men should live with each other in equality, an examination of residential preferences among Jews reveals both subtle and blatant ambiguities. It seems that Jewish desires in regard to housing are outright contradictory. They definitely wish to reside in unsegregated communities. Yet they feel comfortable only when living in close association with other Jews. This, they often feel, necessitates a majority of Jews in their community. In essence, they fundamentally wish to have for neighbors gentiles, but only as a minority. It is as if Jews wished to turn the tables on the gentiles: for so long they had to live as a minority among the gentiles, and now they wish to have the gentiles live among them as a minority. With such tendencies toward withdrawal into a modern American type of ethnic or religious isolation, we cannot easily dismiss the idea that ghetto traditions are still with us; after all, the medieval ghettos were not always imposed on the Jews, but often also chosen by them to preserve their identity.

The question of whether remnants of ghetto attitudes may still be with us and what these remnants may be is the subject of the rest of this essay. Many American Jews have freed themselves of such attitudes, but what is worrisome is that what is true for this select group is not true for all of the Jewish community.

M any authors who have written on the Holocaust use Jewish history to explain the ghetto Jew's failure to grasp what went on in the twentieth century. The historian Raul Hilberg wrote in *The Destruction of the European Jews:**

> Much has been said and much has been written about the Judenraete, the informers, the Jewish police, the kapos—in short, all those persons who deliberately and as a matter of policy cooperated with the Germans. But these collaborators do not interest us so much as the masses of Jews who reacted to every German order by complying with it automatically. To understand the administrative significance of this compliance, we have to see the destruction process as a composite of two kinds of German measures: those which perpetrated something upon the Jews . . . [such as] shooting, or gassing, and those which required the Jews to do something, for instance, the decrees or orders requiring them to register their property . . . report at a designated place for labor

* Published in New York by Quadrangle, 1985.

or deportation or shooting, submit lists of persons . . . deliver up property . . . dig their own graves, and so on. The successful execution of these latter measures depended on action by the Jews. Only when one realizes how large a part of the destruction process consisted of a fulfillment of these measures can one begin to appraise the role of the Jews in their own destruction.

If, therefore, we look at the whole Jewish reaction pattern, we notice that in its salient features it is an attempt to avert action and, failing that, automatic compliance with orders. Why is this so? Why did the Jews act in this way?

Hilberg considers it due to their "two-thousand-year-old experience" and explains that "over a period of centuries the Jews had learned that in order to survive they had to refrain from resistance. . . . The Jews had never really been annihilated. After surveying the damage, the survivors had always proclaimed in affirmation of their strategy the triumphant slogan 'The Jewish people lives.' This experience was so ingrained in the Jewish consciousness as to achieve the force of law."

But though Israel is alive, the Jewish ghetto people—with their unique religion and culture that had survived intact since the Middle Ages—were indeed exterminated by Hitler, along with the Gypsies and a great number of others. Only those who had broken with the ghettos resisted, like those youngsters of the Hashomer Hatzair and those others of Poale Zion, the Bund, and the Communists, who together formed the armed resistance movement. And even they, as their spokesman put it, were still in Poland only by accident. As one Zionist caught in Vilna said: "Our whole life is turned toward the land of Israel; it is only an accident that we are still in exile. European Judaism is undergoing a catastrophe at this time, but we broke with it the day we joined the movement."

By the nineteenth century or perhaps even earlier, but particularly since the start of this century, Eastern ghettos had become an anachronism. After World War I, Buber collected the stories of the Hasidim, very much as anthropologists collect the stories of some primitive people before it becomes too late, because they are either dying out or are dropping their native ways to become Westernized. Long before Chagall became famous for his paintings of nostalgic scenes in the ghetto, or a *Fiddler on the Roof* became successful as a musical play of nostalgic appeal, Sholom Aleichem, Isaac Bashevis Singer, and many others had been writing with nostalgia of a quaint and faraway life in the ghetto. In each case it was a way of life the artist had broken with and could no longer accept for himself, however lovingly he described it. But Chagall, before he could paint his moving ghetto scenes, had to become assimilated, first in Munich, then in Paris. And his odyssey is typical for the ghetto-born of independent spirit.

For about three generations, all took leave of the ghettos who were no longer willing to submit to conditions below a minimum supporting self-respect in the modern world. So did all those who wanted to become part of this modern new world, and all those who wanted to fight for freedom—their own and that of others. Many of these joined or even became leaders of socialist and communist movements and parties, in both Russia and the West, and of course of Zionism.

For as long as escape to the surrounding world had been extremely difficult, those who were impatient with ghetto ways had nevertheless been stuck there. They forced through some reforms to match the changing times, but the last of these inner reforms were those of the Hasidic movement around 1750. Thereafter, it was precisely the fact that the surrounding society became open to Jews which froze much of Eastern Jewry in the ghetto position. From then on, they remained fixed in their antiquated, nonfunctional traditions. Religious doctrine regulated even the most minute aspects of daily living, and the smallest adaptation to change was difficult to effect. It was not just the ghetto Jews' religious life that no longer evolved; their entire outlook, even to matters of dress, education, and language, remained near-medieval. It was a triple tyranny that forced many into leaving: the pogrom-minded gentile world, governmental discrimination (political, economic, and social), and the private Jewish tyranny of a suffocating religious tradition.

It is hard to assess what it does to a people when for three generations all its most active members—those committed to fighting for freedom—leave the group; when only those who lack the courage or imagination to conceive of a different way of life remain behind. The Jewish elite which shows up so well in American cultural life, for example, had for a century been lost to the Jewish communities of Eastern Europe.

It was a totally assimilated Viennese Jew, Herzl, who, after at first advocating total assimilation, including baptism, then began the movement for a Jewish homeland in which a modern Jewish nation could be born. Israel lives because long before the Holocaust, the active elements of ancient Jewry had broken with a medieval culture to create a new and entirely different nation. Ghetto religion had no place in it, save as a small anachronistic minority, suffered there out of nostalgia and sentiment. The Israeli Jew has nothing in common with the Jews of the ghettos but a name.

Nothing can better illustrate the difference in the mentality of Eastern and Western Jewry than the fact that under Hitler about 350,000 Jews fled Germany, Austria, and Czechoslovakia, tens of thousands fled from Belgium and Paris, and the majority of Jews in Communist Russia fled or were evacuated when the Germans invaded, but in Poland, by contrast, though there was an unguarded escape route through the Pripet Marshes, only a few thousand Jews availed themselves of this opportunity. In the main ghetto, Jews looked upon flight with a sense of futility. They had long since lost the active leadership that a victimized population needs for staging any successful resistance or revolt.

It is exactly the absence of this activist element and the many hundreds of years of "compliance" that explain ghetto mentality, not any racial inheritance of the Jews. In some dim fashion the Nazis, who were at first shocked by the compliance of the Jews in their own destruction, later took account of this fact. In his dinner conversation on April 2, 1942, Hitler remarked, "One must not have mercy with people who are destined by fate to perish."

It may, and has, come to pass that a people will die out. But it is never the destiny of a people to be murdered, be they Incas or Indians or Jews. To survive, however, required a clear understanding of what was going on and a well-planned resistance before it was too late to act, before the point of no return had been reached.

The history of mankind, as of the Western world, abounds in persecutions for religious or political reasons. Large numbers of men were exterminated in other centuries too. Germany itself was depopulated by the Thirty Years War, during which millions of civilians died. And if two atomic bombs had not sufficed, maybe as many millions in Japan would have been exterminated as in the German camps. War is horrible, and man's inhumanity to man even more so. Yet the importance of accounts of the extermination camps lies not in their all too familiar story, but in something far more unusual and horrifying. It lies in a new dimension of man: an aspect we all wish to forget about, but can forget only at our own risk. Strange as it may sound, the unique feature of the extermination camps is not that the Germans exterminated millions of people— that this is possible has been accepted in our picture of man, though not for centuries had it happened on that scale, and perhaps never with such callousness. What was new, unique, and terrifying was that millions of people, like lemmings, marched themselves to their own death. This is what is incredible, what we try to understand.

Strangely enough, it was an Austrian who forged the tools for such understanding, and another Austrian whose acts forced an inescapable need to understand them upon us. Years before Hitler sent millions to the gas chambers, Freud insisted that human life is one long struggle against what he called the death drive, and that we must learn to keep these destructive strivings within bounds, lest they send us to our destruction. The twentieth century did away with ancient barriers that once prevented our destructive tendencies from running rampant, both in ourselves and in society. State, family, church, society—all were put to question, and found wanting. So their power to restrain or channel our destructive tendencies was weakened.

The reevaluation of all values which Nietzsche (Hitler's prophet, though Hitler, like others, misunderstood him abysmally) predicted would be required of Western man if he was to survive in the modern machine age has not yet been achieved. Thus the old means of controlling the death drive have lost much of their hold, and the new, higher morality that should replace them is not yet achieved. In this interregnum between an old and a new social organization—between man's obsolete inner organization and the new structure not achieved—little is left to restrain man's destructive tendencies. In this age then, only man's personal ability to control his own death drive can protect him when the destructive forces of others, as in the Hitler state, are running rampant.

Failure to master one's own death drive can take many forms. The form it took in those extermination-camp prisoners who walked themselves into the gas chambers began with their adherence to "business as usual." Those who tried to serve their executioners in what were once their civilian capacities, such as physicians, were merely continuing, if not business, then life as usual. Whereby they opened the door to their death.

Quite different was the reaction of those who did away with business as usual and would not join the SS in the experimentation or extermination. Some of those who reported on the experience desperately asked the question: How was it possible that people denied the existence of the gas chambers when all day long they saw the crematoria burning and smelled the odor of burning flesh? How come they preferred not to believe in the extermination just to prevent themselves from fighting for their very own lives? For example, Olga Lengyel, in *Five Chimneys: The Story of Auschwitz* (Chicago: Ziff Davis, 1947), reports that although she and her fellow prisoners lived just a few hundred yards from the crematoria and the gas chambers and knew what they were all about, after months most prisoners denied knowledge of them. German civilians denied the gas chambers, too, but in them the denial did not have the same meaning. Civilians who faced facts and rebelled invited death. Prisoners at the death camps were already doomed; rebellion could only have saved the life they were going to lose anyway, or the lives of others.

When many other prisoners were selected with Lengyel to be sent to the gas chambers, they did not try to break away, as she successfully did. Worse, the first time she tried it, some of her fellow prisoners called the supervisors, telling them that Lengyel was trying to get away. Lengyel can offer no explanation for this, except that they resented those who might try to save themselves from the common fate, because they lacked enough courage to risk action themselves. I believe they did it because they had given up their will to live and had permitted their death tendencies to flood them. As a result, they now identified more closely with the SS, who were devoting themselves to executing destructive tendencies, than to those fellow prisoners who still held a grip on life and thus managed to escape death.

But this was only a last step in giving up living one's own life, in no longer defying the death instinct, which, in more scientific terms, has been called the principle of inertia. The first step was taken long before anyone entered the death camps. It was inertia that led millions of Jews into the ghettos that the SS created for them. It was inertia that made hundreds of thousands of Jews sit home, waiting for their executioners, when they were restricted to their homes.

Those who did not allow inertia to take over considered the imposition of such restrictions a warning that it was high time to go underground, join resistance movements, provide themselves with forged papers, etc., if they had not done so long ago. Most of them survived. Again, inertia among non-Jews was not the same thing. It was not certain death that stared them in the face, but oppression. Submission and a denial of the crimes of the Gestapo were, in their case, desperate efforts at survival. The remaining margin for a human existence shrank severely, but it existed.

So one and the same pattern of behavior helped survival in one case, did not help it in the other; it was realistic behavior for Germans, self-delusion for Jews and for prisoners in the extermination camps, of whom a majority were Jews. When prisoners began to serve their executioners, to help them speed the death of their own kind, things had gone beyond simple inertia. By then, death instinct running rampant had been added to inertia.

Lengyel mentions Dr. Mengele, one of the protagonists of Auschwitz, in a typical example of the business-as-usual attitude that enabled some prisoners, and certainly the SS, to retain whatever inner balance they could despite what they were doing. She describes how Dr. Mengele took all correct medical precautions during childbirth—rigorously observing all aseptic principles, cutting the umbilical cord with greatest care, etc. But only half an hour later, he sent mother and infant to be burned in the crematorium.

All this would be past history except that the very same business-as-usual attitude is behind many efforts to forget or even deny completely two things: that twentieth-century men like us sent millions into the gas chambers, and that millions of men like us walked to their death without resistance. In Buchenwald, I talked to hundreds of German Jewish prisoners who were brought there in the fall of 1938. I asked them why they had not left Germany because of the utterly degrading and discriminatory conditions they were subjected to. Their answer was: How could we leave? It would have meant giving up our homes, our places of business. Their earthly possessions had so taken possession of them that they could not move; instead of using them, they were run by them. The same business-as-usual attitude enabled millions of Jews to live in ghettos where they not only worked for the Nazis, but selected fellow Jews for them to send to the gas chambers.

Most Jews in Poland who did not believe in business as usual survived World War II. As the Germans approached, they left everything behind and fled to Russia, much as many of them distrusted the Soviet system. But there, while perhaps considered citizens of a second order, they were at least accepted as human beings. Those who stayed on to continue business as usual moved toward their own destruction and perished. Thus in the deepest sense, the walk to the gas chamber was only the last consequence of a philosophy of business as usual. True, the same suicidal behavior has another meaning. It means that man can be pushed so far and no farther; that beyond a certain point he chooses death over an inhuman existence. But the initial step toward this terrible choice was the inertia that preceded it.

I have met many Jews, as well as gentile anti-Nazis, who survived in Germany and in the occupied countries. But they were all people who realized that when a world goes to pieces, when inhumanity reigns supreme, man cannot go on with business as usual. One then has to radically reevaluate all of what one has done, believed in, stood for. In short, one has to take a stand on the new reality, a firm stand, and not one of retirement into even greater privatization.

It would seem like belaboring the obvious to point out that the Jews in Europe could easily have known what lay in store for them, because Hitler again and again told them so. Yet I have received so many statements in response to my published writings, saying they *could not* know, that I find it necessary to review some of the facts.

Harry Golden, for example, in a very sympathetic review of my writings on this subject, said that the reason the Jews did not fight was that "it has never happened before in all history. The anti-Nazis, Christian clergymen, liberals, the men who made jokes about Hitler, and the ambitious who wanted to take things over themselves: they understood that this was no boy's game, but that it was a matter of life and death. Consequently they were morally prepared to offer resistance. The Jews never quite understood this. They did not believe they were going to be killed for the simple reason that they were Jews."

This, exactly, is the point. *Why* did the Jews not quite understand what the anti-Nazis and the Christian clergymen understood well enough? Why could they not believe such developments were possible, nay probable? The answer lies in a way of thinking that shuts out non-ghetto history. Those who think this way thus believe that what has never happened to Jews never happened at all. But a short look at history shows that such racial slaughters have happened many times, and that it had happened in our own time. To know this, and hence to be prepared for it, only one thing was needed: that the world outside the pale be taken seriously, that it be felt worthy of one's careful attention.

The Eichmann trial and continuing trials of newly captured Nazi war criminals, the Kastner affair, a whole library of writings ranging from the artistic achievement of *The Last of the Just* to the hysteria of *Perfidy*—all are signs that the present generation of Jews cannot stop being haunted by the question of how six million Jews could have died. How was it possible that we did not rush to halt the slaughter? These questions will continue to perturb me, as they do all Jews, and also many non-Jews. And for their own protection, now and in the future, Jews must try to find answers, though even if we succeed, those of us who lived through it will never know full peace of mind. This essay represents another effort to seek an answer, though I do not pretend to have found it.

Some time ago I questioned in print why there is such vast admiration for *The Diary of Anne Frank*. I received many reactions, positive and negative, but whether those who let me know their reactions agreed or disagreed, they all shared one feature: a deep compassion for what they called the "innocent" victims of Nazi aggression.

Need I say that I share their compassion and feelings of outrage? And yet about the issue of innocence I cannot follow them. "Innocence" is a word whose connotations we cannot afford to overlook. Webster's first definition is "free from guilt or sin." But this will not do, for who of us is ever wholly free from guilt or sin? The second definition is "free from the guilt of a particular crime." This applies a bit better, but not even the Nazis claimed that the Jews had committed crimes in the ordinary sense. Instead, they identified Jews as an undesirable minority, like the Gypsies or Jehovah's Witnesses, whose continued existence did not fit in with the plans of the master race.

I was further startled to find that in the many communications I received, the adjective "innocent" was applied only by Jews to Jewish victims. Nobody referred to the innocent Gypsies or the innocent Jehovah's Witnesses, though they, like the Jews, were internal minorities, one of which, the Gypsies, was exterminated *in toto*. Maybe I overlooked it, but despite search I can recall no popular references to the innocent Norwegians, for example, whom the Nazis also killed in numbers. Is this because the Norwegians fought back, and he who fights back in self-defense knows what he is doing, and so the term "innocent" does not apply?

This takes me to Webster's third definition of innocence. It is "knowing no evil, guileless, artless, ignorant, simple, ingenuous, naive; hence, foolishly ignorant or trusting, simpleminded." Is this really the feeling of Jews about Jews—that they are simpleminded and naive as a group? If not, and since Jews do not view themselves as free from sin or guilt, why the insistent use of the adjective? Guiltless the Jewish victims certainly were, in the sense of the law, but this was never presented as an issue, as mentioned. So what exactly are Jews asserting about Jews by consistently applying the adjective "innocent"?

I think that what we are trying to assert, by implication, is that those outside Germany who did not stand up and fight are innocent of guilt, though at bottom we know we are guilty of nonparticipation, guilty of not having done all we could have done, and the more we should have done. That is why Jews do not speak of the innocent Gypsies or Poles; we do not have the same feeling of obligation about them—we do not feel we should have fought to save them from destruction. The tacit, and I believe unconscious, argument seems to run: if those Jews who lived directly under the Nazis could be so innocent of what the Nazis were up to, if they could have overlooked what Hitler said he was going to do (and did), then we who were so much farther away are blameless for having kept ourselves in similarly "innocent" ignorance.

What concerns me here is why Jews both inside and outside Germany felt they could afford to remain innocent when mass murder was rampant. When millions are slaughtered, nobody but a guileless child remains innocent. We are all tainted by it. Why did they (and we) not know, not even wish to know? Why were we (and they) not innocent, but intent on keeping ourselves ignorant?

If intelligent, mature persons retain an innocence tinged with ignorance about matters of life and death, then the psychoanalyst cannot simply dismiss it. And if innocence could explain it all, we would be satisfied and cease questioning; we would not ask ourselves over and over again: "How was it possible?"

After discussing this and related problems in print, I received a letter from the widow of a liberal rabbi of one of the oldest Jewish communities in Germany, who now lives in America with her children. She wrote: "I felt so excited, and to a degree relieved, when I read what you said had been so wrong with us German Jews. I lost my husband, the rabbi, as a consequence of his concentration-camp experience. I could not understand that the Jews offered so little resistance, and I remember blushing with shame about the passivity of my fellow Jews who accepted so submissively what the Nazis did to them. I cannot live in peace with myself, thinking how we Jews accepted without resistance what the Germans did, and that we Jews did not do enough to save those whom we could. I too could have done more to save some of my relatives."

To cry "Perfidy" at this or that Jewish or non-Jewish group or organization provides no solution to the problem of their innocence and ours—their innocence, which cloaked a deliberate ignorance, and our ignorance, which was not innocent either. This innocent ignorance, I believe, is part of a phenomenon that, for want of a better term, I call ghetto thinking.

Ghetto thought belongs to the ghetto Jew, and he, let us remind ourselves, is the Jew in exile, dispersed. The other Jew, the Israeli, the one at home in Judea, has a tradition that is different; he is not compliant but fights back, as he does in Israel today.

There are many types of Jewish ghetto thinking and attitudes, and each has good and bad aspects. Some of them we rightly cherish: the closeness of family ties, the warmth of human understanding, the direct communication with God, the humility, the ability to accept hardship with humor and resilience—all of these, and many more, are aspects of ghetto life that have become part of the Jewish heritage, that we wish to see preserved in our lives. But these qualities are not in dispute; they do not endanger us, and hence do not concern me here.

What does concern me is how the heritage of centuries of Jews living in the European ghettos seems to have put blinders on the eyes of many Jews. In order to justify an existence in or out of the ghetto that was contrary to human dignity, Jews provided themselves with psychological excuses that enabled them to bear what was basically intolerable, to live under conditions that were basically unlivable. One made oneself insensitive to debasement by the oppressor so that one might be allowed to survive. Because in the ghetto world the oppressor usually relented in the end, and because the Jew's self-abasement destroyed him as an autonomous human being, he was permitted to survive, even to thrive materially. In short, to be able to survive that particular Jewish condition, the Jews blinded themselves to the universal human condition. Such was the reality of the ghetto existence. To believe the situation was the same with the Nazis was transferring ghetto thinking to the world of the twentieth century, where it no longer had validity.

As a young man I read a then-popular book by a fellow Viennese Jew, Franz Werfel's *The Forty Days of Musa Dagh*. In it, he described how the Turks exterminated the Armenian people. Werfel, who had freed himself of ghetto thinking, knew that the extermination of an entire people was quite possible in our time. Do I need to add: and thus, able to see what was coming, he escaped in time? All of us could also have read how Stalin had exterminated millions of his own people because they didn't fit into the new order of things. Millions of kulaks were killed outright and others starved to death, just as Jews were starved to death in the German camps.

With these modern examples of the mass extermination of internal minorities, tens of thousands of Jews not bound by the ghetto way of thinking believed Hitler when he announced repeatedly that there would not be a Jew left in Europe after the war, and they escaped in time. Most of those who clung to their ghetto thinking perished.

Nor has such thinking vanished with Hitler and with the abolition of ghettos. I am again and again confronted by it. Usually I meet with unbelieving astonishment when I remind American Jews of what should be known to them: that Hitler also destroyed millions of Russians and Poles, and the entire Gypsy population of Europe. It is the same disbelief I encountered earlier among my Jewish friends when I told them that in Dachau and Buchenwald in 1938 and 1939 the majority of my fellow prisoners were not Jews, but German gentiles. To these Jews, bound by ghetto thinking, only what happened to the Jews counted; they were not aware of what happened to others. Lacking interest, they could not learn from others' experiences. Those Jews who were interested and learned from it were able to save themselves. I think it is tragic ghetto thinking that so many Jews still see this greatest tragedy in Jewish history only from the perspective of their own history and not from that of world history, to which it belongs.

As for Europe's Jews not knowing what lay ahead, such a view is equally unfounded. I recall vividly, as I am sure everyone who lived through this period does, the sight of Jews washing the streets where they could be ridiculed and made sport of, after the invasion of Austria. But there is no point in recounting the shameful litany. The facts are well known to all and were reported regularly at the time in the Austrian and German papers, as well as in the back pages of all the foreign press.

Within Germany, the papers were also full of statements in one form or another that there was no longer a place for Jews in the German Reich. Other articles told with jubilation and pride how many Jews had already been forced into emigration and how the rest would have to follow them soon. To ignore these warnings, to remain "innocent" in the jaws of disaster, was to court death.

As a matter of fact, before the outbreak of war, a Jew had a better chance of being discharged from a concentration camp than a German gentile did. When I was in Dachau and Buchenwald in 1938, anti-Semitic feelings occasionally spread within the camp, because prisoners were resentful that all many Jewish prisoners had to do to gain release was to prove they would leave Germany immediately. In Buchenwald, in 1939, the saying went: There are only two ways to leave the camp—as a corpse or as a Jew.

German Jews (and those of Poland, too) permitted themselves to remain innocent, avoided eating from the tree of knowledge, and remained ignorant of the nature of the enemy. They did this because they were afraid that knowing would mean having to take action.

This, then, is my thesis: A certain type of ghetto thinking has as its purpose the avoidance of taking action. It is a type of deadening of the senses and emotions, so that one can bow down to the mujik who pulls one's beard, laugh with the baron at his anti-Semitic stories, degrade oneself so that one will be permitted to survive.

It was part of ghetto thinking when, after the boycott of Jewish places of business, individual Jews and organizations proclaimed, contrary to the truth, that they had not been molested. It was ghetto thinking when German Jews objected to the truth about their mistreatment being made public and when Jewish organizations in Germany objected to the answering American Jewish boycott of German goods. They were motivated by anxiety and a desire to curry favor. That is exactly what ghetto thinking is: to believe that one can ingratiate oneself with a mortal enemy by denying that his lashes sting, to deny one's own degradation in return for a moment's respite, to support one's enemy who will only use his strength the better to destroy one. All this is part of ghetto philosophy.

It is not that German Jews were too well assimilated, as is sometimes asserted, and that this was their undoing; most of the truly assimilated ones—that is, those assimilated not to Germany but to the world of which it is only part—fled Germany long before the Nuremberg laws, long before the Nazis even thought of sending Jews to the concentration camps except as political enemies.

It is true that many Jews could only have emigrated to countries they did not consider very desirable. I witnessed how Jews refused permits to go to the Philippines, because they preferred to wait until a U.S. quota permit became available. For a long time everyone who wanted to, and who could pay the passage, could go to Shanghai, and it was not then at all difficult to get a Cuban visa. There were several other places, deemed undesirable and rejected by many because they could not get themselves to understand the nature of the Nazis. Had they not remained "innocent," no place on earth would have seemed undesirable compared to Buchenwald—not to mention Auschwitz—although the death camps belong to a later period when knowledge would no longer have helped.

Thus it was the Jews' procrastination in the face of their annihilation as self-respecting persons that gave the Nazis time to develop a policy of physical annihilation. The steps of this development can now be traced.

Documents unearthed for the Nuremberg and Eichmann trials show convincingly how Jewish ignorance was preserved when knowledge was easily available. Certainly from 1937 on, it was clear that the Nazi government would not shy away from any method that would eliminate Jews from the Third Reich. As early as 1935, a whole branch of the Gestapo had as its sole purpose forcing the Jews to emigrate. In 1937, Eichmann, in a conversation with the representative of a Jewish organization, told him clearly that the government was dissatisfied because so far only 20 percent of the German Jews had left Germany, and that all of them had to leave. At that time, high Nazi officials raised the question of whether to keep the Jews as hostages in case of war; this suggestion was rejected because the wish that they all emigrate was greater—they were not wanted even as hostages.

Until the invasion of Austria in 1938, the terror measures designed to induce Jewish emigration were not systematized, but this changed with the creation of a central office for Jewish emigration. Individual and well-publicized acts of terror were stepped up; more and more Jews were jailed or sent to concentration camps; and more stringent measures were taken to see that Jews should leave Germany. Some fifty thousand Jews, allegedly once Polish citizens, were deprived of their German citizenship and in October 1938 were transported to the Polish border, where they were turned over to the Polish authorities. Grynszpan belonged to one of the families so expelled, and for this outrage he decided to kill a member of the German embassy in Paris who happened to be vom Rath.

Retaliation for Grynszpan's act, the destruction of Jewish synagogues, homes, and places of business, was only a last and most visible demonstration that the German government would not relent in its intention of eliminating all Jews. Tens of thousands were brought into the concentration camps, and it was made very clear to them that if they would emigrate, leaving their possessions behind, they would be discharged immediately.

We have the record of a meeting between Heydrich and Goering on November 12, 1938, where it was made quite clear that their purpose was still simply to force Jews into emigration. At this meeting Heydrich, with great pride, reported that he had succeeded in forcing out fifty thousand Austrian Jews and that more could be made to emigrate; the difficulty was not so much in getting the poor Jews to go but in getting the wealthy Jews to part with some of their money to finance passage for those without money.

Thus it was not only Jews in foreign countries who did not do enough. It was extremely difficult to get German Jews to help their fellow Jews to emigrate. In the Viennese Kultus Gemeinde I witnessed how officials begged and bargained with wealthy Jews to permit some of the money they had to leave behind to be used for financing the emigration of poor Jews. There was a great deal of haggling, and vast amounts were left behind because they could not be transferred out of the country. But many of the rich or fairly rich would allow only small percentages to be turned over to the Jewish organizations searching for money to pay for the emigration expenses of poorer Jews.

This was not callous self-interest; it was deliberate ignorance of what might be in store for the Jews left behind, and of the fact that their personal fortunes, so hard won, would now be lost. Thus, stubbornly "innocent" about themselves and those who would have to stay, these Jews became inhuman, not because they were evil, but because they permitted themselves not to know.

I have devoted most of my life to studying why some men embrace bondage to mental illness rather than struggle for mental freedom. I have also concerned myself extensively with the problem of why millions of Jews did not flinch from death, but shrank from fighting for their lives. I wrote a book on the question which I called *The Informed Heart,* in part to indicate that while many people have warm hearts, they can, unfortunately, be poorly informed hearts.

Of the consequences of ignorance, Hillel said two thousand years ago: "He who does not increase his knowledge decreases it; he who does not learn is worthy of death." But it was not only lack of knowledge that led millions to their doom; it was also an unwillingness to fight for themselves, fight for their lives and for the lives of those they loved. This unwillingness to fight was a direct consequence of ignorant innocence—ghetto thinking. In the ghetto, one complied and waited for the tempest to subside. The Jews had not troubled to learn that things had changed, so they could not know that this tempest was of a wholly new order.

But if we do not fight for ourselves, nobody will fight for us. Those Jews under Hitler who did not fight for themselves perished; most of those who did fight for their lives survived, even under Hitler. Since so many Jews did not fight, no one fought for them. Because, as Hillel asked, "If I am not for myself, who is for me?"

If any doubt this, the survivors of Warsaw do not. There a small handful not beholden to ghetto thinking tried desperately and almost from the beginning to mobilize resistance. They met with blind refusal from within, and with hostility or indifference without. It is all the more instructive and awesome how Polish aid from outside the wall materialized almost at the instant that signs of resistance, of self-defense, began to be heard from the starving remnant within.

But according to Raul Hilberg's authoritative report, *The Destruction of the European Jews:* "Measured in German casualties, Jewish opposition shrinks into insignificance. The most important engagement was fought in the Warsaw ghetto," whence nearly four hundred thousand were taken to their death. At the time of the uprising there were only about seventy thousand Jews left in the ghetto, and their armed strength was fifteen hundred. The total strength of the vastly better equipped German forces was two thousand to three thousand. In the end there were "sixteen dead and eighty-five wounded on the German side, including collaborators. In Galicia, sporadic resistance resulted in some losses to the SS and police. Eight dead, twelve wounded. It is doubtful that the Germans and their collaborators lost more than a few hundred men, dead and wounded, in the course of the destructive process." That is, less than a hundred German dead to over four million Jews dead. That is the true proportion of what happened.

In disputing my thesis, it has been claimed that passivity in the face of persecution is an essential Jewish virtue. I could, of course, counter with stories of the struggle for Palestine in ancient times, and of Israel's battles today. Others have said: True, in ancient times Jews were fighters, but since then, Jewish morality has become more refined; the newer Jewish tradition is one of passive suffering of violence, and this is morally superior to responding to violence with violence—it represents a higher morality to submit to death rather than to kill.

Unfortunately for that thesis, Jewish behavior lends it little credence as a guide for explaining the behavior of millions of European Jews. Often those who passively submitted to extermination by the Nazis— and who did so, I am told, because of their conviction that it is better to die than to kill—were the very same ones who had bravely fought and killed in the imperial armies of the Kaiser or the czar only a couple of decades before. If millions of Jews did not resist their extermination because they preferred to suffer rather than resort to violence, where were the millions of Jewish conscientious objectors in World War I?

I believe it was not rejection of violence that explains Jewish passivity under the Nazis, but rather an inability to act in self-defense on one's own, as a Jew. The same persons were capable of acting violently and aggressively when ordered to do so by the authority of a state. But submission to a state—killing others when it so decrees, and permitting oneself to be killed when it so demands—is entirely different from non-violence.

This basic contradiction between Jewish reactions is posed in Jean-François Steiner's book on the revolt at Treblinka,* without ever being recognized as such. Yet from the very first, it nullifies the thesis of this fictionalized account. On the one hand, Steiner admires and identifies all of Jewry with those Jews who accepted life under ghetto conditions, where "Jews never defended themselves, never revolted. The most pious saw [pogroms] as punishment from God, the others as a natural phenomenon comparable to hail in vineyard country. . . . They had learned one thing: the gentile is stronger, to resist only fans his anger. . . . This right to lynch was a kind of unwritten law which nobody dreamed of contesting."

At the same time, Steiner also admires those who, like his own father, did indeed contest the unwritten law by voting with their feet, leaving the ghetto behind. Later he contrasts the two types of Jews: those who had accepted the laws of the ghetto, and those others who rejected it, either through assimilation or through embracing Zionism or Russian Communism. How differently these two reacted he shows by movingly describing how the Jews of Vilna betrayed the leader of the resistance movement, the Communist Wittenberg. Out of fear for their lives, which they should have known by then could not be saved by compliance, these Jews of the ghetto turned Wittenberg over to the Gestapo as commanded.

Steiner also retells the story of the first group of thousands of Jews who were taken from Vilna to their extermination. Among this group was a Jewish officer of the Red Army, who had stayed behind at the time of the Russian retreat to organize guerrilla fighters, but had been caught. As he and the others marched to their death, he told them: "It's now or never." He knew that this was the point of no return, and acted on it by jumping on the nearest guard, grabbing his gun, and shouting to the others to revolt. But all the men bowed their heads and murmured the Sh'ma Yisroel. "For if God exists nothing can happen that he has not

*Treblinka (New York: Simon & Schuster, 1967).

willed." And one of the few guards who was herding the column of prisoners found no one to oppose him as he shot down the Red Army soldier.

It was only those who had long before broken away from ghetto life and ways, as had this Russian officer, who could decide not to submit passively to the "will of God" but to fight actively for a new life, both long before the German invasion and after it.

Steiner, having grown up with values close to those of this Russian officer, cannot help embracing them, hence his true heroes are those who fight, and die fighting. All those, in fact, who were active in the Vilna resistance and most of the key rebels at Treblinka had long since broken with the ghetto. Kleinman, who had such an important role in the revolt as foreman of the camouflage commando, and who defeated the Germans in the first armed encounter after the break, "had been formed in the hard school of the Hashomer Hatzair, one of the toughest Zionist youth movements."

Djielo, another hero of the revolt, had been "Captain Bloch of the Czech Army." Adolf left home at sixteen, served in the French Foreign Legion, and returned to Lodz to urge his family to escape to Russia. But he could not persuade his father to flee, so he stayed to organize a resistance movement and was eventually caught.

Meir Berliner, the only Jew in this story who single-handedly killed an SS man inside the camp, left Warsaw and his family at the age of thirteen, making his way to Argentina. He was caught in the Warsaw ghetto, to which he had traveled in search of his parents. He killed an SS guard with a ritual knife after he had seen him beat his father, and seen both his parents taken to the gas chambers.

It was also an assimilated Jew, a former reserve officer, who, when asked to serve as Jewish commander of the camp by the SS, refused, saying he would rather commit suicide than be a slave driver for the Nazis. For his refusal, he was instantly killed. So was Berliner, and all others who resisted individually. But so were all the Jews, once caught by the Nazi machine. Successful resistance would have required the Jews to rise in large masses, and at once, before deportation.

Steiner's book was highly recommended by Simone de Beauvoir, who writes in her introduction that this story of one revolt in the face of mass extermination is a story "of pride." But I cannot accept it as sufficient cause for pride that of eight hundred thousand prisoners who passively went to their death at Treblinka, only the very last thousand, and only when their death was imminent, finally tried to break out of this human slaughterhouse.

According to David Ben-Gurion, one of the purposes in smuggling Eichmann out of Argentina to stand trial in Israel was to give the generation born after the Nazi Holocaust a closer understanding of its victims, and to promote some identification with them. I doubt that it had this result. As a matter of fact, Israeli children, when told about the extermination of millions of Jews by Hitler, were incredulous. Their response was: "These can't have been Jews. A Jew does not allow himself to be slaughtered; he would never walk passively to his death." This is the attitude of a generation whose parents risked their lives to fight for life and freedom, a new generation that knows nothing of ghetto thinking.

It is not a question of lack of courage. In European and American armies, Jewish soldiers fought as well as any under arms; in Israel they fought better than most. Why, then, did the European Jews not fight against Hitler? I believe the reason stemmed from within: because their view of themselves was a ghetto view; they saw themselves as an impotent minority, surrounded by an overwhelming enemy. A minority they were, and also surrounded by an enemy. But they were neither impotent nor helpless to resist.

The reason they could not and did not fight back lay in their inner feelings of resignation, in the careful eradication, over centuries, of tendencies to rebel, in the ingrained habit of believing that those who bend do not break. Witness the heroes of the Warsaw ghetto, the few thousand who, however late, fought and died fighting—though some of them also survived and escaped. Their heroism shows that not fighting back had nothing to do with the odds against winning. They fought when the odds to win and survive were nil, while hundreds of thousands did not resist when the odds for winning and surviving were far greater.

These heroes who fought were Jews, too, but they were Jews who had shaken off an internal ghetto. So also had those who left Europe as soon as Hitlerism threatened their human dignity, left their earthly possessions behind to save life and self-respect. It was possible to free oneself of ghetto thinking. Unfortunately, the majority stayed and died because they clung to an antiquated notion of reality. Convinced that the ghetto oppressor relents in the end, they allowed secondary anxieties to dominate; they ignored the possibility of death, and feared most of all to risk a foreign sun. Dependence on and devotion to the fleshpots of Egypt was ghetto thinking before an earlier exile, but we modern Jews had no Moses. Without prophets to lead us by the hand, we must each fight on our own any tendencies within ourselves to ghetto thinking. Hence the urgency of my concern with whatever remnants of it still flourish among us.

It is the same concern that led Israel's attorney general, Gideon Hausner, to ask death-camp survivors again and again, as they took the stand in the Eichmann trial: "Why did you not revolt?"

As on so many other days of the trial, the attorney general put the question also to Dr. Moshe Bejski, who had described how some fifteen thousand Jews were forced to watch a fifteen-year-old boy being hanged for the crime of singing a Russian tune. "Why," the attorney general asked, "when there were fifteen thousand people like you facing a mere ten, or at best hundred, men of the police, why did you not storm them? Why did you not revolt?" The newspaper reports that the witness was staggered by the question and had to sit down. We, too, are staggered, and try to forget. But we cannot.

That same day another witness, Yaacov Gurfein, was questioned. He had escaped from a train of Jews being shipped to the gas chambers. Judge Benjamin Halevi asked why there had been no resistance, and the witness replied that they had no will to resist. "So why did you jump from the window of the train?" asked the judge. And Gurfein replied: "I wouldn't have jumped if my mother hadn't pushed me." The question that haunts us is: why could these Jews not jump on their own?

One final example I owe to Hannah Arendt. She tells how several thousand Jewish women were rounded up in a French camp before being handed over to the Germans. On their second day in the camp, which was just being organized, French members of the underground entered the not yet walled-in compound, offering forged papers and a chance to get away to all who wished it. Though what lay in store for them had been vividly described, the vast majority of the women were incredulous and showed no interest in this chance to save their lives. Only a handful, less than 5 percent, took advantage of the offer, among them Hannah Arendt. All of them made good their escape, and most are still alive. The rest wanted to think things over, were not so sure that escape was the best course of action, etc. A day later it was too late; the camp was encircled. All who had hesitated to take action went to the gas chambers.

All people, Jews or gentiles, who dare not defend themselves when they know they are in the right, who submit to punishment not because of what they have done but because of who they are, are already dead by their own decision; and whether or not they survive physically depends on chance. If circumstances are not favorable, they end up in the gas chambers. How utter submission in the face of brutal violence means death, though one may still continue to breathe for a long time, was best described by Simone Weil, a Jewish woman who knew both persecution and the value of life. In a brilliant essay, "The Iliad, or the Poem of Force," composed after the fall of France in 1940, she wrote of what Homer too understood: How

> the force that does not kill, i.e., that does not kill just yet, [that] merely hangs poised and ready over the head of the creature it can kill at any moment, turns a man into a stone, turns a human being into a thing while he is still alive.
>
> A man stands disarmed and naked with a weapon pointing at him; this person becomes a corpse before anybody or anything touches him.
>
> If a stranger completely disabled, disarmed, strengthless, throws himself on the mercy of a warrior, he is not by this very act condemned to death; but a moment of impatience on the warrior's part will suffice to relieve him of his life. . . . Alone of all living things the suppliant we have just described neither quivers nor trembles. He has lost the right to do so.
>
> So when Priam entered Achilles' tent and "stopped, clasped the knees of Achilles, kissed his hands," he had reduced himself to a thing which could be disposed of in short order. Achilles realized this, and "taking the old man's arm, he pushed him away." As long as he was clasping Achilles' knees, Priam was an inert object; only by lifting him up off his knees could Achilles restore him to living manhood.

It is precisely this issue that led me to be critical, not of the Frank family, nor of Anne Frank, but of the universally positive reception given her diary in the Western world. I would like to stress once again that I have no quarrel with the Franks, least of all with poor Anne. But I am highly critical of the ghetto philosophy that seems to have pervaded not only the Jewish intelligentsia but large segments of the free world. We seem to find human grandeur in submitting passively to the sword, in bending the neck, which, as Weil said so poignantly, degrades a human being to a mere thing.

The Frank family created a ghetto in the annex, the Hinter Haus, where they went to live; it was an intellectual ghetto, a sensitive one, but a ghetto nevertheless. I think we should contrast their story with those of other Jewish families who went into hiding in Holland. These families, from the moment they dug in, planned escape routes for the time when the police might come looking for them. Unlike the Franks, they did not barricade themselves in rooms without exits; they did not wish to be trapped. In preparation, some of them planned and rehearsed how the father, if the police should come, would try to argue with them or resist in order to give his wife and children time to escape. Sometimes when the police came the parents physically attacked them, knowing they would be killed but thus saving a child. In at least one case, we know of a tragic variation. Both parents stayed on passively, convinced that "it can't happen to me." Only the girl, a mere child, had the initiative to run away, though that had not been her parents' original intention. This is the story of Marga Minco, who lived to tell it in her book *Bitter Herbs* (New York: Oxford University Press, 1960).

The glorification of the Franks is part of a ghetto thinking that denies a reality which would otherwise compel us to take action. It suggests how widespread is the tendency to deny reality, among Jews and gentiles alike, in the Western world, and this though Anne's story itself demonstrates how denial can hasten our own destruction.

If the ghetto Jew is dead, and the Israeli Jew is born to resistance, what remains of world Jewry now stands at midstream. These Jews who are neither ghetto Jews nor Israelis are in between, nowhere truly at home. They, like the author, are inwardly torn. It was a blessing that the most vital segment of the Jewish people had prepared for the birth of a new and different nation. But that Israel is very much alive does not alter the fact that the Jewish people of the ghetto were exterminated by Hitler.

The unfortunate victims are dead; nothing we can do will change the shame of the century, of which we all are a part. It was not my intention here to judge either Anne Frank or the six million other Jews who perished. I do not wish to criticize nor to whitewash, but to understand and to learn. What I plead for is that we do not despise the lesson the six million victims unwittingly taught us, at the cost of their lives. Ghetto thinking is not a crime; it is a fatal mistake.

Perhaps the time has come again when the Jews, because of their peculiar experience, have something of the greatest importance to teach. In many ways, the Western world itself seems to be embracing a ghetto philosophy of not wishing to know, not wishing to understand what is going on in the rest of the world. If we are not careful, the white Western world, which is already a minority of mankind, will wall itself up in its own ghetto, by instruments of so-called deterrence. Within such a protective girdle—which is also a constrictive one—many contemplate digging into their shelters. Like the Jews who remained in their Eastern ghettos even after the Nazis arrived, we seem concerned only that business should go well in our big shtetl, and never mind what goes on in the rest of the world.

As we Jews succeed in freeing ourselves of whatever remnants of ghetto thinking we still harbor, it may fall to us to teach the Western world that it must, as we all must, enlarge the feeling of community beyond our own group, beyond iron curtains—not because all men are basically good, but because violence is as natural to man as the tendency toward order.

Index

Acosta, Uriel (Gabriel), 244
advertisements, 135
  television commercials, 154
aggression, 54
  childhood, 151–2
  see also violence
Aichhorn, August, 18, 19
All in the Family (television program),
  153–4
Amala and Kamala (wild children),
  166 *n.*, 167–8, 169–70, 171,
  172–80
American Foundation for the Blind, 163
American Jewish Committee: Rivertown
  study, 246 and *n.*
Anagnos, Michael, 158, 160
analyst(s)
  Bettelheim as, 98
  as doctors (or not), 31
  reasons for choosing career, 54–5
  role and relation to patient, 29–31
anima (Jungian concept), 60, 61
Anna (wild/autistic child), 181–5
anti-Semitism
  Freud and, 46, 47
  of Nazis, *see* Jews and Nazis
  in Vienna, 244
  see also Jews
Arendt, Hannah, 89, 268
Aristides the Just, 129
Aristotle, 151

art
  appreciated in old age, 101–2
  children's, 6
  vs. dream and neurosis (Trilling), 92
  and entertainment, 121–2
  Expressionism, 109
  motion pictures as, 112–26
  popular and elite, 121, 122
  in Vienna, 15–16
art museums, 146–7; *see also* museums
Athens, 130
Auschwitz (concentration camp), 254,
  261
Austria
  and Germany (19th century), 7; World
  War II, 208, 262
  history, cultural and political, 4–5
  see also Vienna
autistic children
  animal-like behavior and comparisons,
  171–2, 180
  Anna, 181–5
  Joe, 185–7
  parents' relationship to, 170
  and wild children, compared, 166–88

Babel, Isaac, 84, 88
Bacon, Francis, viscount St. Albans,
  142–3
Balzac, Honoré de, 136

poetry
  Freud and (Trilling), 86
  Frost's definition, 126
Polish Jews in World War II, 181–4, 249,
    251, 255, 259, 260, 263–4
Potemkin (motion picture), 115
Preiswick, Helene, 68
primers and readers for children, urban
    images in, 138–40
Proust, Marcel, 135, 136
psychoanalysis
  Bettelheim and, 24–38, 105
  as science, 49
  Trilling and, 82–94
  Vienna's influence on development of,
    3–4, 6, 10–17
  see also psychoanalytic movement
psychoanalyst(s)
  Bettelheim as, 98
  as doctors (or not), 31
  reasons for choosing career, 54–5
  role and relation to patient, 29–31
psychoanalytic movement
  Freud's relationship to his followers in,
    42, 50–1
  Fromm on, 51–6
psychotics and psychosis, 34–7, 178

Rank, Otto, 44
Rath, Ernst vom, 262
readers and primers for children, urban
    images in, 138–40
reality principle, 91, 93
regression, motion pictures and, 116
religion
  declining cultural role of, 117, 118,
    121
  Freud and, 51
  see also Christianity
Rembrandt Harmenszoon van Rijn, 101
repression, sexual, 54, 105
righteous people, 191–2

Rilke, Rainer Maria: *Tale of Love and
    Death of Cornet Christoph Rilke,* 14
ritual(s) and ritualism, Jewish, 246, 247
Rolland, Romain: *Jean Christophe,* 99,
    203
Rosegger, Peter: *When I Was Still a Poor
    Peasant Boy in the Mountains,* 134–
    5
Rousseau, Jean Jacques, 106, 204
Rozengard, Claudine, *see* Vegh, Claudine
Rudolf, archduke of Austria, 10
Ruskin, John, 148
Russians and Nazi persecution, 251, 259

Sakel, Manfred, 4
Sansei (Japanese-Americans), 245
Scheftel, Pavel, 78
Scheftel, Renate, 78, 81
Schiele, Egon, 15–16
Schiller, Johann Christoph Friedrich
    von, 109
Schimkovitz, Othmar, 16
schizophrenia, 4, 179
Schmidt, F. V., 11
Schnitzler, Arthur, 13–14
  "Enormous Country, The," 13
  "Little Love Affair, A," 13
  Miss Else, 9, 13–14
Scholem, Gershom, 108
Schönberg, Arnold, 16
Schopenhauer, Arthur, 148
Schramm, Wilbur, 152
Schwarz-Bart, André: *Last of the Just,
    The,* 256
science fiction films, 125
Sesame Street (television program), 154
sex drive
  and death drive, 10–11, 12, 14, 15, 60
  Freud on, 14, 84, 85
sex education, 145
sexuality
  Freud on, 25, 54, 105

Permissions
Acknowledgments

Some of the essays in this work were originally published in *American Journal of Sociology, Channels, Commentary, Harper's, Midstream, The New York Review of Books, The New York Times, The New Yorker,* and *The Washington Times.*

Grateful acknowledgment is made to the following for permission to reprint previously published material:

Basic Books, Inc., Publishers and *Chatto & Windus Ltd.*: Excerpts from the Introduction by Lionel Trilling from *The Life and Work of Sigmund Freud*, edited and abridged by Lionel Trilling and Steven Marcus. Copyright © 1961 by Basic Books, Inc., Publishers. Rights outside the U.S. administered by Chatto & Windus Ltd. Reprinted by permission of Basic Books, Inc., Publishers and Chatto & Windus Ltd.

Farrar, Straus & Giroux, Inc.: Introduction (portion from "Janusz Korczak: A Tale for Our Time") by Bruno Bettelheim to *King Matt the First* by Janusz Korczak. Introduction copyright © 1986 by Bruno Bettelheim. Reprinted by permission of Farrar, Straus & Giroux, Inc.

Harcourt Brace Jovanovich, Inc.: Excerpts from *Beyond Culture* by Lionel Trilling. Copyright © 1965 by Lionel Trilling. Excerpts from *A Gathering of Fugitives* by Lionel Trilling. Copyright © 1956 by Lionel Trilling and renewed 1984 by Diana Trilling. Reprinted by permission of Harcourt Brace Jovanovich, Inc.

The Levy Humanities Series, The University of Southwestern Louisiana: "Lionel Trilling on Literature and Psychoanalysis" by Bruno Bettelheim (*Explorations*, Summer 1989, Vol. 3). Copyright © 1989 by The Levy Humanities Series, The University of Southwestern Louisiana. Reprinted by permission of The Levy Humanities Series, The University of Southwestern Louisiana.

The New Leader: "Two Views of Freud," Part II, by Bruno Bettelheim (May 19, 1958). Reprinted by permission of *The New Leader.*

Rutgers University Press: "The Child's Perception of the City" by

A NOTE ON THE TYPE

This book was set in a digitized version of a face called Primer, designed by Rudolph Ruzicka (1883–1978). Mr. Ruzicka was earlier responsible for the design of Fairfield and Fairfield Medium, Linotype faces whose virtues have for some time been accorded wide recognition.

The complete range of sizes of Primer was first made available in 1954, although the pilot size of 12-point was ready as early as 1951. The design of the face makes general reference to Linotype Century—long a serviceable type, totally lacking in manner or frills of any kind—but brilliantly corrects its characterless quality.

Composed by Graphic Composition, Inc., Athens, Georgia
Printed and bound by the Haddon Craftsmen, Inc.,
Scranton, Pennsylvania.

Designed by Anthea Lingeman